Homeward Bound

Homeward Bound

The Demobilization of the Union & Confederate Armies, 1865–66

William B. Holberton

STACKPOLE
BOOKS

Published by
STACKPOLE BOOKS
5067 Ritter Road
Mechanicsburg, PA 17055
www.stackpolebooks.com

Photographs: All copies made by author, with credit to:
Massachusetts Commandery Military Order of the Loyal Legion and
the U.S. Army Military History Institute.

Printed in the United States of America

10 9 8 7 6 5 4 3 2 1

FIRST EDITION

Library of Congress Cataloging-in-Publication Data
Holberton, William B.
    Homeward bound : the demobilization of the Union and Confederate armies,
        1865–1866
 / William B. Holberton.—1st ed.
        p. cm.
    Includes bibliographical references and index.
    ISBN 0-8117-0788-1
    1. United States. Army—History—Civil War, 1861–1865. 2. Confederate States of
America. Army—History. 3. United States. Army—Demobilization. 4. Confederate
States of America. Army—Demobilization. 5. United States—History—Civil War,
1861–1865. I. Title.

E491 .H66 2000
973.7'4—dc21   99-089758

with gratitude and appreciation to

Dennis E. Frye
Gary W. Gallagher
A. Wilson Greene
John J. Hennessy
Robert K. Krick

CONTENTS

ACKNOWLEDGMENTS

Most of the research phase for this book has been accomplished at the United States Army Military History Institute (USAMHI), Carlisle Barracks, Carlisle, Pennsylvania, and the Virginia Historical Society, Richmond. I am indebted to the personnel of both institutions for their helpful guidance and generous assistance. Dr. Richard Sommers, David Kehoe, and Pamela Cheney at USAMHI contributed far more than they will ever realize to the book. For their contributions I am especially grateful. The personnel in the photographic section of the archives, Michael Winey and Randolph Hackenburg, gave me all kinds of helpful assistance, which I gratefully acknowledge.

In connection with my research in Richmond, Dr. Michael Valente was always the gracious, hospitable host. Putting up with me and putting me up provided a welcome respite from the often tedious work of research. His kindness is appreciated.

An ever-present and constant guide has been Dr. John H. Ellis, professor emeritus of history at Lehigh University, Bethlehem, Pennsylvania. John acted as my advisor during my work on my master's degree, which I received in 1993. His encouragement, delightful sense of humor, and thorough knowledge of his field have been of untold assistance to me. Dr. Roger Simons, Dr. William Shade, and Dr. Joseph Dowling, under whom I studied during my master's stint, are definitely represented in this work. Dr. James S. Saeger, also of Lehigh University's Department of History, has played a part, too, in that I enjoyed his course in American Military History.

The members of the Civil War Round Table of Eastern Pennsylvania have, perhaps unknowingly, provided me with welcome encouragement and assistance. In addition, William Frankenfield, Jeffrey Stocker, Leo Ward,

Edward Root, James Sikorski, and Jeffrey Gates have graciously loaned me books from their extensive personal libraries. Jeff Stocker read through my initial draft and made many helpful suggestions and comments. Almost invariably, his suggestions found their way into the final product.

William G. Shade of Lehigh University loaned me an especially helpful book, while Tom Broadfoot, a well-known figure in Civil War publishing, surprised and pleased me by presenting me with his last copy of a reprinted book, now out of print once again. It is a prized item in my library. Another prized book in my collection came into my possession through the gracious and generous hands of Dr. Michael Stevens. My sincere thanks to each of you.

Robert E. L. Krick, who should not be confused with the well-known Civil War historian by the same name, but who is an outstanding historian in his own right, has encouraged me with his smile, wit, and the titles of a couple of sources. Thanks, Bobby!

Civil War historians—those in academia, those who are members of the National Park Service, and the many members of the legal profession who seem to find respite in Civil War history—are a breed unto themselves, with their never-failing eagerness and readiness to help a struggling neophyte. I am happy and proud to be able to call many in this special category my close personal friends. At the risk of omitting someone who should be included, I am dedicating this book to Dennis E. Frye, Gary W. Gallagher, A. Wilson Greene, John J. Hennessy, and Robert K. Krick. Over the years, through many symposia, field trips, bull sessions, and other pleasant social contacts, the members of this quintet have been the stalwart backers of this book. They have never failed to help when asked, and often help has been forthcoming even without my asking. Thank you, one and all.

Paul Reitmeier and Michael Demyan led me gently through the intricacies of the camera and computer. Without their professional expertise, I would still be back at square one. To say I am indebted is an understatement.

My publishers at Stackpole Books have far exceeded their responsibilities to a first-time author, I am sure. The enthusiasm and confidence of my editor, Michelle M. Simmons, gave my morale a tremendous surge. As she outlined the steps preliminary to the publishing phase, I could almost see the book in its finished state. When she began to speak of the possibility of book signings and appearances, my head began to whirl. Such support and encouragement are greatly appreciated by beginners in the field, and I shall always be grateful.

Father William B. Holberton passed away on March 6, 2000, prior to the final editing and publication of *Homeward Bound*. Father Bill was a veteran of the Second World War, serving as an infantry officer in the European theater where his service earned him the Bronze Star. He was also a lifelong student of the Civil War. It was his passion for Civil War history coupled with his personal experience of demobilization at the end of World War II that inspired him to write this book.

Father Bill was ordained a Roman Catholic priest in the Diocese of Rochester, New York, in 1961, serving for eighteen years as Catholic chaplain at Strong Memorial Hospital in Rochester. More recently, he returned to his alma mater, Lehigh University, in Bethlehem, Pennsylvania, where he held a position as assistant Catholic chaplain from 1991 until his death. In 1993 he earned a master's degree in history from Lehigh, fifty years after he had received his bachelor's degree in business administration. During this period he developed strong ties with the Lehigh Army ROTC unit and became actively involved with alumni affairs. He was also extremely active in the Lehigh Valley chapter of the Civil War Roundtable.

Above all his accomplishments, Father Bill will be remembered as a kind, thoughtful, generous, and devoted priest, family member, and friend. The completion of *Homeward Bound* was undertaken by a group of Father Bill's friends as a loving tribute to his memory. Among those who contributed, Dr. John H. Ellis, Professor Emeritus of History at Lehigh University, deserves special recognition for his dedication and technical assistance.

Mark D'Agostini
December 2000

INTRODUCTION

Youth is the time when hearts are large,
And stirring wars
Appeal to the spirit which appeals in turn
To the blade it draws.
— Herman Melville

Regardless of the name that is applied, whether it be the Civil War, the War Between the States, the War of the Rebellion, the War for Southern Independence, or one of the other many titles used over the years, the United States' fratricidal war of 1861–1865 continues to be the source of constant and prolonged attention on the part of thousands of historians, scholars, reenactors, buffs, authors, and students. Fascination with "our greatest national crisis, an event which at once split us apart and forged a single nation," has resulted in an outpouring of books, monographs, journals, pamphlets, videocassettes, computer games, and models.[1]

One author describes this effort of more than a century in graphic terms, such as "explosion" and "eruption," neither of which is an exaggeration.[2] The output of Civil War titles has indeed been staggering. It is said that the number of items published, including biographies, unit histories, reference works, specialized studies, articles, and documents is equal to the number of days elapsed since the war ended.

Even foreign military historians, observers, and commentators recognized the unique properties of the Civil War. Capt. Justus Scheibert, a captain of engineers in the Prussian Army, observed operations during late 1862 and early 1863. For many years subsequent to the war, he wrote widely on it, commenting on many different aspects of the conflict. In an effort to explain the seemingly unending appeal of the war, Scheibert wrote that the Civil War would "remain for centuries an inexhaustible mine." Vigo Roussillon, a professor of military administration at the French staff school, did extensive postwar research on the Civil War by studying reports of French military observers. He called the Civil War the "first of modern wars" and said it was "a major war of almost unprecedented dimensions."[3]

But despite all of the research, there are still some rather important gaps in writings on the subject. Certain aspects of the war were long neglected; today many of them are in the forefront of scholarly research and publication. The role of African-Americans in the war, including those in the military and naval services of the opposing forces, and the role of women, both free and slave, on the North and South home fronts, are but two examples. Some other aspects of the war are still neglected in large part, perhaps due to the overwhelming publicity given to closely related events or places. Events that occurred in Richmond and the surrender at Appomattox often overshadow the lengthy siege of Petersburg, for example.

One almost totally ignored war-related topic is the demobilization of the Union and Confederate forces. Two articles by Ida M. Tarbell, published in *McClure's Magazine* in 1901, were reprinted in *Civil War Times Illustrated* in December 1967 and January 1968. One other mention of demobilization is a brief article, "Epilogue: America Looks to the Future," included in a special August 1990 issue of this same magazine, entitled "The War's Last Days." The only other publication I have located is a 1952 Department of the Army manual, "History of Personnel Demobilization in the United States Army." This booklet had a limited circulation, however, and it devoted a few pages to each of the wars of our country's history, tracing in broad outlines the procedures used to return civilian soldiers from the front to their homes.

This omission seems to be a serious lacuna, as the mobilization of volunteer units throughout the country, as well as the Military Conscription Acts of the Confederacy in 1862 and the Union in 1863, are subjects of numerous monographs and journal articles. One author stated: "An efficient mobilization plan is an essential ingredient in the successful conduct of any war. It requires the assembly and the organization of troops, material and equipment for active military service in time of war or other national emergency."[4] All army personnel would agree with this statement, and it seems eminently logical to expect that an equally efficient demobilization plan would be an essential ingredient at the close of the conflict.

Almost all books and journal articles leave the reader with the impression that everything important to the war came to a complete halt with the various surrenders, primarily that of April 9, 1865, at Appomattox Court House. At times one is led to believe that this was *the* surrender, as there is no mention of subsequent ones. A few books do briefly mention the Grand Review, held in Washington, during which the two main Union armies, the Army of the Potomac and the Army of the West, passed in review during a two-day period in May 1865. If this review is mentioned at all, it is almost invariably as the final episode of the war. If the book continues beyond this point, Reconstruction becomes the main theme.

And yet many of the men in both armies had miles to travel before they were discharged from service. The passage of these miles included some interesting situations and experiences, all of which properly belong to the story of the war. There were, unfortunately, some tragic accidents along the way, such as the *Sultana* disaster, and some of the homeward-bound soldiers never arrived at their destinations. Despite all the obstacles and hindrances—and there were many—demobilization did occur. It is a fact of the history of the Civil War, just as it is for all wars.

Aside from the official and formal statements of procedures to be followed by the Union forces in their disbandment (there was no comparable formality for the Confederate forces), the best sources of material are the postwar memoirs, diaries, and letters of the soldiers. Despite all the material that has been lost over the years, an impressive quantity of personal accounts still exists. Much of this material lies in state archives, historical society stacks, and especially rich lodes of material like those at the U.S. Army Military History Institute and the Virginia Historical Society.

The term *demobilization* meant something quite different to the Federal and Confederate veterans. The man in blue was returning to a land that was essentially untouched by war. Changes had occurred there but these were mostly due to greater production on the farms and in the mills and mines, as well as the unbelievably increased utilization of railroad facilities. All of this stemmed from the nation's wartime needs for food, horses and mules, munitions, coal, iron, uniforms, and other items. His family had likely experienced the wounding or death of one or more family members, but he was home. He had been outfitted with a new uniform, he had been well fed, he had been transported home, and he had just been paid for his wartime services, although in many instances the payrolls had gone unpaid for long periods. Back on familiar turf, among family, friends, and neighbors, he could look forward to good prospects of employment on the farm, in a factory or mine, or in his chosen profession. Over and above these possibilities, there were almost unlimited opportunities in the newly opened land in the West. He could enter into this final phase of his gainful service to his country with much enthusiasm, optimism, and hope.

"The Confederacy was born in chaos and never fully outgrew it." So wrote a much-respected author in a recent biography of Stonewall Jackson.[5] These words are just as applicable to the demise of the Confederacy, with all the confusion and tumult of the final days in and around Petersburg and Richmond, the flight of the government, the retreat to Appomattox, Lee's surrender, and the submission of the remaining armies of the Confederacy. Most certainly, they describe perfectly the final chapter of that demise—demobilization.

The Confederate veteran thus entered into his final phase of service in defeat and rejection, hungry, nearly naked, with no definite travel provisions, penniless, and with the prospects of destruction and despair waiting for him on the home front. This state of want was intensified in many instances by cataclysmic changes, as the returning soldier found that his previous way of life had been swept away by the ravages of war and the abolition of slavery. Dramatic changes had occurred in his absence in the social and economic structures and in his family's lifestyle. Where once he might have had many people to provide for his needs and pleasures, he now had to fend for himself. Some of these men were woefully incapable when faced with the necessity of earning a living by physical endeavors or by planning and implementing programs for the plantation, farm, mill, store, or home. Nevertheless, despite the adversities they encountered, many of the returning soldiers were able to provide for themselves and their families, albeit with great difficulty.

Historians and authors tend to make comparisons between the Union and Confederate personnel, equipment, strategy and tactics, armament and munitions, and so forth. Demobilization can be analyzed in the same way. The Union approach to demobilization was one of structure, regulation, supervision, and relatively good administration. In comparison, the Confederates had no system, no structure, no supervision, no program at all; the men just went home. The Union forces used well-defined and specified travel routes and means, while the Southerners just flowed across the landscape like an out-of-control stream. It is relatively easy to pinpoint on a map the routes and points of assembly and dispersal for the Federal forces; the corresponding picture for the Confederates would be a separate mark and line on the map for practically each individual soldier.

One rather graphic comparison points up the wide discrepancy between the Union and Confederate resources and capabilities, which also carried over into the demobilization phase. During 1862, while the Civil

War was being prosecuted by the Union with all its means of manpower and materiel, the Federal government was still able to mount three important war-related projects: the Homestead Act, which opened up vast areas of virgin land for settlement; the Morrill Land Grant Act, which enabled states to sell land and use the proceeds to endow colleges that would offer, in addition to the regular academic courses, ones in agriculture, engineering, and home economics; and perhaps the most important—and the most far-reaching—project, the transcontinental railroad.[6]

Although there was certainly a war-related advantage for the North to obtain more expeditious communication with the Pacific Coast states, for the most part, the transcontinental railroad held little war-waging benefits for the North. Yet the North was able to invest time, talent, and money in a program that had been discussed and argued for years and still carry on the war, despite the knowledge that the railroad would be a long time in the construction phase.

During this same period, the Confederates' supply of crucial materials was so limited that they were collecting the contents of chamber pots and outhouses to be leached for niter or saltpeter, a principal ingredient of gunpowder. In addition, the government requested housewives to salvage their kitchen fats for use in providing lubrication grease, especially for use on the railroads. The extreme imbalance between these activities of the North and South illustrates most vividly the differences in resources.[7]

Another rather graphic picture was drawn by Margaret Mitchell in her popular epic novel of the South, *Gone with the Wind*. She describes the homecoming of one returning Confederate soldier:

> A familiar sight, a bearded man coming slowly up the avenue under the cedars, a man clad in a ragged mixture of blue and gray uniforms, head bowed tiredly, feet dragging slowly. . . . The man lifted a face covered with a dirty blond beard and stopped still, looking toward the house as if he was too weary to take another step.[8]

So Ashley Wilkes returned to Tara—not to his own home, which now consisted of gaunt, stark chimneys, but to his family, who lived at Tara, to the neighborhood that he had always known and now could not recognize.

This brief excerpt could be the description of the homecomings of most of the returning, defeated Rebels. Yet there are many intimate, personal accounts of the experiences faced by the returning veterans, and these stories are all different. Together they provide a tapestrylike view of the postsurrender days.

To sketch in sharp lines the experiences of both the victor and the vanquished on their homeward journeys is the purpose of this book. Quite simply, this Civil War book begins where most other Civil War books end.

CHAPTER ONE

The Surrenders

Shot and fire have passed us by,
We the fortunate ones do qualify
To resume our lives at hearth and home,
Never more to leave or roam.

Just as there are many claimants to the honor of being the first Union or Confederate military unit to enter the war or the first soldier to be wounded, killed, or captured, so too the lists are long at the end of the war. Who was the last enlisted man or officer killed or wounded? Which Confederate was the last one to capitulate?

There were several surrenders of the Confederate forces, although most consider that at Appomattox Court House on Palm Sunday, April 9, 1865, to have been the final surrender of the Civil War. It was here that Gen. Robert E. Lee surrendered the forces remaining in the Confederate Army of Northern Virginia to Lt. Gen. Ulysses S. Grant. Lee, immaculately uniformed in his military finery, presented an imposing figure even in defeat. Grant, on the other hand, had just returned from an inspection of lines and troops and, in his dusty, mud-spattered uniform, more resembled a humble private than the commander in chief of the Union armies.[1]

The once-powerful Army of Northern Virginia, reduced in number through combat losses as well as significant desertions during the last few days of the war, mustered only about 26,000 men for the actual surrender.[2] The details of the surrender negotiations, the reaction of the Southern soldiers when they learned the news, the actual surrender ceremony with the rendering of reciprocal military honors by Gen. Joshua L. Chamberlain, with the Army of the Potomac, and Gen. John B. Gordon, with the remnant of the Army of Northern Virginia, have been recounted many times.

McClean House, Appomattox Court House, Virginia: scene of surrender of the Army of Northern Virginia, April 9, 1865.

The generosity of General Grant's surrender terms and the spirit in which they were given were matched by General Lee's acceptance of the terms and his humble gratitude for the emergency rations that were provided his hungry men.

Over the next few days, other Confederate forces throughout the South surrendered and were disbanded. Some of these events were formal in nature; others just seemed to happen rather informally.

One of the earliest Confederate leaders to cease operations following Appomattox was the man who had been far more than a mere thorn in the side of the Union forces for two years or more—John Mosby. On April 21, 1865, he disbanded his Rangers, applied for a parole, and began practicing law in what had been the "Mosby Confederacy."[3]

On April 18, 1865, at the Bennett House, near Durham Station, North Carolina, Gen. Joseph E. Johnston concluded an armistice with Gen. William T. Sherman. The terms of this initial agreement were not acceptable to the administration officials in Washington, as it included matters of a political nature that were considered to be beyond the scope of responsibility of the military commander. A revised agreement was worked out, and the actual surrender occurred on April 26. By this act, Johnston, who had taken over command of three departments of the Confederate military organization, surrendered some 30,000 men in the Army of Tennessee.[4]

The next important element of the Confederate Army to surrender was that of Gen. Richard Taylor. Taylor had control of the Departments of Alabama and Mississippi and East Louisiana, with an army of 42,293 men.[5] On May 2, Taylor accepted the terms proposed by Gen. Edward R. S. Canby, commander of the Military Division of West Mississippi. The terms of this agreement were essentially the same as Grant had given Lee. In addition, General Taylor was permitted to use the railroads and available transport ships in order to facilitate the return of his men to their homes. Two days later, Taylor met Canby in order to make the surrender official. The paroles were accepted on May 8, and for some reason, Taylor always referred to this date when writing about the surrender. (A minor point, but puzzling when one is attempting to establish the sequence of events during those hectic days.) This act of surrender occurred at Citronelle, Alabama.

The following day, Lt. Gen. Nathan B. Forrest disbanded the troops of his independent command, although technically his troops were included in Taylor's surrender. Forrest, defeated in his final battle in the neighborhood of Selma, Alabama, on April 2, rather eloquently addressed his men in a farewell message from Gainesville, Alabama, saying, "You have been good soldiers, you can be good citizens." Gen. Robert E. Lee allegedly called this larger-than-life figure among Confederate generals, a man who rose from private to lieutenant general, "the greatest soldier in his command."[6] High praise, indeed, especially as Lee had never laid eyes on Forrest. According to John Allan Wyeth, a trooper in Forrest's command who became his postwar biographer, Gen. Joseph E. Johnston rated Forrest as "the war's greatest soldier" and maintained that with military education and training, Forrest would have been "the great central figure of the Civil War."[7]

Next in line to formalize surrender proceedings was Maj. Gen. Samuel Jones. As commander of the Department of South Georgia and Florida, he surrendered his forces at Tallahassee, Florida, on May 10, to Brig. Gen. Edward M. McCook, who commanded a cavalry division in the Military Division of Mississippi and who took part in surrenders in Alabama and Florida.[8]

At Chalk Bluff, Arkansas, on May 11, Brig. Gen. Merriwether Jeff Thompson ended the service of his brigade, under the same terms as those granted at Appomattox the previous month, after a rather prolonged exchange of questions, answers, proposals, and counterproposals, by surrendering to Maj. Gen. Grenville M. Dodge, commander of the Department of Missouri. This surrender pertained to the troops of the Northern Subdistrict of Arkansas, the District of Arkansas, and West Louisiana in the

Trans-Mississippi Department. Thompson's parole stated that he was a general in the Missouri State Guard; some sources list him as a Confederate general, but although he often petitioned President Davis for promotion to the grade of brigadier general in the Confederate Army, Davis repeatedly refused to approve the promotion. The mayor of St. Joseph, Missouri, in the troubled, hectic days of 1861, Thompson became "a very competent cavalry commander" and even occasionally held division command.[9]

At this point, the sequence of surrenders was interrupted by what one author calls, "the last significant land battle of the war"—a two-day skirmish on May 12 and 13, 1865, at Palmito Ranch, near Brownsville, Texas, on the Rio Grande. On both days, the Union forces, under Col. Theodore H. Barrett, at first prevailed but then were beaten back by Confederate counterattacks headed by Col. John S. Ford, also known as "RIP" or "Rest in Peace" Ford, who had the distinction of leading the Confederates to a last-gasp sort of victory. This last battle involved the 62nd U.S. Colored Infantry, and thus the last man to be wounded in a Civil War land engagement was a black sergeant named Crockett.[10]

At this late date, the troops of the Trans-Mississippi Department had not yet surrendered. The governors of Arkansas, Mississippi, and Louisiana advised Gen. E. Kirby Smith, commander of this department, to give up and formalize a surrender agreement. In addition, according to one member of the 3rd Texas Cavalry, "the Trans-Mississippi Department's command began a spontaneous disintegration in the middle of May."[11]

Lt. Gen. S. B. Buckner, acting on behalf of Kirby Smith, "entered into a military convention" with Union major general Peter J. Osterhaus, who was acting for Maj. Gen. Edward R. S. Canby. This "military convention" was agreed upon in New Orleans on May 26, 1865. General Smith, a general in the Provisional Army of the Confederacy, approved the terms of the agreement in Galveston, Texas, on June 2. Once again, there is a difference in the dating of this surrender of the last major Confederate force, with some historians opting for the earlier date and others using the final acceptance date as the official date of surrender.

Even more interesting is the action, at the time of this surrender, on the part of Confederate brigadier general Joseph O. ("Jo") Shelby, whose promotion on orders of the Trans-Mississippi Department Headquarters to the rank of major general was never confirmed by the Confederate government. At Corsicana, Texas, in June 1865, Shelby told his force of 200 men that he would never surrender and then headed for Mexico, his troops

Brig. Gen. Stand Watie, C.S.A.,
Cherokee chief

dwindling to the size of "a small brigade" along the way. Abandoning their battle flag in the Rio Grande, Shelby and his men crossed into Mexico where they allied themselves with Maximilian. In payment, they were given a plot of land near Vera Cruz where they established a short-lived settlement called Carlota. Eventually, Shelby and some of his men returned to the United States. Others of Kirby Smith's command, which totaled 17,686 men, also refused the terms of surrender and scattered, some to Mexico or the Far West, while others simply went home.[12]

Little by little, the isolated pockets of guerrillalike troops were being overwhelmed. Some small groups of "unreconstructed" Rebels remained at large, but these groups more or less withered on the vine. In later years, such groups of resistance have been the subject of novels and motion pictures, but their effect on the war's ending and subsequent demobilization was negligible.

Finally, on June 23, 1865, two and a half months after the surrender at Appomattox Court House, the last formal submission of any sizable body of Confederate troops took place. Here another minority combatant, this time a Native American, played a major role. Confederate brigadier Stand Watie, the highest-ranking Indian officer on either side of the conflict, surrendered at Doaksville, near Fort Towson in the Indian Territory (present-day Oklahoma). Watie had under his command the members of the Cherokee, Creek, and Seminole tribes, as well as the Osage Battalion. Lt. Col. Asa Mathews accepted the surrender on behalf of the Union Army.[13]

The Federal government declared the war officially at an end on August 20, 1865. Such a declaration was necessary from a legal standpoint in order to establish an ending point for various wartime measures, contracts, and regulations.[14]

Although the Confederate Navy surrendered on May 4, 1865, the last active Confederate cruiser, *Shenandoah,* a commerce raider that had been especially effective against Union shipping, did not strike its colors until November 6 in Liverpool, England.[15]

A summary of the troops surrendered was prepared and submitted by Maj. Gen. E. A. Hitchcock, the Union commissary general of prisoners, dated December 6, 1865. This consolidated report of the exchanged and paroled prisoners of war lists the following statistics:

Total Surrendered:
Army of Northern Virginia 27,805
Army of Tennessee 31,243
Depts. of South Georgia/Florida 7,978
Depts. of Alabama/Mississippi/East Louisiana 42,293
Trans-Mississippi Department 17,686
Other smaller units/detachments 47,218
Total surrendered 174,223
Paroled during the war 155,740
Total Surrendered/Paroled 329,963[16]

With the surrenders either accomplished or about to occur, the demobilization process began for both the Union and Confederate armies.

CHAPTER TWO

Blueprints for Demobilization

Melt, melt away ye armies—disperse ye blue clad soldiers,
Resolve ye back again, give up for good your deadly arms,
Other the arms the fields henceforth for you, or South or
*   North,*
With saner wars, sweet wars, life-giving wars.
                                        —Walt Whitman

With the great advantages the North had over the South in the areas of manpower, materiel, and transportation facilities, there were glaring discrepancies between the two in their demobilization processes. On the part of the Union, demobilization was well thought-out and carefully organized, but the Confederate government had no plans. The Union government provided the men in blue with many different advantages during demobilization, but the men in gray had to fend for themselves as they made their long, weary way home from the various surrender locations. The Union veterans received almost every consideration imaginable, truly VIP treatment, while the Confederate survivors were given practically nothing in the way of clothing, pay, or transportation. Although some of the Union victors had some adverse experiences along the way to their home areas, these were relatively minor inconveniences compared with the struggles and hardships the vanquished Confederates had to undergo.

In a letter dated May 1, 1865, Col. Thomas M. Vincent, the primary aide to the U.S. adjutant general, presented to the secretary of war a procedure for mustering out and discharging from service volunteer soldiers in the armies of the United States. This proposal, which required significant prior planning, was submitted just three weeks after the surrender at Appomattox Court House and well in advance of most of the subsequent surrenders. The plan may have already been drawn up in anticipation of the total defeat of the Rebel states, in the terminology used throughout the official correspondence. Secretary of War Edwin M. Stanton, however, directed that the plan be submitted to the lieutenant general commanding the armies for his opinion. If he approved the program, wrote Stanton, appropriate orders were to be issued. On May 11, Lt. Gen. Ulysses S. Grant endorsed the demobilization plan.[1]

Briefly stated, the general intent was to maintain the integrity of major units—that is, corps or at least divisions, and to move them to locations convenient to the particular armies. These convenient locations were termed "field rendezvous points," and it was in these places that the paperwork would begin in earnest. Considering the tendency of army units to take a casual attitude toward record keeping during combat, there would now have to be a strict accounting of the unit records. Indeed, the records of individual soldiers would be, in part, based upon information found in the unit records. Thus, "a critical inspection of the regimental and company records was to be made" at the unit rendezvous points. The muster-out rolls and the payrolls were to be prepared there, and this important and necessary work was to be directed by assistant commissaries of musters for the divisions. Their work, in turn, was to be superintended by the commissaries of the various corps. Corps commanders, together with their staff officers, were directed to push the procedure "with energy" so that the paperwork might be accomplished accurately and promptly.[2]

Certainly the paperwork was formidable. Even more formidable was the sheer number of men to be processed in the demobilization phase. On May 1, 1865, just a few weeks after Lee's surrender at Appomattox, there were slightly more than a million men in the Union Army; by the third week of November, 801,000 had been mustered out and discharged. Demobilization, indeed, was "an extraordinary exhibit of work, performed chiefly within the three months of June, July and August." As Secretary of War Stanton put it, "No similar work of like magnitude regarding its immensity and the small limit of time in which it has been performed, has . . . any parallel in the history of armies."[3]

The mobilization process had been spread out over a four-year period, but in the demobilization phase, the push was on. On the Union side, there was constant pressure to expedite the entire process, from the upper echelons of the War Department, the state politicians, the soldiers themselves, and their families at home.[4] Every aspect of the Union effort was geared to speed without sacrificing efficiency. For the Confederates, the appropriate facilities were lacking for the most part, and the pace was necessarily slower.

The governor of Wisconsin had written to the secretary of war to urge the speedy discharge of the Wisconsin regiments, and the letter reached Maj. Gen. John Pope, the commander of the Department of the Missouri. On August 19, he wrote to Maj. Gen. William T. Sherman, then in command of the Military Division of the Mississippi:

> To gratify this and similar requests would mean abandoning the whole country and all our supplies west of the Missouri River to the Indians. . . . This department would be left without troops. [At the end of two months, by October 15] . . . nearly the entire force in the department will be mustered out. . . . After three years' service, two months seem a short time to wait patiently.[5]

In any war, soldiers, especially citizen-soldiers (and most of the Union men, and all of the Confederate soldiers, fell in this category), are always eager to return to their loved ones, their farms, homes, and places of employment. Alexis de Tocqueville expressed this characteristic quite accurately in his comments about democracy in America:

> Among the soldiers of a democratic army . . . the majority, being enlisted against their will and ever ready to go back to their homes, do not consider themselves as seriously engaged in the military profession and are always thinking of quitting it. They adapt themselves to their military duties, but their minds are still attached to the interests and the duties that engaged them in civil life. Among democratic nations the private soldiers remain most like civilians.[6]

In addition, once the combat phase of any war is completed, the government looks upon volunteer soldiers as expensive luxuries that constitute an obvious and immediate area for cost reduction.

In the early days of demobilization, the Union Army's disbandment was done on a unit basis, much as mobilization had occurred on a local, territorial basis. Before the units could be started on their way to their home states, the muster, payrolls, and other final papers had to be completed. When a unit arrived at the demobilization point, often the same place as mobilization, the program came under the control of the state's chief mustering officer. This

official was responsible for the smooth operation of the final phases of demobilization. The paymasters appeared near the end of the process; the government had wisely determined that no troops would be paid until final
demobilization, and this was almost always at or near the home site of the
unit. This was done to protect the troops from swindlers and confidence
men, well-known breeds of camp followers, as well as to reduce the com-
monplace temptations to gamble. Either could consume a soldier's pay, and
he would reach home with empty pockets after years of combat service.

Since the units traveled to their home states with their arms, colors, and
other equipment, the appropriate officials were to receive these accou-
trements for storage and disposal. The soldiers could retain their weapons,
however, if they chose. A War Department letter from the adjutant general's
office, dated June 10, 1865, established a price schedule for arms: muskets,
with or without related equipment, $6; Spencer carbines, $10; all other car-
bines, $8; sabers and swords, with or without belts, $3. The men could also
keep, without charge, their knapsacks, haversacks, and canteens.[7] This display of generosity on the part of the government made possible a relatively
easy disposition of army surplus property, an inventory problem that has
invariably beset victorious governments in war's aftermath.

Two other important matters also had to be considered, and the War
Department addressed both of them. One was the necessity of feeding the
men during the period of record processing and preparation for discharge.
The men were provided adequate rations, although the food in some
instances was less than popular. Another, somewhat more serious consideration was the matter of discipline. The chief mustering officer, together
with the unit officers, was responsible for the maintenance of proper discipline during these impatient days. Not providing military units with specified duties and activities would be inviting difficulties, scrapes, and
disciplinary infractions. Except for a few unrelated incidents, the whole
process went off remarkably well.

Special care and attention were necessary in the final phase of the
demobilization process: paying off the troops. The government owed the
men their accrued base pay plus any bonuses due, less various charges against
them, such as those for retained weapons. In many instances, the paymaster's
system of payment was woefully behind. General Sherman's army and General Thomas's command in the West had not been paid since August 1864,
while the Army of the Potomac and other troops in and around Richmond
at the end of hostilities had last been paid at the end of 1864. In answer to a

Gen. Samuel Cooper, C.S.A.,
inspector/adjutant general

May 19 query from Grant's chief of staff, the paymaster general replied that the Treasury was in the process of paying Sherman's and Meade's armies and that approximately 123,000 men would receive some $50,000,000.[8]

The position of the adjutant general of the army was the keystone of the entire recruiting and discharging system. Shortly before the 1861 bombardment of Fort Sumter, the adjutant general of the Federal Army was Col. Samuel Cooper, a career officer who had spent many years in that position. From his days as secretary of war in Franklin Pierce's cabinet, Jefferson Davis had come to know Cooper and to appreciate his abilities. Cooper, although a native of New York State, had married into the prominent Mason family of Virginia and thus left Federal service to support his adopted state and the newly organized Confederacy. When Virginia seceded, Davis was quick to offer Cooper the key role of adjutant and inspector general of the Confederate Army. As such, Cooper was the ranking general officer of the Confederacy. In addition to the duties of his office, the adjutant general acted as chief of staff at the very highest level. This position in each army was crucial to a smooth operation of military affairs.[9]

Shortly after the beginning of the war, Lorenzo Thomas, a colonel who was in charge of the U.S. adjutant general's office, became the adjutant general and received the rank of brigadier general in the Union Army. Given

Col. Edward D. Townsend, U.S.A.,
acting adjutant general,
(postwar photo)

the tremendous expansion of the army in a few short months, the adjutant general's duties expanded accordingly. Some authors portray Thomas as being slow to respond to the military exigencies of the crisis. Whatever the case may have been, when Edwin Stanton took over as secretary of war in January 1862, following the rather disastrous and corruption-riddled term of the Pennsylvania politician Simon Cameron, he openly displayed an intense dislike for General Thomas and a low estimation of his ability. One author stated that Stanton "detested [Thomas] on sight." In addition, there were rumors of a certain "lukewarmness" on the part of the adjutant general toward the war, and Stanton is said even to have had doubts about Thomas's loyalty.

Although there appears to have been no basis for these suspicions, Stanton nonetheless managed to isolate Thomas and thus keep him at a distance from the War Department in the nation's capital. This rather strange and unique situation continued as Thomas was sent on frequent field inspection trips and, eventually, to the Mississippi River Valley to supervise the recruitment of black soldiers and the enlistment and transfer of white officers for the colored regiments. Some historians believe that Thomas was assigned the additional duty of "watching Grant," even though Thomas was considered by many to be an eccentric person, one who was addicted to

Capt. Thomas McCurdy Vincent,
U.S.A., assistant adjutant general,
(postwar photo)

strong drink (a strange choice to "watch Grant"), and also a man of limited ability and narrow views. As things turned out, General Thomas was shunted off in such a way that he took little active part in either the vast expansion of the army or its demobilization.[10] With all the effort necessary to organize most effectively the recruitment of soldiers in the early days of the war, and with the knowledge that the office of the adjutant general was central to this particular phase of the war, it is difficult to understand why such a situation was allowed to continue and why Thomas was not replaced with a qualified man of appropriate rank.

Who, then, did control the operations of this crucially important position in the Federal Army? Two officers stood out by virtue of their intense and diligent efforts to undertake the duties of adjutant general: Col. Edward Davis Townsend and Capt. Thomas McCurdy Vincent.

Colonel Townsend, whose maternal grandfather was Elbridge Gerry, vice president in Pres. James Madison's second administration, was senior assistant in the Adjutant General's Department.[11] In this capacity, much of the burden of organization and supervision of the programs fell on his shoulders. Townsend, with his quiet and confident manner, became a close confidant of President Lincoln and was an efficient administrator. He also had a remarkable knowledge of departmental files and army procedures.

In short, Townsend got results. At the conclusion of the war, Townsend was first brevetted brigadier general and then major general for his outstanding services.[12]

Thomas McCurdy Vincent, a first lieutenant in June 1861 and a colonel by the end of the war, had seen combat against the Seminole Indians in Florida (1853–55) and also had taken part in the First Battle of Bull Run (July 21, 1861). During the Civil War, he was "in charge of the organization, muster out, and other details of the volunteer troops." A younger man than Townsend, he remained in service, retiring in 1896 as a colonel in the Regular Army with the brevet rank of brigadier general in the U.S. Army.[13] It was Townsend and Vincent who drew up the plans for both the recruiting and demobilizing phases of the army, supervised their execution, and provided skillful and professional expertise to the president and the secretary of war.

With the cessation of hostilities, toleration of wartime laxity in unit and individual paperwork came to a halt. The War Department began to require complete and accurate records. Despite the urgency to release troops to their civilian status, it was necessary to retain the volunteers in service long enough to verify their records. It was good that such emphasis was placed early in the process, as the resulting information was extremely valuable in later years in connection with applications for pensions and disability allowances. Even with the renewed emphasis on records, veterans often had to contact fellow soldiers from their units in order to substantiate their claims. The detailed history for each man required the following information: name, age, rank, date enrolled and location, date mustered in and by whom, distance traveled, subsistence/forage (furnished by soldier or issued), equipment/clothing (furnished by soldier or issued), absences, special duty, promotions, wounds, illnesses.

After printing and distributing the forms for recording the data, the processing of volunteers began. Adequate transportation was essential to the entire program, and so the officers in charge mobilized rail and water facilities to move the volunteer soldiers back to their home states. Some of the troops began their homeward journey in the time-tested manner of soldiers of all ages—they marched. Ultimately, every railroad and waterway of the North was involved. Facilities on the Ohio and Mississippi Rivers, as well as the Great Lakes, transported large numbers of men. In addition, many units moved by steamer on the high seas, and even Long Island Sound was active as a waterway in the program. Due to the large concentrations of troops passing through New York City, Cleveland, and Chicago, temporary barracks were necessary to provide shelter for troops during transfer procedures in those cities.[14]

With the volunteer soldiers on their way to the field rendezvous points, sufficient mustering out and payroll forms available, competent administrative personnel ready and waiting, and the necessary transportation laid on, the long-awaited demobilization of the Union forces could begin. And begin it did, first with the Grand Review, which effectively was the initial phase of demobilization for the armies in the East at war's end, and then with the actual movement of troops, primarily by rail, toward their common destination—home.

While all this was going on in the North, the Confederates were taking no steps to plan and prepare for demobilization. The Southern approach was characterized by informality and a lack of organization. The informal nature of the Confederate demobilization is perhaps best exemplified by the rather casual dismissal of troops by their commanders and by the high rate of desertions. Events in two widely separated areas, one in Virginia and the other in the Trans-Mississippi Department, reflect the character of Confederate demobilization.

A lieutenant on the commissary staff of the prison commission, Charles R. Chewing, originally a private in Company E, 9th Virginia Cavalry, had reached Danville, Virginia, on April 5, 1865, along with other members of the fleeing Confederate government. His morale must have been somewhat deflated, since he mentioned that the "poor train [was] so overloaded it can hardly move, but moving we are." Considering that they had departed from Richmond on April 2, the train must have been creeping along at a snail's pace, as the distance between the two sites is only about 150 miles. Finding no fuel or food at "this misserable little town," he and the others waited out the situation. After learning of the "great tragedy which has befallen us," referring to the surrender at Appomattox, Chewing and his companions were dismissed on April 11 by Brig. Gen. William M. Gardner, commandant of prisons in the Richmond area, who told his men "to go home as best you can as there is no longer any reason to stay."[15]

At much the same time, out in Texas, Edward W. Cade, an Ohio-born surgeon in the 16th Texas Volunteer Infantry, described the reaction of the troops when they learned of Lee's submission to Grant at Appomattox. Confident that the war would continue west of the Mississippi River, they maintained a semblance of military organization while at Piedmont Springs.

Their confidence gave way to discouragement when they learned that Gen. Kirby Smith had followed the lead of General Lee. At first angry at the surrenders, the men turned to despair; the strain and burden of three years' service outweighed their feelings for their unit. Despite the pleading of their division commander to wait for a properly administered discharge, the men took off, "either with or without a furlough or discharge."[16]

Such desertions reduced the paperwork for the Confederate authorities at the surrender sites. Paroles for all personnel had to be completed and verified against the rolls before the men could be released. These administrative hurdles were not necessary for the men who deserted. Some of the deserters later obtained paroles from Federal authorities in their home areas; some never bothered to go through the formality.

CHAPTER THREE

Desertions:
A Plague on Both Houses

The cloud lifts, after all. They bring him the news.
He is sure of being President four years more.
He thinks about it. He says, "Well I guess they thought
They'd better not swap horses, crossing a stream."
The deserters begin to leave the Confederate armies. . . .
—Stephen Vincent Benét

Desertions commonly occurred on both sides in the conflict. One author considers the bounty system "partly responsible for the high desertion rate of the Union Army, totaling 268,000 men." As three-year enlistments began to expire in 1864, the U.S. government offered a bonus, or "bounty," of $400 and a thirty-day furlough for a reenlistment of three years, or 'for the duration.' By mid-April 136,000 men had reenlisted. The "bounty jumper" would reenlist and get his bounty, desert, change his name, go to another district or state and reenlist, collect the bounty, desert again, and so on until caught. Perhaps some sort of record, one man confessed to thirty-two instances of desertion; for these offenses, he drew four years in prison. The Confederate side of the desertion picture was even more depressing: "By the end of 1864, almost half the men on Confederate rolls were absent; the majority had deserted." In the four months preceding February 1865, 72,000 men had deserted from the Confederate armies east of the Mississippi River alone. Toward the end of that month, General Lee stated that "hundreds of men are deserting nightly." As the Army of Northern Virginia drew near Appomattox, a Confederate sergeant summed up the situation rather concisely and accurately: "For the last six or eight months, our men have deserted by the thousands. Our army has been melting away. It's all over for the Confederacy."[1]

Desertion from the ranks of the Confederate Army represented "a symptom of a deeper and more general cancer in the body of the Confederacy." The reality of desertion had reached alarming proportions. "By the autumn of 1864 it was estimated that some hundred thousand men had seceded, a figure which, as General Lee had warned, brought calamity." One brigade in the First Corps of the Army of Northern Virginia was left with only eight men, according to J. F. J. Caldwell, an officer and brigade historian of McGowan's South Carolina brigade. Gen. George Pickett had approximately 9,500 men in his division present for duty on April 1, 1865, the day prior to Lee's evacuation of Richmond and Petersburg, but only 500 on April 9, the surrender date at Appomattox. Comparable figures for Gen. Bushrod Johnson's division were 1,500 and 300.[2]

Initially, desertion was punished by branding, imprisonment, solitary confinement, or flogging. As the war progressed, punishment for desertion became increasingly more severe, ultimately resulting in death sentences, although many condemned soldiers received reprieves and less severe punishment. The Union Army executed at least 267 of its soldiers for desertion, representing a side of warfare not often mentioned. Even as late as March 1865 at Selma, Alabama, Gen. Nathan Bedford Forrest had two deserters shot. If any joined the ranks of the enemy and then became prisoners of war, they could expect no pardon.

The numbers of deserters were significant. One estimate is that of 1,082,119 Confederate enlistments, 105,000 desertions were recorded, slightly less than 10 percent. On the Union side, out of 1,556,678 enlistments, there were 278,644 instances of desertion, almost 18 percent. These figures, at least for the enlistments, are somewhat suspect, especially for the Confederate Army. Record keeping was not yet refined, so such calculations are, at best, rough approximations. Another historian reported that there were 201,000 desertions in the Union Army and added that "fewer than 76,000 were ever apprehended."[3]

As the final days of the Confederacy were drawing to a close, the superintendent of the Bureau of Conscription asked Secretary of War John C. Breckinridge to request the civil authorities of the states to take a greater role in the apprehension and trial of deserters "in order to reduce desertions and provide needed manpower." Brig. Gen. John S. Preston went on to state that desertion "has become a common crime . . . the criminals are everywhere shielded by their families and by the sympathies of many communities. They form the numerical majorities in many localities." Pressures from families suffering from food shortages, inflation, and scarcity of consumer goods must have been strong indeed.[4]

A member of the 8th Virginia Infantry, John E. Divine, declared that most of the regiment had died at Sayler's Creek on April 6, 1865. He wrote, "Several of those who escaped started home, not waiting for the final humiliation, but others struggled on with the army partly because they had no other place to go." A British observer, Francis Lawley, mentioned that in addition to the armed soldiers who surrendered and stacked their arms at Appomattox Court House, there were "about 18,000 stragglers . . . who claimed to be included in the capitulation."

Members of the Jeff Davis Artillery, along with thousands of their comrades in the Army of Northern Virginia, were dismayed to learn that no food was available at Amelia Court House, about forty miles east of Appomattox, but only ordnance supplies. This disclosure had "a devastating effect on the army. . . . A number of men, who were no longer able to cope with the hardships of the campaign, left the ranks and disappeared." Some men in this unit, which probably fired the last artillery salvos of the Army of Northern Virginia, "not wishing to wait to hear the terms of capitulation . . . decided to take advantage of the cease-fire, to leave the field." Perhaps these soldiers headed for North Carolina and Gen. Joseph E. Johnston's army. The line between outright desertion and decamping in order to join another army is a tenuous one at best.[5]

At war's end, some men from the 4th Texas Infantry of Hood's Brigade were in Kentucky in an effort to recruit new soldiers. Valerius C. Giles, a member of this regiment, reported that "a great majority of the young Kentuckians lit out for home and never surrendered and were never paroled." The remainder of the unit surrendered at Louisville, and then slowly the paroled veterans made their way home to Texas.[6]

Lt. Gen. Richard Taylor's army was not immune to this type of desertion, according to an account of the actions of soldiers in the 34th Texas Infantry of Maj. Gen. John H. Forney's division. On May 24, 1865, Brig. Gen. James E. Harrison, who had succeeded Prince de Polignac as brigade commander, issued orders for the regiments to march as near to their homes as possible and then to discharge their members. "Most of the men in Forney's Division, which included the 34th Texas, had accepted ultimate defeat by May 19 and had gone home of their own accord."[7]

Maj. Gen. Harry T. Hays, transferred from the Army of Northern Virginia to the Trans-Mississippi Department in the fall of 1864, was quoted as saying that in one night 150 men left their units, mostly from the 29th Infantry Regiment. Maj. Silas T. Grisamore of the 18th Louisiana Infantry Regiment reminisced in his postwar memoirs that "desertions began to become frequent" as the soldiers deliberately left for home, realizing that there was no favorable prospect for them in the future, and that there was "universal pillaging" on their part. The pillaging, however, was limited to government property and supplies; no private property was disturbed. According to W. H. Tunnard, of the 3rd Regiment of Louisiana Infantry, at Shreveport, Louisiana, "the majority of men gone or preparing to leave" were "permitted to take government horses, mules and wagons, clothes, leather, thread, buttons, cotton and linen." From this it appears that the men cleaned out the supply dumps of any and all movable goods, all of which were in short supply in the civilian economy to which they were returning.

On May 18, 1865, W. W. Heartsill of the 1st Texas Cavalry Brigade noted in his journal, "From what I can learn, a great many of the soldiers have laid down their arms, and have gone home." After citing figures of desertions from some of the units, Heartsill said that "desertions will lead us to a surrender." A few days later, his prophecy was fulfilled when the Army of the Trans-Mississippi Department formally surrendered.[8]

Apparently the problems of desertion and early departure were pandemic in the Confederate Army. Gen. Johnson Hagood stated in his memoirs that as of April 26, 1865, "in the last ten days desertion had reduced one brigade [in General Johnston's army] from 1600 to 300 men. . . . Officers as high as colonels not only countenanced, but participated in the shameful conduct." Another observer in this same army described the surrender as no surprise to the soldiers, as "they had witnessed thousands of their discouraged comrades quitting the army." A member of the 19th Tennessee Regiment, W. J. Worsham, recorded that "men began slipping out to leave for home, and in order to quiet the unrest, Johnston ordered daily drill and inspection. This gave the men something to do and to think about."

Even general officers took advantage of the situation to disappear quietly. Gen. Joseph Wheeler did not include himself in the surrender of April 26, but started out for home with a few of his old comrades in arms.[9]

But even in the matter of desertions, there were exceptions that proved the rule. One highly disciplined unit amid the increasing storm of desertions was the Palmetto Sharpshooters, a part of John Bratton's brigade in Charles William Field's division. Not only was this particular unit outstanding for its discipline, so too were the brigade and the division. Bratton's brigade was cited as follows: "Of the brigades which composed the Army of Northern Virginia at Appomattox, his was the most completely manned and was the only which left the field as an organized unit." Apparently the discipline of the sharpshooters and the brigade reflected the overall discipline of the division, as Field's division, Hood's old Texas division, also received high praise: "At Appomattox his division, the only thoroughly organized and effective body of troops in the Army of Northern Virginia, [with] its nearly 5,000 men compris[ed] more than half of the infantry surrendered by General Lee."[10]

Responses to a questionnaire distributed among its Civil War veterans by the state of Tennessee, with answers received between 1915 and 1922, provide insight into the problem of desertion toward the end of the conflict. One veteran commented that "throughout the spring of 1865, Confederate veterans drifted homeward." "Drifted" seems to imply that the men were merely turning away from what they perceived to be a lost situation, one that they could in no way change or affect, and for which there was no logical solution except to go home. A Tennessee soldier in the Army of Northern Virginia returned his form with the notation that "our men lost heart . . . and were going home every night." He himself deserted March 1, 1865. It is interesting to observe that "many veterans refused to discuss their discharges from the army." A significant number of these men may have feared losing their state pension rights. Since pensions were awarded only for honorable service, any admission to desertion would result in forfeiting one's pension. Thus the comments these veterans made concerning desertion were of a general nature.[11]

Numbers alone do not reflect the true impact of desertions on the opposing forces of the Union and Confederate Armies. Even though the Northern desertions were roughly two and a half times the Confederate departures, the Union war effort was not crippled by the desertions, whereas the Southern desertions "helped destroy any chance of a Confederate victory." Similarly, the Union desertions neither demoralized Northern society nor resulted in the formation of outlaw bands of guerrilla raiders, who often controlled sizeable territories. Confederate desertions led to both results in the South.[12]

CHAPTER FOUR

The Grand Review and Its Confederate Counterpart

I read last night of the Grand Review
in Washington's chiefest avenue,
Two hundred thousand men in blue,
I think they said was the number.
—Bret Harte

Proclaimed "a benediction on the Civil War" and "the noblest pageant the country had ever witnessed," the Grand Review of the Union forces, at least for the armies of Gen. George G. Meade and Gen. William T. Sherman, was a significant component of demobilization. It was the first major step in the process for many of the troops who participated. The distances traveled northward by these two armies, moving some of the troops directly into the pipeline of demobilization, meshed smoothly into the overall program.

Both armies marched to Washington, with Meade's coming from the Richmond area and Sherman's men marching from Raleigh, North Carolina, by way of Richmond. Through rail service did not exist, even in peacetime, and there was such widespread destruction of railroad facilities in that much-fought-over area of the South that movement by foot was the only practical means to use. These men were veterans of hundreds of miles of such road marches. They had gone through the routine of breaking camp, marching all day, setting up camp, and preparing rations countless times. Since peace had descended upon the land, there was no danger of enemy action, so local security was at a minimum, thus simplifying the march routine.

Grand Review, Washington, D.C., May 1865

The armies moved swiftly and efficiently toward their goal of Washington. Sherman's army marched from Raleigh to Richmond, a distance of 156 miles, in five and a half days. From Richmond, the Army of the West went on to Washington in four columns, divided in such fashion as to minimize confusion en route and to maximize effective use of the road network. In so doing, the army passed through almost every battle site in northern Virginia, of which there were quite a few.[1]

During the march, Pvt. Robert Hale Strong of the 105th Illinois Infantry Regiment described the scene on the Wilderness battlefield: "We marched for hours over the battlefield. The dead had been buried where they fell, and the burial consisted only of throwing a little dirt over the dead men. Here and there an arm or leg would stick out."[2] Such gruesome sights may have been familiar to hardened veterans, but especially with the seasonally high temperatures, the charnel atmosphere must have been unpleasant. Even so, to those western soldiers for whom eastern battle sites had been only names in newspapers, the march was something of a sight-seeing tour. Even General Sherman himself rode with the four columns intermittently in order to see as much as he could.[3]

Despite the cessation of hostilities, the brutality of war manifested in yet another way during the march. In a letter written May 11, John Brobst of the 25th Wisconsin Volunteer Regiment described the marching conditions in "very warm weather": "Many men melted on the march, some fell dead, some died soon after, and some are getting well."

Private Strong offered a possible explanation for the devastating forced marches that occurred en route to Washington. According to the Illinois infantryman, it was rumored that the commanding general of the XX Corps, Maj. Gen. Joseph A. Mower, and other corps commanders had laid wagers as to which outfit would reach Washington first. Though this may have been just a rumor, in fact, the march did turn into a destructive race. "The first half of the march was not hard," wrote Private Strong, "but then the race began. The march we were on wore out the best of us. . . . I have seen men dying from exhaustion, lying in fence corners, whose deaths were simply murder. . . . When we left Richmond, some of the hardest marching began."[4]

Whether they moved by "hard" road marches or by ship from City Point to Alexandria via Chesapeake Bay, as did the 57th Massachusetts Volunteer Infantry, not all troops considered the journey "a happy occasion," even though the Bay State soldiers "all knew now that they were on the first leg of the road home."[5] Indeed, the chronicler of the 16th Maine Regiment, writing some twenty years after the war, termed the road march to Arlington the "most inhuman tramp for display" and said that the Grand Review was "the last ounce of suffering needed to break the health of . . . veterans."[6] Despite the obvious hardships and maximum efforts needed to move the troops to the Washington area, most accounts tend to minimize the discomfort and focus on the major goal of the marching: the trek toward discharge and home.

When the armies finally reached the Washington environs, a *New York Times* correspondent described the scene as "an impressive and exhilarating pageant." "South of the Potomac," a staff officer in Sheridan's cavalry noted, "the country was for miles a vast camp." Considering that there were approximately 200,000 men in the area, the logistical problems were almost overwhelming. Provision of bare essentials, water, food, sanitary facilities, forage, and even disposal of manure from the thousands of animals tried the ingenuity, skill, and zeal of the Quartermaster, Commissary, and Engineer Corps. Logistical problems notwithstanding, the food was good. According to Private Strong of the 105th Illinois, "While in Washington we drew the best of rations, soft bread instead of hard crackers, fresh meat and vegetables."[7]

Drilling and other "keep-busy" measures continued in order to prepare for the Grand Review itself. The commanding officer of the 18th New

Hampshire Infantry Regiment, Col. Thomas L. Livermore, had risen through the ranks from private and thus was an experienced and qualified soldier who had cleaned his rifle countless times. He seemed not to think too highly of one aspect of his regiment's training and drill in preparation for the Grand Review. The division to which his regiment was assigned paraded one evening in a "torch light review . . . with lighted candles in the muzzles of the rifles." If the purpose of such a drill was to keep the troops occupied, the plan almost certainly succeeded, as rifles crusted with melted wax would have been extremely difficult to clean.[8]

The Army of the Potomac and the Army of the West together represented about 20 percent of the total armed forces at the end of the war. Entirely different in their experiences, areas of campaign, style of fighting, and manner of marching on parade, these two forces were to pass in review before the president and his cabinet, the general of the armies, U. S. Grant and his staff, members of the Supreme Court and Congress, the diplomatic corps, state governors, and the general public. The differences between the two armies even extended to what Gen. Joshua L. Chamberlain termed "hostile competition, hard feelings, dislike and discord." Originally camped adjacent to each other on the south side of the Potomac River, the two armies expressed their rivalry by exchanging insults, taunts, and even blows. Sherman's troops called the men of the Army of the Potomac "feather bed soldiers," "white collars," and "soft breads," and they in turn were labeled "water fowls" and "Sherman's mules."

The enmity coupled with fatigue, short tempers, and hot, humid weather, virtually ensured that violence would erupt. Gunfire broke out on one occasion, leaving two men dead and several wounded. This incident went far beyond mere rivalry, and the commanders withdrew all ammunition but two rounds per man. Finally, Sherman's army was moved across the Potomac River in the interest of maintaining order in the encampments. So bitter were the feelings between the two armies, according to a Wisconsin volunteer, that the soldiers in Sherman's army got along better with the Confederates than they did with General Meade's men.[9]

Once order was restored, the Grand Review was finally staged. It was spectacular, impressing all who witnessed it, even the military personnel, who had seen many parades during their careers. Colonel Livermore wrote that the "sight was worth coming from the ends of the world to see . . . a novel and impressive spectacle." Lyman Daniel Ames, a chaplain of the 29th Ohio Volunteer Infantry regiment, Army of the Potomac, assigned to duty at the hospital of the 2nd Division, XX Corps, near Alexandria, Virginia, was more restrained in his comments about the first day's activities: "A fair display of military power, a creditable performance."

Most civilians, however well informed about the war and the army, had no concept of the magnitude of the forces. When told that the troops taking part in the two-day review were only a relatively small part of the entire army, they could not comprehend the total reality. Warren Wilkinson, a volunteer in the 57th Massachusetts Infantry, wrote home that it was "the greatest assemblage of soldiers and equipment the nation had ever known."[10]

Review officials erected stands on Pennsylvania Avenue in front of the White House, with the one on the south side reserved for the main reviewing party, including President Johnson, General Grant, and other important guests, such as the diplomatic corps. The stand oppposite was for the judiciary, members of Congress, and other ticket holders. In addition, two stands were reserved by private citizens to accommodate recuperating sick and wounded soldiers.[11]

Overall, the review took two days. The Army of the Potomac marched past the first day, May 23, taking six hours, and the Army of the West the second day, taking seven hours. The parade began at 9 A.M. each day.

Pvt. John F. Brobst of the 25th Wisconsin Infantry said that "Sherman's vandals did better and made a better appearance than the famed Army of the Potomac," hardly an unbiased report, since his regiment was part of the Army of the West. If Sherman's soldiers did outshine Meade's, however, it was not for any lack of trying on the part of the Army of the Potomac. The men were sized in order to present a uniform appearance; this meant that the shorter men were kept in camp as guards, according to Pvt. John Haley, one of the shorter men in the 17th Maine Infantry.[12]

After the units passed the reviewing stands, they were moved out of the area as quickly as possible in order to provide road space for the seemingly endless columns of troops yet to pass in review. In some cases, the units went back to their assembly areas, but in other instances, they moved to new sites close to the railhead so that their homeward journeys could begin. Two examples of such camp changes involved the 73rd and the 55th Ohio Volunteer Infantry Regiments. Both regiments started out from Alexandria the day of the Grand Review. The 73rd went into a new camp on the Baltimore Turnpike after it passed in review; the 55th moved into camp north of Washington, near Fort Lincoln, on the Anacostia River. As a result of these moves, each regiment was in a better position to start its homeward journey.[13]

One characteristic of the Grand Review that is seldom mentioned is the total absence of black troops, who made up nearly 10 percent of the Union Army at war's end. Their absence from the festivities celebrating the victorious conclusion of the war appears to have been deliberately planned. An article in the *New York Times* a few days after the review denied that the exclusion was an attempt "to spare the sensitive feelings of the rebels, which might have been wounded" by inclusion of black troops. African-American soldiers were no more excluded, the article contended, than were white troops who were not present to participate. Many soldiers of both races were needed to garrison critical areas in the South, Southwest, and the West. The men who were absent, especially the black troops, were praised by the *Times* for their contribution to the war effort and for their devotion to their country. The inclusion of African-American troops in the review would have been appropriate, since they made such a forceful contribution to winning the war.[14]

On the Confederate side, it is difficult to imagine any sort of review or parade under the circumstances described by George Cary Eggleston, a member of Gen. "Jeb" Stuart's cavalry: "When at last the beginning of the end came, in the evacuation of Richmond and the effort to retreat, everything seemed to go to pieces at once. . . . The best troops became disorganized and hardly any command marched in a body." Eggleston, brother of nineteenth-century author Edward Eggleston, went on to say that after Appomattox there was "utter disorganization."[15]

Gen. James Longstreet described the troops of the Army of Northern Virginia in stark words: "The army . . . walked empty-handed to find their distant, blighted homes." Another of Stuart's men recalled that following the surrender, "suddenly they were free—free from starvation, free from restless nights of trying to sleep under blankets of rain and snow, free from death itself, free to go home, and free to start rebuilding for the future."[16]

The contrast between the troops that had marched off to war four years earlier and "the weary scarecrow survivors" who began to filter toward their homes from the surrender sites was dramatic. The men who had left for service amid a "waving, cheering throng" were now "gaunt, sunburnt, dirty, and ragged" and returned to find "no bands to greet them, no orations, no shouts." Many of them "had nothing but the ragged clothing on their backs." A correspondent for the *New York Tribune* wrote that he was "daily touched to the heart by seeing these poor homesick boys and exhausted men [surrendered and paroled Confederate soldiers] wandering about in threadbare uniforms, with scanty outfit of slender haversack and blanket roll hung over their shoulders, seeking the nearest route home; they have a care-worn and anxious look, a played-out manner."[17]

Despite the returning veterans' feelings of "rage, anguish at failure and defeat, bewilderment and helplessness, and uncertainty as to who they were, what were their rights or position or property," and although they had serious questions about the future, all was not completely grim.[18] In Georgia, the men of the 1st Kentucky Brigade marched into the town of Washington "in closed column, flags flying in their tatters, arms at the parade position," as the townspeople looked on. Thus for a few moments, in one small, isolated spot in the ex-Confederacy, there was a review of sorts.[19]

Another type of review was provided by the Union troops in honor of Lt. Col. John Cheves Haskell, who had been in command of the artillery of the Army of Northern Virginia. As this one-armed veteran made his way home, "the Union troops were very friendly, in fact almost oppressively so, turning out the guard constantly as I would ride by, cheering and talking to my couriers as though they were the best of friends. I never saw them together for five minutes that the Union soldiers failed to say, 'Never mind, boys, we will all get together and go down with Uncle Bob [Robert E. Lee] to lead us and drive the French out of Mexico.'"[20] Such military honors may not have been rendered on a very wide scale, but they certainly had to be heartwarming to the men who received them.

One soldier, George Henry Alderson of Summersville, near Lewisburg, West Virginia, received a different sort of welcome. He was the first Confederate soldier to return to his home in the area, shortly after the surrender at Appomattox Court House. When he arrived in Lewisburg with the dramatic news of the surrender, he was immediately jailed as a deserter. Not only does this incident reflect the difficulty of communication, but it also shows that some intense feelings on behalf of the faltering Confederacy still remained among the civilian population. Alderson's story was verified as other soldiers returned and he regained his freedom.[21]

Not a parade or a review, but an escort of sorts was provided Brig. Gen. Daniel C. Govan's brigade of Gen. Joseph E. Johnston's Army of Tennessee. Govan's troops, 998 enlisted men and 73 officers, were from Arkansas, and in connection with their return to their native state, a Union officer in the Headquarters of the Department of the Cumberland requested an escort from Rear Adm. S. P. Lee. "Govan's rebel brigade is to be sent to some point on [the] Mississippi River. To prevent treachery, had not one or two gunboats better be sent with them? There will be three transports." The next day, May 19, Admiral Lee replied that two gunboats would be sent as near as possible to Nashville in order to accompany the returning Rebels. Just what sort of treachery was anticipated is not known, but it is clear that the Union authorities provided for most eventualities that could upset the relative calm that existed following the several surrenders.[22]

The Grand Review, according to Gen. Joshua Lawrence Chamberlain, represented "an army . . . marching to its dissolution."[23] This dissolution process, demobilization, was now ready to begin for both the victors and the vanquished.

CHAPTER FIVE

Demobilization

And when he sleeps,
He does not dream of Grant or Lee or Lincoln.
He only dreams that he is back at home
With a heroic wound that does not hurt,
A Uniform that never stings with lice,
And a sword like Henry Fairfield's to show Ellen Baker.
—Stephen Vincent Benét

To learn the details of demobilization, one must go to the *Official Records,* to the voluminous correspondence, orders, circulars, instructions, letters, and even reprimands, to trace the mustering out and discharge activity as it occurred. These sources are largely available for the Union side of demobilization; they are available for the Confederates to a lesser degree, as many of their official papers were destroyed at the time of the evacuation of Richmond and its subsequent occupation by Union troops. Letters, diaries, memoirs, and unit histories are perhaps better sources to use in tracing the Confederate contribution to demobilization. Memoirs, mostly written postwar, in some instances after many years had elapsed, are the least reliable source. Unit histories, though written after the war, often have the benefit of the combined memories of several people, rather than just one.

An excerpt from a May 18, 1865, War Department letter to chief mustering officers in the loyal states provides insight into considerations of timing, scope, and selection: "All volunteer organizations of white troops in General Sherman's army and the Army of the Potomac, whose service expires prior to October 1, 1865, have been ordered mustered out." This shows that white and black soldiers were not treated equally. Note also the inconsistent manner of designating the armies, one by the name of the commanding general and the other by its official name. This letter goes on

31

to specify categories of men to be processed: "Three-year regiments mustered in July 2, 1862 and prior to October 1, 1862; three-year recruits mustered in for old regiments between the same dates; one-year recruits mustered in for old and new units, who entered service prior to October 1, 1864." From these distinctions in length of service, it is clear that both soldiers and units with greater lengths of service, whose service was due to expire by October 1, were given priority for discharge.[1]

And then the gates opened! There was a veritable flood of orders and new regulations that placed more and more men into the system, all heading for discharge and, best of all, home. Perhaps a directive included in the adjutant general's letter to the governors of the loyal states best expressed the program's overall objective: "Troops about to be discharged should go out of service promptly, should be properly cared for, and their interests fully protected."[2] It was the duty of the adjutant general's office to carry these aims into effect by executing the policy laid down by the secretary of war.

In general, the speed of the process was astonishing. When certain units of Union infantry, artillery, or cavalry were selected for discharge from particular armies, it often seemed that the ink was hardly dry on one set of orders when new orders appeared. Indeed, a constant stream of new orders accelerated the reduction of the volunteer forces. For example, a letter sent out on May 30, 1865, said, "All volunteer artillery in the armies of the Potomac, the Tennessee, and Georgia are to be mustered out and discharged immediately." Within days, on June 2, another order was issued for "batteries of volunteer artillery to be reduced at once to the number absolutely required under existing circumstances by the necessities of service."

Occasionally, orders for the discharge of troops in a particular department required certain other units to remain in service for an extended time due to a particular assignment. In Maj. Gen. Joseph Hooker's Northern Department, which included Ohio and other Great Lakes states, the 88th and the 128th Ohio Volunteers were held back because they were on duty at Camp Chase and Johnson's Island, two camps for Confederate prisoners of war.[3] Odd as it may seem, the Federal forces were being discharged faster than the Confederate prisoners were being released and repatriated, so special provisions were necessary to ensure sufficient security at the prisoner-of-war facilities.

Soldiers in hospitals, recovering from wounds and diseases, were also subject to mustering out and discharge, their physical condition permitting, as were men on special duty away from their regular units. Pvt. Wilbur Fisk, a member of the 2nd Vermont Infantry Regiment, had been detailed to special duty as part of the guard force for a large base hospital of VI Corps. As the patients' health improved, the men were moved into the demobilization system, while the guards remained behind. Fisk wrote:

> We are getting dreadfully out of patience at the delay that keeps us here doing nothing. It is impossible for Uncle Sam to discharge everybody at once, and we must wait our turn, but we are decidedly opposed to waiting any longer than that. All are anxious to be discharged at the earliest possible moment.

He went on to say, "We must be patient, the Government cannot do everything at once. Some troops must be kept, and somebody must be those troops." Fisk's practical wisdom, so well expressed, must nevertheless have been difficult to accept. The letter was written June 4, 1865; finally he rejoined his outfit, which left Virginia on July 16 and arrived at Burlington, Vermont, on July 19. July 25 was the date of the final step in the process— payday. Fisk's patience ultimately brought him home.[4]

Underlying the torrent of orders and telegrams, there was always a note of urgency. On May 18, a week prior to the Grand Review, the adjutant general sent a telegram to General Meade and to the commanding generals of the Armies of the Tennessee and of Georgia, all other armies, and military departments, except the Departments of the East, the Pacific, New Mexico, and the Northern Department. Its instruction read, "Muster-out rolls should be ready in the shortest time possible." Extra clerks and additional space were to be assigned in order to facilitate the process. Army commanders were directed to use hospital and wall tents to provide the space necessary for the clerical work to be completed.[5]

The dates on the various orders reveal clearly that demobilization required sustained efforts. Undoubtedly, the midnight oil burned in the office of the adjutant general night after night. And so the process continued, with orders for regiments to "be immediately mustered out and discharged."[6] At times it must have seemed that there was no end in sight, for hundreds of thousands of volunteer soldiers were involved.

Moreover, there were vast geographical areas for which the army was concerned and responsible. Not only were its major responsibilities varied, including the Mexican frontier and the West, in addition to the occupied Confederacy, but movements of troops were complicated by the great distances within areas. After the War Department had nearly exhausted the supply of still-serving volunteer units, the orders became all-inclusive, as if some units might have been overlooked. On July 7, 1865, telegrams were sent to the commanding generals of the Army of the Tennessee and the Army of the Potomac, now styled the Provisional Corps, ordering them to disband the Tennessee command completely and to muster out all remaining volunteer regiments in the Provisional Corps.[7] One way or another, the two armies were to be stripped of their volunteer units and personnel.

The Quartermaster General's Department was responsible for planning, coordinating, assembling, and directing maximum utilization of the country's transportation resources. These resources consisted of the civilian railroad network; inland water transportation, both river and lake; and ocean transport. In addition, in some limited areas, military rail lines were still in operation. These means necessarily included what was available in the Confederacy, as large numbers of troops in the South had to be transported to their homes in the North or West, and Confederates were returning to their homes too. Durring much of the discharge process, there was also a significant volume of traffic going in the opposite direction, as thousands of freed Rebel prisoners, refugees, and ex-slaves returned to the South, using ocean transports and some railroads.[8]

With the large number of men to be transported and the constant pressures from all sides for speed, the undertaking presented problems of formidable proportions. Yet the steps taken by the Quartermaster General's Transportation Branch in solving those problems were nothing less than ingenious.

The field rendezvous points designated by the War Department for mustering out troops were well chosen. Consideration was given to proximity of sites to the troops as well as to the available transportation facilities, in the interest of facilitating movement of volunteers from the field to state rendezvous points and from these to the soldiers' homes. A complete list of field rendezvous points by army department or military division is included in appendix A; the state rendezvous points are listed in appendix B.

The entire demobilization program thus went into action: completion of required paperwork, initial mustering out at relatively close field rendezvous points, movement by a combination of means to state rendezvous points, final payoff, and the official discharge. It is noteworthy that the program proceeded at a rapid pace. Between the first of May and mid-November 1865, 801,000 officers and men were mustered out and discharged. The bulk of the processing occurred between May 1 and August 7, when 641,000 men went through the pipeline. Sherman's Army of the West and Meade's Army of the Potomac were the first units to complete the mustering out of volunteers. The last regiment of the Army of the Potomac started for home on July 19, and on August 1, the last regiment of the Army of the West was mustered out. These two armies accounted for 279,000 of the total processed.[9]

The Union troops ultimately received their back pay, although generally not until the very last minute of their service time. Even though the paymasters were well in arrears in paying the troops, they men did finally receive the money that was due them. Paper money, legal tender notes, or "greenbacks," had been authorized in the North in 1862. Despite the slow acceptance of this new style of currency on the part of the people, the notes were legal tender and did circulate. While the ratio of the greenbacks to specie varied along with the fortunes of war, at war's end payment of $1.46 in paper money was necessary to buy a dollar's worth of gold.

The overall Confederate financial picture was not encouraging, and its negative effect on military pay was marked. With the idea that they were becoming a new nation, the Confederate authorities had begun to circulate money that had very dubious backing at best. Inflation took hold, thanks to the monetary policy or, perhaps more accurately, the lack of one, and practically wiped out the value of the currency in circulation. At the end of the war, in order to buy a dollar's worth of gold, $60 to $70 of Confederate money was needed.[10]

Confederate soldiers had long gone without any pay, thus adding to the hardships suffered by their families. Some money was available in the last few minutes of the Confederacy's existence, but it was hardly more than a token amount. Each man present at the surrender in North Carolina by General Johnston received a pro rata share of the available funds. Gen. Johnson Hagood described the distribution of funds to the men in his brigade, each of whom received $1.25. Maj. Gen. Matthew C. Butler said his men received $1.75. Still at the same surrender, troops of Maj. Gen. Joseph B. Kershaw were said to have been given $1.29 each, while the 12th Louisiana Infantry had to settle for $1.15 per man. Troops in the artillery apparently did not rate a comparable amount, as the Chatham Artillery unit each received $1 in silver.[11]

Despite all the confusion and turmoil of the last hours of the Confederacy, it appears that proximity to the highest echelon of government paid rather handsomely. A member of Pres. Jefferson Davis's escort, John Will Dyer, was present when the treasury fund was distributed to the officers and men of the escort, each of whom received $26.40 in gold and silver.[12]

Before looking at the Confederate version of demobilization, it would be good to examine just what it was that the returning Confederate veteran was going to find at the end of his demobilization experience. A New Jersey–born Confederate major general, Samuel G. French, describes the Confederacy at war's end:

> A once beautiful country, almost desolate and silent; the busy hum of industry had ceased; the daily smoke of burning buildings, the marching of armies, and the dull sound of distant cannon terminated; railroads had been destroyed, bridges were burned, many wagon roads were impassable; agriculture had nearly ceased, draft animals had been taken for war purposes; the flower of the South . . . had fallen . . . in the fight; the noble women were almost paralyzed in mind . . . ; four million slaves sat idle . . . ; provisions were scarce, and the whole scene was a picture of war's desolation and misery.[13]

If the paroled Confederate could have made his way to Richmond, he might have been surprised at what he found. A letter from Dr. James Madison Brannock, a paroled surgeon of the 5th Tennessee Regiment, to his wife in Jackson, Tennessee, on May 7, 1865, was included in a postwar issue of the *Richmond News Leader,* in an article entitled "Post-War Excitement." The picture drawn by Doctor Brannock is far different from the scene described by General French:

> Richmond is all bustle and excitement. Trade of every kind is going ahead again as it was before the war. The theaters and other places of amusement are under full headway, and you can get without difficulty almost every luxury in the world.[14]

From his description of life in Richmond a bare month after the demise of the Confederacy, well before some of the later surrenders, it would appear that in many respects the South recovered rather quickly.

For the Confederate veterans, although there was no structure to the process, there were many similarities in their approaches to the problems of transportation, food en route, funds, and varying reactions on the part of the civilian population. Generally speaking, the Confederates had little or no money of any kind; they were weary from marching and fighting and had been poorly nourished by inadequate rations; and like returning veterans of all wars, they were eager to complete their journeys in order to rejoin their families and friends. However, while most men were no doubt happy to be homeward bound, one unnamed private noted in his pocket diary that "it required more nerve to go home . . . than to count any danger or endure any sacrifice."[15]

The pace of the homeward journey depended on the mode of transportation used. All too frequently, it was the old-fashioned foot march, and then the pace was a slow one. One veteran wrote of the 3rd Mississippi Infantry, "The weary scarecrow survivors slowly made their way homeward over back country roads from the Carolinas and Alabama."[16]

Communication systems, painfully slow by today's standards, were even more so in the last days of the conflict. The area in and around Athens, Georgia, had manned and equipped the Troup Artillery. The local citizens' first intimation of the Confederate defeat came as a surprise: "Suddenly, without warning, soldiers thought to be near Petersburg began to appear in town. Gaunt, sunburnt, dirty, and ragged, they came by train, by wagon, on horseback and on foot." And so the men of the Troup Artillery returned home.[17] It is difficult even to look at such an informal disorganized reality as demobilization.

The paroled veterans returning to Tennessee faced a unique problem that resulted from the split loyalties of the population of the state, especially in the eastern portion. Soldiers of Tennessee units surrendered near Greensboro, North Carolina, under Gen. Joseph E. Johnston, were generally from the central and western portions of Tennessee and thus had to travel through the pro-Union eastern part of the state in order to reach home. Their reception by the local population was far from warm, running the gauntlet from threats of revenge to outright challenges and armed opposition. Men from the same units tended to band together on the long march home, and since many soldiers still had their horses and other animals, and approximately 20 percent of them were permitted by Union authorities at the surrender sites to retain rifles for protection and hunting along the march, many civilians reacted adversely to what they perceived as active and equipped Confederate military units. Since the local people, loyal to the Union, considered these groups of armed Confederates to be potentially dangerous, they pressured the local military authorities to force the Confederates to give up their weapons and animals.

Thus, at Strawberry Plains, northeast of Knoxville; at Sweetwater, between Knoxville and Chattanooga; and at Chattanooga itself, the veterans boarded freight trains only after they had been stripped of all military equipage. At Strawberry Plains, some of the soldiers threw their weapons into the Holston River as an alternative to turning them in to the Union troops. Others bypassed the Union troops at Sweetwater by swimming the Tennessee River and thus avoiding the checkpoints. The men may have been defeated, but they had not lost their initiative.[18]

CHAPTER SIX

Demobilization and the Railroads

I see trains of cars swiftly speeding along railroad tracks
drawn by the locomotives,
I see the stores, depots, of Boston, Baltimore, Charleston,
New Orleans.

—Walt Whitman

Central to the demobilizations of both the Northern and Southern veterans was the railroad system, a term that might most accurately be restricted to the North and those portions of the occupied South in which the railroads were maintained by the Union armies. Throughout the rest of the South, only remnants of a system still existed.

The greatest number of returning Union veterans were transported by railroad. For the returning Union soldiers, no matter how remote the location of the military unit or how great the distance to the state rendezvous point, the longest portion of the journey home was made by rail. Be it slow or fast—and some trains were excruciatingly slow—by boxcar, coal car, flatcar, or passenger coach, with or without food and water, rail movement of troops was an integral part of demobilization. Confederate veterans, on the other hand, availed themselves of any means of conveyance they could find. In the few areas where the limited facilities were still functioning in the South, railroad transportation was preferred primarily because of its relative speed. Otherwise the men turned to slower modes such as steamboat or wagon, and if these were not available, they marched on foot.

At the time of the Civil War, American railroads were local in nature; they were feeders for specific population centers rather than direct connections between cities. Generally, these railroads facilitated the movement of specific goods or products from their sources to ports along the coast. In the South, therefore, cotton, which ruled so much of the area's activities, determined the railroad routes. Likewise, tobacco, rice, and sugar all had their well-defined routes, which translated into railroad lines. At the outbreak of the war, the principal trunk lines in the South were the steamboat lines, and most of these were Northern owned. Historically, most of the funding for development of railroads in the South had come from the North and from Europe. Even in the North, commerce was one of the major determining factors in the location of the railroads, but in addition, the railroads indirectly linked major cities, as well as inland waterways and the coastal ports. It took the war to expand the concept of American railroads as the framework of a national transportation system.[1]

American railroads at this time had a variety of gauges. This was especially so in the South, where in 1861 there were 113 independent railroads using at least three different gauges: 4' 8$^1/_2$", 5', and 5' 6". In the North, gauge differences were not as much of a problem, as railroad lines were fast becoming independent systems and thus extended longer distances than in the South. Since a national railroad system had not yet been envisioned, the potpourri of gauges made little difference. It was the requirements of war that finally led to standardization of gauge at 4' 8$^1/_2$", although this goal was not reached until 1886, when, as was said at the time, "the South [finally] joined the Union."[2]

From the viewpoint of the Union, the Civil War occurred at a peak moment in the development of railroads in this country. Had the war broken out ten years earlier, the country's railroads, both North and South, would not have been able to handle the wartime increases in the transportation of men, materiel, and foodstuffs. In 1840, there were but 2,800 miles of railroad track; at the end of that decade, this had increased to 9,000 miles; by 1860 the mileage was more than three times that. These 30,000 miles of railroad track, roughly one-third in the South and two-thirds in the North, ultimately became the framework of a national network. The explosion of railroad construction during 1850 to 1860, despite the adverse effects of the depression and panic of 1857, in part related to what was considered the "overbuilding of railroads," was ultimately crucial to the war and its outcome, affecting both the North and the South in varying degrees and ways.[3] The railroads played an important role in the mobilization and operational phases of the war and were a significant element in demobilization.

In the North, there were four major railroad lines or systems that carried traffic from the East Coast to the Midwest. Three of these four lines were wholly in the North: the Pennsylvania, the Erie, and the New York Central, as they were later called. These three main lines suffered no war-related destruction at the hands of the Confederates. The fourth line, the Baltimore and Ohio, began and ended in the North, but three-quarters of the railroad lay in Virginia, and the entire system was within slaveholding territory. The B & O, therefore, though strictly speaking a Northern railroad, had so much of its activity in seceded Virginia that it was often treated as a hostile facility by the Union. Even so, this railroad was especially important to the Union war effort, particularly the U.S. Navy. The B & O was one of the prime haulers of high-grade steam coal, necessary as fuel for the ships and thus important to the blockade of the Southern ports and to naval activities in general. Thus Confederate strategists made this railroad the target of many raids, which temporarily interrupted traffic.

Throughout the war, the B & O developed an amazing ability to rebound, repair, replace, and restore damaged facilities. At times, it seemed that the Union could rebuild bridges faster than the Confederates could destroy them. This ability greatly diminished the negative effect the men in gray were trying to create.

Because of the variety of gauges, the problem of through service was seriously complicated in the South. There was only one connection of each of at least three gauges between Virginia and the rest of the Confederacy.[4] Two major railroad routes in the South connected Richmond and the western areas of the Confederacy, Mississippi and Louisiana, but only one was completely operational. The first route ran in a northeasterly direction, from Memphis, Tennnessee, through Corinth, Mississippi, on to Chattanooga, Tennessee, then to Bristol, Virginia, and thus on to Richmond. A count of the different railroads involved in this route reveals that seven lines were necessary. The other route, unfinished as it was, consisted of eleven lines and ran a more southerly path, from Vicksburg, Mississippi, to Meridian, Mississippi, then on to Montgomery, Alabama, to Atlanta then Augusta, Georgia, on to Wilmington, North Carolina, and north to Petersburg and Richmond. There were crucial, time-consuming gaps in this route; construction was under way in some spots, and in others, steamboats supplemented the track deficiency.

Just prior to the war, in 1860, in the East and in what later came to be known as the Midwest, excluding the Mississippi River Valley, there were no through rail lines connecting the North and the South. The only way such passage could be achieved was by steamboat on the Ohio River or a ferry across the Potomac River between Washington and Alexandria,

Virginia. Within the first year of the war, however, the Union had constructed the Long Bridge across the Potomac River.[5]

Though Washington was the capital of what was now a large, vigorously expanding nation, it was one of the most isolated points for rail service in the East. There was only one connection, and that a single track for most of the war, between the capital and the main line of the Baltimore and Ohio Railroad. The Washington Branch, as it was known, ran from Relay House, on the main line, some nine miles west and a bit south of Baltimore, to the capital; there it stopped, as there was no rail connection on into Virginia. Confederate destruction of the portions of the main line of the B & O at various times prevented expansion of this branch to double track until December 1864. It seemed that as the company accumulated sufficient ties and track for the proposed expansion, the Confederates raided and destroyed such extensive sections of the main line that the materials had to be diverted to the restoration of the main line.

There was another interchange on the same branch line, however. At Annapolis Junction, the Annapolis and Elk Ridge Railroad came into the Washington Branch, thus connecting Washington and Annapolis. This apparently modest and inconspicuous, eighteen-mile-long railroad really saved the day when, early in the war, Confederate sympathizers in and around Baltimore destroyed bridges and portions of track on the B & O, following the famous mob action involving the 6th Massachusetts Infantry Regiment. The line from Annapolis permitted troops and materiel to be shipped by train to the mouth of the Susquehanna River, thence by boat and barge on the Chesapeake Bay to Annapolis, and by train to Washington via the interchange at Annapolis Junction. Not only did this detour enable rail transportation to continue, albeit in lesser amounts and with greater delay, but it was the beginning of what turned out to be a most valuable and extensive wartime innovation, the United States Military Railroad System.[6] This railroad system performed yeoman service during the conflict, and its contribution to the demobilization of troops was also significant.

The Confederate capital of Richmond was in a somewhat better position regarding railroads. Five different lines came into Richmond, but none of these lines connected. The result was that all through shipments, be they personnel, horses, armament, ammunition, foodstuffs, or other war materiel, had to be unloaded, moved through the streets by cart and wagon, and then reloaded on the ongoing trains. In time, temporary tracks were laid on the streets in order to facilitate through shipments, and teams of horses and mules hauled the cars. The steep slopes and hills in Richmond taxed the ingenuity of the local engineering staff. Obviously, such a makeshift arrangement could not even begin to handle efficiently the volume of traffic that was involved.

In the Mississippi River Valley and its environs, rail travel between the North and South was easier than in the East. Lines ran from Mobile, Alabama, north into Kentucky and to the Ohio River, as well as from New Orleans to Grenada, Mississippi, and then on to Memphis.

In addition to the confusion, delay, and potential problems of scheduling as a result of several relatively short lines operating independently between New York City and Washington, there was the need for ferry service at points on the Hudson, Delaware, and Susquehanna Rivers. Ferries were a necessary part of the through service. One improvement occurred in November 1861, when car ferries were placed into operation at the Susquehanna River, eliminating the need to change cars. Little by little, improvements were made that benefited not only the passenger traffic, but also the transportation of goods and materials.

Along these same lines, especially in the North, significant improvements were made during the war in the track system and in the rolling equipment. Trains were run on better and tighter schedules, in large measure due to telegraph dispatching. Single track was expanded to double in many areas, additional sidings were constructed, bridges were ultimately built over the Susquehanna and Delaware Rivers, and the design of the rails themselves was improved. In addition, specialized rolling equipment was designed and put into operation for the transportation of iron ore, oil, and grain. Railway post office cars, hospital cars and trains, and armored cars also entered into use during the war.[7] Most technological improvements occurred in the North, although the South managed to stay abreast of change despite the perennial shortages of material.

The Southern outlook for efficient operation of its existing railroads was rather grim at the beginning of the war and remained so throughout the conflict. Southern railroads operated with rolling stock that became progressively more battered; the depots were crammed with loaded freight cars that were left standing while troops were desperately in need of food and munitions. Fuel, cordwood throughout most of the war in both the North and the South, became scarce because of a lack of labor to cut the wood and because of pilfering of fuel stocks by soldiers in need of firewood. Likewise, wood for crossties became increasingly difficult to obtain.

In general, the South did not have sufficient resources to maintain its prewar level of business, much less the wherewithal to accommodate wartime increases in demand. One significant gap in the South's railroad operations was the perennial lack of a universal system of freight car interchange. Railroads jealously protected their own stock and were loath to release it to other lines. Replacement of worn rolling stock was practically impossible. In Texas, one railroad had a single engine; when this engine was beyond any useful repair, the line was forced to resort to oxen. As a result, a fifty-mile journey took about three days.[8]

The wartime technological advances in equipment were more than matched by the development of tactical and strategic uses of the railroads in the war. Early in the war, two men who in subsequent months became high-ranking generals showed great foresight in their assessment of railroads from a military viewpoint. On April 29, 1861, with the war just hours old, Thomas J. Jackson telegraphed Gov. John Letcher of Virginia: "Recommend construction of a railroad from Strasburg to Winchester for strategic purposes." Jackson had just completed the roundabout route from central Virginia to Harpers Ferry and became aware of the drastic need for a continuous line down the Shenandoah Valley. His recommendation reveals an early appreciation of railroads in the forthcoming war.[9]

In May to June 1861, in western Virginia, Gen. George B. McClellan "became the first field commander to attempt the use of a railroad in combat maneuver."[10] He expressed the importance of railroads in warfare in an August 4, 1861, memorandum to President Abraham Lincoln:

> It cannot be ignored that the construction of railroads has introduced a new and very important element into war, by the great facilities thus given for concentrating at particular positions large masses of troops from remote sections, and by creating new strategic points and lines of operations. . . . We must endeavor to seize places on the railways in the rear of the enemy's points of concentration. . . . By seizing and repairing the railroads as we advance the difficulties of transportation will be materially diminished.[11]

One rather striking difference between the Northern and Southern rail systems, one that remains largely unexplored and unanalyzed, is the disparity between the North and the South in the number of trained, experienced railroad personnel available at the highest governmental and military

Thomas A. Scott,
assistant secretary of war,
Pennsylvania Railroad executive

levels. Here the North came out well ahead of the South. The list of Union generals and other personnel who had had experience of various types involving railroads, their planning, construction, and operation is impressive. McClellan himself had been the chief engineer of the Illinois Central Railroad and subsequently president of the Ohio and Mississippi. For a short time in 1861, Nathaniel Banks had been president of the Illinois Central, which had also employed Ambrose E. Burnside for a time. Simon Cameron, Lincoln's first secretary of war, had a controlling interest in the Northern Central Railroad, and his son was a vice president. This association was such that the line was known as "Cameron's road."[12] Thomas A. Scott was a vice president of the Pennsylvania Railroad before becoming an assistant secretary of war in charge of coordinating connections and schedules. P. H. Watson, also an assistant secretary of war, had been a railroad executive, as had Maj. Gen. John A. Dix, who, in the 1850s, had been president of two different railroads. Maj. Gen. Grenville M. Dodge had pursued a career that involved much hands-on work in railroad engineering and surveying in Illinois, Iowa, and Nebraska. And Abraham Lincoln and Edwin M. Stanton had both been railroad lawyers.

In the South, there were several Northern-born railroad operating personnel. The superintendents of three of the major Virginia railroads, the

Daniel C. McCallum, U.S.A.,
director of military railroads,
breveted major general towards
end of war

South Side Railroad, the Virginia Central, and the Richmond, Fredericks-burg, and Potomac Railroad, all came from the North. Samuel Ruth, the superintendent of the Richmond, Fredericksburg, and Potomac Railroad in the Confederacy, was not only a native of Pennsylvania, but he was, in fact, a Union spy. How much he contributed to the success of the Union war effort is unknown, but it was sufficient for the Confederates to arrest him as hostilities were ending.[13]

Daniel C. McCallum, of Rochester, New York, was general superin-tendent of the New York and Erie Railroad when he accepted an appoint-ment as military director and superintendent of railroads in the United States, with sweeping authority over the entire Northern railroad network. Initially, his control only affected the eastern theater of operations, but by war's end, it included the western theater also. His primary function was that of liaison between the government and the railroads, and between the railroads and the manufacturers of railroad engines and rolling stock. Such a centralization of authority was a significant advantage for the North.[14]

Perhaps the most important Union railroad-experienced man, who accomplished unbelievable feats of engineering, repairs, and operations, was Herman Haupt. His contribution was immeasurable; the list of his accom-plishments is lengthy. One outstanding example should provide the measure

Brig. Gen. Herman Haupt, U.S.A.,
railroad engineering genius

of the man. In the Gettysburg Campaign, Haupt was able, in the short space of four days, to repair broken lines, extend existing facilities, and coordinate trains to the point of supplying General Meade's army with well beyond the daily requirements. General Lee's army, during this same period, was functioning without sufficient rations, fodder, or ammunition. This situation had existed well before the campaign began; the matter of supplies of food and fodder was an objective in planning the campaign. Yet for some four months prior to Gettysburg, the Confederate supply and rail system had been unable to move even minimum requirements of supplies. Thus Haupt did in four days what the Confederacy could not do in four months.

Railroad experience among Confederate generals and civilian leaders was in much shorter supply. The rather meager list includes William Mahone, Isaac Trimble, and Robert Rodes, each of whom ultimately became a major general. Mahone had been the engineering officer of several Virginia railroads and president and superintendent of the Norfolk and Petersburg Railroad. Trimble had helped develop Eastern and Southern railroads and had served as an engineer during the construction of these railroads. Later he was a railroad executive in Baltimore. Rodes had worked for several Southern railroads as a civil engineer. The one Confederate who seemed to have the most railroad experience was Joseph E. Johnston.[15]

Johnston's railroad experience prior to the war was quite extensive. He had displayed an interest in railroads in the 1850s, while stationed in Texas. He was interested in planning their routes; in constructing roadbeds, tracks, and trestles; and especially in the bridging of streams and gullies. Jeffrey N. Lash's *Destroyer of the Iron Horse: General Joseph E. Johnston and Confederate Rail Transport, 1861–1865,* gives insight into the rather casual, sometimes almost criminally incompetent, manner of using or misusing the Southern railroads on the part of several Confederate commanders, including Johnston.

> Thus, before the Civil War Johnston had received a thorough grounding in railroad technology, gained an appreciation of the great financial value of railway property, and acquired some experience as a railroad surveyor. Nevertheless, his apparent indifference to and lack of understanding of the technical improvements subsequently introduced in railroad construction and the increasing costs of railroad equipment, his remarkable forgetfulness with advancing years, and his severely limited imagination about the potential military value of the railroad left him largely unprepared to use the railroad as an instrument of war in 1861.[16]

According to Lash, the situation never improved during the remainder of the war. Lash also accused most of the other top Confederate military figures of having failed "to use the railroad effectively." The only exceptions he made were Gen. Robert E. Lee and Lt. Gen. Leonidas Polk, whom he called "easily the Confederacy's ablest railroad general."[17] This lauding of Polk makes one wonder about the entire thesis of the book, as Polk's military abilities were "judged to be hardly commensurate with his rank." On one occasion, he was severely censured by Gen. Braxton Bragg for "dilatory tactics at Chickamauga."[18] Both Bragg and Polk were Jefferson Davis's close friends and associates, and it is unusual to find Davis's friends at odds with one another.

In November 1862, the Confederate government offered the position of railroad superintendent for the Confederacy to New Hampshire native William M. Wadley, an ex-blacksmith who was extremely tall and powerfully built. He entered military service as a colonel, but as later events proved, he never received confirmation in the rank; in fact, the Confederate Congress rejected him. Wadley was probably the most experienced railroad man in the South, having functioned in ranking positions of several railroads. As an assistant, he chose Frederick W. Sims, who later succeeded Wadley in the post. Wadley, efficient and loyal as he was, was nonetheless caught up in jurisdictional squabbles between the Office of Adjutant General and the quartermaster general. When centralized control of the Confederate railroads became law on May 1, 1863, the quartermaster general assumed direction, and Wadley was relieved of his duties as coordinator.[19]

Though the position of superintendent of railroad transportation in the Confederacy may seem to imply firm, centralized control of all railroad capacity and facilities, such was not the case. The only pressures the government could bring to bear on the railroads were recommendation, suggestion, and request; the position, essentially an empty title, did not permit any compulsion. The policy of states' rights carried over into the field of transportation, and no effective centralized governmental authority was ever established. This situation was allowed to exist throughout almost all of the conflict, despite Gen. Robert E. Lee's recommendation in March 1862 that it was "absolutely essential that the movements of railroad trains should be under one undivided control."[20]

Just as the preponderance of experience among the Union personnel far outweighed that of the Confederates, a great gap also existed between the approaches to railroading by the two governments. It was not until the last few months of the war that the Confederate legislature passed a bill giving the president authority to take over control of the property and operations of the railroads. By this late date, February 1865, there were but three railroads left in operation, and their potential was indeed feeble. In contrast, the United States Congress had enacted a similar law early in 1862.[21]

Historically, Northern firms had constructed almost all engines for the Southern railroads; that source ceased with the firing on Fort Sumter. Southern rolling stock became less and less effective as the war progressed. New cars were built in limited quantities, but no new engines were placed in service. Southern railroads attempted to use very shallow roadbeds for heavy trains; in some instances, the roadbeds did not even exist, as the rails were merely laid on the ground surface. Because all production and processing of heavy metals was allocated to armaments, "not a single bar of railroad iron [was] rolled in the Confederacy since the war [began]," wrote Lt. Col. Frederick W. Sims, superintendent of railroad transportation, to Secretary of War John C. Breckinridge on February 16, 1865.[22] This, together with the lack of construction of any new engines, meant that some rail lines were forced to sacrifice their facilities in order to keep other, more important lines in operation. If this bitterly contested policy had continued indefinitely, the South would have totally consumed its own railroads. Actually, several of the railroad shops had the capacity to produce new locomotives and, in fact, had done so in the decade prior to the war. These shops had assembled already cast items that had been shipped in from other areas of the country or from Europe. It was not possible for these relatively small shops to produce the castings of the various parts needed for new engines. Some railroad track was imported, and some quantities were obtained by conquest, but these two sources hardly made a dent in the overall requirements of the Southern transportation system.

One author has stated that the railroads in the South between 1850 and 1890 were "poor in capital, in managerial talents, in the type traffic that permitted railroads in the North to prosper, in genius for the combination and subordination of individual egos demanded by a logical, rational system."[23] This broad statement provides much of the explanation for the superiority of the Northern railroads during the war and in subsequent years.

During the war, both armies had rather extensive experience in moving brigades and even divisions of troops over relatively long distances, but in the fall of 1863, two troop movements occurred—one Union, the other Confederate—that far exceeded all previous transfers in numbers of men moved, speed of the movements, and distances traveled. These two troop transfers highlight the coming of age of railroads in the country. Who knows when the nation's railroads would have achieved a similar point had there not been the exigencies of war as a spur.

One of the most involved railroad troop movements of the Civil War, and possibly for any war up to that time, was undertaken in September 1863, when upward of 20,000 men, together with thousands of horses and related equipment, moved to the support of the Union forces in the Chickamauga, Tennessee, area. The XI and XII Corps traveled from the Army of the Potomac, utilizing seven railroads, as well as ferries, river steamers, and the traditional road march. Another 20,000 soldiers arrived in the same area, also by rail, from Maj. Gen. W. T. Sherman's army in Mississippi. Undertaken and completed in complete secrecy, the entire strategy "became a model for military planners for decades to come."[24] The experience, problems, and logistical fine-tuning involved in executing these two Union troop operations were extremely valuable when the time came to implement the demobilization program, which relied so heavily on rail transportation for its completion.

Although the almost total destruction of the railroads in the South negated much of the postwar value of the Confederate wartime railroad experiences, the Confederacy still benefited from its extensive movement of troops. In the summer of 1862, well before the Union troop transfer, the Army of the Mississippi transferred from Tupelo, Mississippi, to Chattanooga, Tennessee. At least 25,000 men moved by rail, using six different rail lines, while all the horse-drawn elements of the army moved overland. The major move, however, occurred in September 1863, when Gen. James Longstreet moved his First Corps, some 12,000 soldiers, from northern Virginia to Chickamauga. This transfer was seriously complicated by breaks in rail lines—so much so that the entire move used sixteen separate railroads.[25] These two 1863 movements of troops, possible only because of the available railroad capabilities, stand out as definite patterns for postwar demobilization troop transfers.

By the end of the war in Virginia in early April 1865, the Northern railroads were far stronger than at the war's beginning in 1861. In the South, on the other hand, except for those taken over and rehabilitated by the Union forces, the railroads were essentially a mass of wreckage and ruin.[26] This scenario is what faced those coordinating the Union demobilization as well as the homeward-bound Confederate soldiers.

Effective use of the existing rail systems was extremely important in the demobilization procedure. Union troops in Washington destined for the southern parts of the middle states, the Western states, and Tennessee and Kentucky loaded on railroad cars in Washington and traveled north toward Baltimore to Relay House. From here they moved via the Baltimore and Ohio main line to Parkersburg, West Virginia, or Bellaire, Ohio. At this point, they detrained and embarked on river steamers bound for Cincinnati, Louisville, the camps in southern Ohio and Indiana, and St. Louis.

Federal units heading for the Northern states, however, marched to Baltimore, roughly forty miles, in order to avoid congestion at Relay House. The Washington Branch, even though double-tracked by this time, just could not handle the extra volume. Once at Baltimore, the troops proceeded either to Philadelphia via the Philadelphia, Wilmington, and Baltimore Railroad, and on to New York City, or to Harrisburg via the Northern Railroad, connecting with the Pennsylvania Railroad. If the soldiers were destined for the northern parts of Ohio, Indiana, or Illinois, they went from Harrisburg to Pittsburgh, some going on to Chicago by rail, and others going to Cleveland to board lake steamers for travel to various lake ports that would put them close to their state rendezvous points.

Some soldiers going to New England went by rail to Harrisburg, then northward via Elmira, New York, and on to their destinations. Others heading in the same direction went by rail from Baltimore to Philadelphia, then to New York City and on to New England. For this last leg of the journey, they took steamships on Long Island Sound or on the open sea to ports along the New England coast.[27] Use of all of these routes involved an enormous amount of coordination and planning to accomplish the troop movements.

The quartermaster general had envisioned the physical aspects of such large and lengthy troop movements. On May 19, 1865, he wrote to the director of the military railroads, the officer who coordinated travel on private railroads, to take "every possible precaution to insure the safety and comfort of the men." The cars were "to be carefully fitted up and provided with water and other necessary conveniences." In addition to appropriate meal stops, the trains were also to halt "at proper points to enable the soldiers to attend to the calls of nature." Altogether, the entire troop movement was to take place "with the least inconvenience, fatigue, suffering and danger."[28]

Even so, according to an item in the *New York Times,* sufficient potable water on troop trains was a problem that constantly plagued both the government and railroad officials, to say nothing of the troops themselves. Quartermaster General Montgomery C. Meigs clipped this newspaper article and sent it to the editor, along with extracts from his May 19, 1865, directive quoted above and a letter saying that "possibly if [the order is] published in your paper, it would enable the officers of the troops to know their rights, and report any neglect of the railroad officials." The original news account reported that the soldiers "are often nearly famished, and actually drink the muddy water along the road when the cars stop." As the official correspondence shows, proper water supplies were required; how well railroad personnel followed the directives was a different matter.[29]

The combinations of road marches, train travel, river ferries, lake or ocean steamers, and then train yet again must have been grueling, but no doubt the men were willing to put up with the inconveniences and discomfort. Their war experiences had been far worse. Now they were on their way home.

CHAPTER SEVEN

Union Demobilization: The Reality

I saw the interminable corps, I saw the processions of armies,
I saw them approaching, defiling by with divisions,
Streaming northward, their work done, camping awhile in
  clusters of mighty camps.

—Walt Whitman

The majority of men enlisted during the war were in volunteer units, and thus volunteer soldiers were the focus of the demobilization program. In some instances, the system appears to have worked quite well. The 15th New Jersey Infantry Regiment left Washington by train on June 23, 1865, for Trenton, arriving the next day. After a reception of speeches, a meal, and a review, the regiment went into camp just east of Trenton. The regimental historian concluded his account tersely: "The following week we were paid off, and disbanded." Similarly, Battery B, 1st New Jersey Artillery departed from the nation's capital June 2 for Trenton, "where the muster out and pay rolls were made out." Two weeks later, on June 16, the battery was mustered out.[1]

Men of two other New Jersey units, the 12th and 13th New Jersey Volunteer Infantry Regiments, experienced a rather rapid processing through the demobilization pipeline. The 12th was at Appomattox, and the 13th was in North Carolina at the time of Johnston's surrender to Sherman. Both units participated in the Grand Review and then headed for New Jersey. The 12th Regiment arrived in Trenton on June 12, and the soldiers were guests of the governor at a dinner the next evening. This regiment was paid off and discharged June 17. The 13th Regiment departed from their camp northwest of Washington on June 9, en route to Newark. The troops

were paid and discharged on June 10, and they took part in a formal parade
and review in Newark on June 15. In approximately sixty days, both regiments had been moved from their positions at the surrender sites to the
Washington area, had taken part in the Grand Review, and then had proceeded to their home areas by the most direct and rapid means available.
For these two units, the demobilization process worked well.[2]

The Irish Brigade, one of the most renowned brigades in the Army of
the Potomac, took part in the Grand Review and then entered the demobilization process with a smoothness that matched its military prowess. Early
in July 1865, the brigade returned to New York City, as three of its original regiments—the 69th, the 63rd, and the 88th New York Volunteers—
hailed from the area. The three regiments participated in the local Fourth
of July celebration and then were mustered out.[3] The process apparently
functioned well for units in and around Washington.

Other regiments ended the war far removed from Washington. Part of
the 18th Indiana Light Artillery, commanded by Eli Lilly, who later
founded a pharmaceutical company, was deep in Georgia at the end of the
war. By means of road marches, the unit traveled to Atlanta and then Chattanooga. There the 18th Indiana, together with all its equipment and animals, loaded on railroad cars for the trip to Nashville. At this point, the unit
turned in its horses and equipment, and the men left two weeks later, arriving June 25, 1865, in Indianapolis. Five days later, the regiment was paid off
and discharged.[4]

Farther east, Bentley Kutz, a member of the 195th Pennsylvania
Infantry Regiment, was at Summits Point, West Virginia, which is located
on the Winchester and Potomac Railroad and therefore within easy striking distance of the main line of the B & O Railroad. Kutz was only about
twenty miles from Harpers Ferry, patiently awaiting his discharge. Despite
the proximity to a main rail line, April and May went by; finally, on June
21, 1865, the unit was mustered out of service. Two days later, the regiment
was paid off. As Kutz wrote in his diary, "So that ends this book."[5] He
mentioned nothing about his trip back to Reading, Pennsylvania; apparently, it was anticlimactic to the discharge itself.

In a letter to his brother Charles, John McGowan of the Independent
Pennsylvania Battery E, Headquarters, 2nd Division, XII Corps, wrote on
April 22, 1865, from Raleigh, North Carolina, "We have another long
march before us and then for home. We will have to march from here to
some place in Maryland to be discharged and paid off." Here, rumor took

over. The latest information from some uncertain source said that the unit would be on the road for twenty-five to thirty days to cover the approximately 300 miles between Raleigh and Frederick City, Maryland. Whether the road march took place is not discussed in McGowan's letters. That a soldier could so calmly discuss the very real possibility of a month of road marching is an indication of how desperately the men wanted to go home, as well as how crowded the rail facilities were along the East Coast. The rather matter-of-fact mention of the prospective road march also reflected the physical condition and capabilities of the troops.[6]

Not every unit stationed at a distance from its home area experienced long delays. The 76th Pennsylvania Volunteer Infantry was near Raleigh, North Carolina, when Gen. Joseph E. Johnston surrendered. On May 18, 1865, the men of this unit were mustered out. They turned in their tents and other equipment and were ready to begin the trip back to the Keystone State. Simon Bennage of Company E and another soldier "were detailed to take care of . . . [the] discharge papers . . . [which were] in a large box." The papers were to accompany the troops to Harrisburg in order to accomplish the final discharges. Beginning on May 19, the trip was long and varied and not without its dangers and excitement. The returning soldiers traveled from Raleigh to Morehead City, North Carolina, by way of Smithfield, Goldsboro, Kingston, and New Bern. At Morehead City, they boarded the steamer *Ellen Knight* and, together with another boat loaded with troops, started north the next day. On the way, they ran into rough seas, and they had difficulty crossing the bar into the open sea as they left Morehead City. The accompanying boat struck an underwater obstacle and sank, with the loss of some thirty men. On May 21, they arrived at Fortress Monroe, Virginia, and went on to Baltimore. Here, they boarded a train and began the trip to Harrisburg, arriving on May 23. On May 28, 1865, Bennage wrote in his diary, "At noon I was paid and at 2 o'clock I started on my last trip home."[7] The trip from Raleigh, North Carolina, with the proper papers all prepared and ready, to Harrisburg, Pennsylvania, where the unit was finally discharged ten days after the process began, represents an efficient operation of the demobilization process.

Another Pennsylvania outfit, the 207th Pennsylvania Infantry Regiment, required a much longer period to accomplish the same procedure, and they even had an advantage of starting from a position on the South Side Railroad near Appomattox Court House. Despite the shorter distance, the time factor was considerably greater, amounting to almost two months.

Daniel Brion, a soldier in this unit, maintained a diary, with entries that were extremely brief and cryptic, sometimes just consisting of one word or a short phrase. On April 9, 1865, the day that General Lee went to Wilmer McLean's house in Appomattox to surrender to General Grant, the 207th Infantry marched to Burkesville. In camps for a few days and marching several days, they arrived at Petersburg, Virginia, on April 22. The next day, the troops moved to City Point and boarded a boat for the trip to Alexandria, which they reached on April 25. On the last day of April 1865, they mustered for pay, and for the next three weeks they were in camp, on guard duty, undergoing inspections, passing in review, washing clothing, and even fishing one day. Finally, they moved on into Washington, where they participated in the Grand Review on May 23. The last day of May found the unit in Baltimore, and they were in Harrisburg the next day. After turning in their weapons and equipment, they did nothing for a few days. At long last, June 5 saw the men discharged and paid off, although Brion mentions that the "last installment of bounty [was] not paid." June 6, 1865, was Brion's long-awaited day: "Arrived home."[8]

An escaped prisoner of war, Capt. James B. Thompson of Company F, 190th Pennsylvanian Volunteer Infantry Regiment, had returned to Union lines at Atlanta in October 1864. Captured the previous May at Bethesda Church, Virginia, at the time of the assault on Cold Harbor, he returned to his unit. Thompson served throughout the spring campaign of 1865, ending at Appomattox Court House on April 9, 1865. His experiences from that point on must have been fairly typical of the time, as his memoirs barely mention events until the time of his mustering out at Harrisburg, July 6, 1865.[9]

Another Pennsylvania native, John Levy of Company H, 95th Pennsylvania Volunteer Infantry Regiment, wrote to his wife from Dansville, Virginia, on April 29, 1865: "No more use for us in this part of Virginia." He expected to start back to Richmond or Petersburg soon. "Likely tomorrow as nearly all Army movements are commenced on Sunday. . . . The war is considered to be over." He wrote about the salutes that had been rendered the previous day, together with bands playing and people cheering upon receipt of the news of Johnston's surrender. "I think we will not be kept long. I expect to be home by fall. All danger of war is over."[10]

Reese H. Egbert of Company E, 74th Pennsylvania Volunteer Infantry Regiment, gave his impressions of those exciting and climactic days in letters to his family dated April 21 and May 3, from Beverly, Virginia:

The Rebs is played out and if you should here tell of us being on the home road in about three weeks you should not be surprised for things look very favorable. . . . Thier is a rumor that we will move very soon and the cornel of our rigament sayes if we did move it would be towards Harrisburg and onced we get thier again we will be home pretty soon. . . . Here the whole talk is about home but you must not be to shure fore things might tak a different turn but the new is here rite from Washington that Lee and Johnston have bothe surrendered to Grant with thier whole forces.

Egbert went on to mention that their principal activity during this time was drill, two hours in the morning and one hour each afternoon, together with a dress parade daily at 5 P.M.[11]

Soldiers' diaries have two advantages: The entries are necessarily brief, and the soldiers write them soon after the events, thus providing a relatively high degree of accuracy. Pvt. Jacob Yarger of the 16th Pennsylvania Cavalry Regiment was in and around Petersburg early in June 1865. The unit was transferred to Lynchburg, and five days later, at Manchester, the regiment was mustered out of service. The journey home from Manchester was via Richmond, Baltimore, Harrisburg, and Camp Curtin, outside Harrisburg. His entry for June 18, 1865, says it all: "We was payed." The next day, Yarger arrived at his home in Fremont, Pennsylvania.[12]

Not everyone was unhappy with the current situation of waiting for the final paperwork, accounting for property and equipment, and a final movement toward home. John H. Burrill of the 2nd New Hampshire Infantry Regiment wrote from Manchester, Virginia, on May 19, 1865, to his parents in New Hampshire that "it is probable we will be home sometime this summer—do not care how soon." This rather low-key statement was followed by "I do not think I shall ever wish to join the Army again." Then he adds a condition: "Under some circumstances, perhaps." About two weeks later, still at Manchester, Burrill reported:

We are quite pleasantly situated here, not much of anything to do. I have made a request to be released from the Regiment as I have to stay out here sometime and I mean to get along as easily as possible. About our coming home—to me it is a doubtful . . . [possibility] and I will not attempt now to judge when we will come. There must be an army kept here a while yet as there is no other law.

Still at Manchester on June 18, he wrote to his parents:

I have no news worth telling, only am away from the Regiment
and intend to keep it so. Am in the Quartermaster Department,
3rd Division. Am having an easy time with not much to do and a
great deal of liberty which is a big thing.

Burrill apparently intended to make his remaining service time as comfortable and effortless as possible. By mid-August, he was at Fredericksburg,
Virginia, boarding with a private family. He not only contributed his
rations, but also paid the family a certain amount each week. Late in
August, he wrote from Fredericksburg that he did not care particularly
when he got home, as he was "having a nice good time. Have a nice job.
Like it very much." He does add that "this is still not the kind of life one
wants to live always."

In the middle of September, this contented soldier wrote in a letter
home that he had been performing the duties of the commissary sergeant
but was then working in an office, helping one of the clerks. In this same
letter to his parents, he does admit that he hopes to be home soon but adds,
"True, am having it easy here but had rather be with friends than here."

Another letter, apparently the last in the series, was written in Fredericksburg on November 27. In this letter, Burrill admits to being "so very
lonesome, do not know what to do with myself." Then he adds, "Am very
anxious to get home and what is more, have now a good prospect of soon
getting home." Apparently his "good prospect" materialized, as nothing
more is available concerning his progress through the demobilization
pipeline.[13]

Capt. James W. Cartwright and 1st Lt. Edwin A. Wallace, both in the
56th Massachusetts Infantry Regiment, wrote a series of letters to John
Cartwright, either James's brother or a mutual friend, presumably located
back in Massachusetts. On April 20, 1865, Wallace wrote, "We have been
resting on our oars [a nautical metaphor stemming perhaps from his Nantucket Island background] near this station [Burkesville, Virginia]." Four
days later, from City Point, Virginia, Cartwright wrote that they were to
leave for Washington that day with the corps. He also mentioned that the
government owed him $600 in back pay. Following a "delightful trip" on
the steamer *Montauk*, Cartwright wrote from Alexandria that he knew not
how long the unit would remain there or where they were going next.
"I have now as much as I can attend to, to muster my company for pay and

Docks at City Point, Virginia, transshipment point for Petersburg front, 1864–65, via U.S. Military Railroad

make returns to Washington." By the end of May, he was "tired of playing soldier and so are most of our officers." On June 1, still in Alexandria, he wrote for funds: "I have not a red [cent], and if you could send me $50, it would be acceptable." He went on to say that the amount owed to him by the government had risen to "over $1,000."

By June 14, 1865, still in the same location, Cartwright wrote, "It was easy enough to get into the Service but d——d hard to get out." (This truism has been repeated countless times by servicemen throughout history.) He adds, "We see no signs of a move or of pay." The wheels of demobilization finally must have turned for the 56th Massachusetts Infantry, as Cartwright wrote from Nantucket Island, Massachusetts, on July 29, 1865, "At home."[14]

Another Massachusetts native, Corp. Arthur B. Wyman, Company K, 57th Massachusetts Volunteer Infantry Regiment, had been a prisoner of war and had been paroled. He was at his home in Woburn, Massachusetts, on furlough, and then went to Readville. On April 14, he left home for Boston and then went on by train to New York City, Philadelphia, Baltimore, and Annapolis. By the sixteenth, he was in the parole camp. Next he was involved in a series of transfers and movements that resembled a game of checkers—first to Washington, then to Alexandria, Fortress Monroe, City Point, Fortress Monroe again, then back to Alexandria. Finally he arrived at his regiment at Georgetown Heights. He took part in the Grand Review, which he termed "a tiresome march." At the end of May, he felt that he had "no very good prospects of going home for some time yet." Things began to look up when, on June 22, the unit received an order to discharge all returned prisoners. "I suppose that I shall at last get out of Uncle Sam's clutches." By June 25, he had completed the paperwork for his mustering out, and he wrote in his diary that he had "hopes to bid farewell to hardtack and salt pork forever, in a few days." Much to his surprise, on June 27, an order came through that countermanded the mustering out, and the next thing Wyman knew, he was on picket duty between Tennallytown and Georgetown. Moved to Washington, he was on duty at the Aqueduct Bridge. His July 13 entry is the final one in his diary: "Went down to Washington today to see about getting discharged."[15] Presumably he was successful in his efforts.

The 22nd Massachusetts Infantry Regiment, together with the 2nd Company of Sharpshooters and the 3rd Light Battery (Artillery), marched from Burkesville, Virginia, and on May 12, 1865, reached the environs of Washington. The next several days provided a respite from their long march, as they visited friends in other units and prepared for the Grand Review. On June 29, more than a month after the magnificent parade, the units started for home. Arriving in Boston on July 1, the national holiday gave them some time off. Soon afterward, on July 6, the men assembled and moved to an island in the Boston Harbor, Galluppe's Island, sometimes shown as Gallop, Gallop's, or Gallup's Island, the last stopping place for local soldiers before they resumed their civilian lives. Five days later, they became full-fledged civilians; their wartime service was a matter of history.[16]

On the same day that the 22nd Massachusetts Infantry reached Galluppe's Island, the men of the 38th Massachusetts Infantry Regiment went there upon their arrival in Boston. Their journey had been easier on the feet, however, as the unit had moved by steamer from Savannah, Georgia, to Boston, having started their homeward trek from Goldsboro, North Carolina. Once at Galluppe's Island, according to Lewis Josselyn's memoirs, the troops were discharged and allowed to go home until July 13. On that day, the city of Cambridge gave the regiment "a glorious reception."[17]

Not all of the Massachusetts troops passed through Galluppe's Island, however; some troops used Faneuil Hall, in downtown Boston. The 1st

Massachusetts Infantry Regiment was mustered out in Boston, and "at the end of a few weeks, the men were paid off at Faneuil Hall." The 12th Regiment of New Hampshire Volunteers quartered overnight in the same facility on their way back to their native state. They had boarded the steamer *State of Maine* at Rockett's Landing in Richmond on June 22. By way of New York City, the men went on to Boston and Concord, New Hampshire, where they were paid in full and discharged.[18]

The 5th Regiment New Hampshire Volunteers followed somewhat the same pattern of demobilization movements. Leaving Burksville, Virginia, where the men received a "ration of whiskey," this unit went on to the Washington area and participated in the Grand Review. According to the regimental historian, the men received a "1/2 ration of whiskey" in camp the evening of the review. It was a month before the troops moved to Concord, New Hampshire, where they were paid, mustered out, and "became again civilians."[19]

Another New England unit, the 19th Maine Regiment of Volunteer Infantry, made even better time in its demobilization proceedings. On May 13, the troops arrived twelve miles from Washington. They pitched their last camp at Bailey's Crossroads, outside Washington, on May 15. Two weeks later, they were mustered out, and they started for home the next day. Their train trip followed the usual route: Washington; Baltimore; Philadelphia; South Amboy, New Jersey; and then across the Hudson River to New York City. They reached Portland on June 3 and Augusta the following day. Here they were paid off on June 7 and, as their historian wrote, "broke ranks forever."[20]

The railroads all along the East Coast, and especially in the Portland, Maine, area, were busy during those early days of June 1865. Having begun their journey at Bailey's Crossroads, only a few days behind the 19th Infantry, the 17th Maine Volunteer Infantry Regiment arrived in Portland on June 8, just hours behind the famous 20th Maine Infantry Regiment. The troops of the two units shared a reception, which included "a generous collation." On June 10, the regiment was paid off and discharged. Following these acts of demobilization, the "regiment . . . ceased to exist."[21]

Not all of the Maine units were as fortunate to be discharged so quickly. Lt. Henry W. Gay, 15th Maine Infantry Regiment, wrote to his parents from Georgetown, South Carolina, on August 11, 1865, in the harsh language of his day:

What we are doing here now. . . . We are keeping the niggers from killing the whites. The niggers are of a notion that the white men have not any right to come on the plantation and we have to go and settle it and the niggers sine the agreement between them and their former owners. They are to give them one half of what is raised on the plaice and give them their alowances just the same as before the war and the niggers are so ignorant that they will not signe the papers unless a soldier goes and makes them do it. . . . I tell you it is not much like the soldiering that we had last year, but I do not like to be a soldier in the peacable time. There is not any fun in it.

Yet another Maine unit, the 11th Maine Infantry Regiment, was not mustered out until February 2, 1866, at City Point, Virginia. Traveling by steamer, the troops made their way to New London, Connecticut, and then went on to their home area in Maine. Upon their arrival in New London, they at least received "a hearty welcome," which no doubt helped soften their disappointment at such a delayed demobilization.[22]

Three New York State units, one from Rochester, another from the North Country (generally, the Watertown-Ogdensburg-Plattsburg area), and the third from western New York, along Lake Erie, were in the demobilization pipeline at essentially the same time. The comments and observations of individuals in each of the outfits tell us about the morale of the troops, their hopes and desires, and their final assessments of their service.

Writing from Raleigh, North Carolina, to his sister at home, William Henry Walling of the 142nd New York Volunteer Infantry Regiment, the North Country regiment, expressed the hope that the unit would remain in the Raleigh area until it was completely ready to go directly home without stopping in Albany or having to go via Ogdensburg. His last letter, dated June 1, 1865, stated that the order for mustering out had been received, together with the necessary governmental forms.

Capt. Andrew Boyd of Company H, 108th Regiment New York Volunteers, was home in Brockport, outside Rochester, a week after the Grand Review had occurred. The speed of this demobilization was really quite remarkable, although Boyd seems to have taken it in his stride, as his only diary entry when he was finally paid off for his services was "a citizen once more."

After receiving the news of General Johnston's surrender, Theodore W. Skinner, 112th New York Infantry Regiment, wrote on April 30 from

Raleigh to friends in Westfield, New York, that he did "not expect to have more fighting to do. I think the war is about wound up. . . . I guess by that time [June] Uncle Sam will not need any soldiers than what regulars he has got in the service." About a month later, still at Raleigh, he stated that he had "made up [his] mind to be at home by the 1st of July" and that he would "not give up but what [he] shall be there by that time."[23]

Besides those suggesting a tour of duty on the Mexican border, many other rumors were circulating. On May 17, 1865, a corporal in the 117th Illinois Volunteer Infantry Regiment, Adolphus P. Wolf, wrote from Montgomery, Alabama, his reaction to the news of the capture of Jefferson Davis and the arrest of Confederate vice president Alexander H. Stephens:

> I think the war is over and the armies will be mustered out as soon as possible. I am heartily glad of it for it has been going on long enough. The rumor is circulated through camp, that we are to move North in 13 days, to be mustered out. I do not place much reliance in such rumors, I only hope they may be true.

As it turned out, his hopes were in vain; the regiment was not mustered out until August 5, 1865.[24]

The 46th Illinois Volunteer Infantry Regiment took a circuitous route home. At the end of the hostilities, this unit was at Mobile, Alabama. In his diary, Edward H. Reynolds of Company H tells of working day after day on the payrolls. On May 5, 1865, each man turned in half his ammunition, retaining twenty rounds. On May 11, five companies received their pay; early in the afternoon, however, higher headquarters issued orders for each man "to draw an extra pair of shoes, all other necessary clothing and 100 rounds of ammunition"—this less than a week after the order that had them turn in ammunition. In addition, new weapons were to be drawn to replace unserviceable ones. The next day, the rest of the regiment was paid off. The day following, the regiment boarded cars on the Mobile & Ohio Railroad and headed north. Reynolds described the streets of the towns they passed through, and also the southbound trains, as being "grey with Confederates . . . all anxious to reach their homes."

The trip was interrupted for a few days at Gainesville, Alabama, where the regiment relieved "a force of Confederates who were guarding the arsenal, cotton warehouses, commissary stores, etc. They were very glad to see us, being anxious to turn over this duty and get away to their homes." Here is another instance of the vanquished being demobilized in advance of the victors. The unit changed direction on May 20 and headed back to Mobile, accompanied by rumors that it would soon move out again, this time to "either home or Texas."

Five days later, the men of the 46th Illinois boarded steamers and departed for New Orleans, "presumably to be sent to the West in pursuit of General Kirby Smith." Upon arriving at New Orleans the following day, they learned of Smith's surrender and then went back on the steamers en route to Baton Rouge, Louisiana, and points north. The amount of paperwork that was required, as well as the shortage of qualified personnel to handle it, is revealed in Reynolds's comment that "all who can write then read it, are busy on our last set of muster papers."

In June 1865, the regiment was established along the Red River at Grand Encore, Louisiana. Among its duties was the requirement to hail all vessels in order to examine the boats' papers. A battery of two guns was established on the riverbank as a powerful incentive for the boats to stop. Here the unit remained until December 27.

It was not until January 20, 1866, that the unit was mustered out at Baton Rouge and embarked on riverboats for Cairo, Illinois. After a five-day trip, the troops switched over to the Illinois Central Railroad, reaching Camp Butler on January 27. There, five days were necessary to prepare the final papers and discharges. The men received their discharges on February 1, 1866, and once again the troops boarded trains, this time headed home.[25]

Apparently Lt. James F. Greathouse, the regimental quartermaster of the 99th Illinois Infantry Regiment, did not know of the lengthy and time-consuming process the 46th Illinois was undergoing when he wrote on July 11, 1865, to an army comrade, Lt. George S. Marks, who had been discharged the previous December. "We expect to be mustered out soon, but I do not know before our time expires or not; it can't be long, if we have to stay our full term."[26]

Another unit that experienced a delay in its demobilization was the 20th New York State Militia, also known as the Ulster Guard. Soon after the surrender at Appomattox, this unit was on duty as the provost guard in Richmond. It was not until November 27, 1865, that the Ulster Guard embarked on steamers at Richmond, bound for Norfolk. Apparently their service as provost guards had been satisfactory, as they received a similar assignment at Norfolk, the Portsmouth Navy Yard, and the hard-labor naval prison. Late in January 1866, the men were mustered out, received their back pay in New York City, and then returned home to Ulster County.[27]

A combination of transportation means served the 3rd Regiment of Wisconsin Veteran Volunteer Infantry well on its homeward journey. A nine-day road march took the unit to Richmond, and then the troops moved on through that much-fought-over area of battlefields. Like the troops before them, they too viewed the human remains on the Spotsylvania grounds. The 3rd Regiment set up camp opposite Washington and took part in the Grand Review. Like many other units, the regiment then moved into a new camp area, northeast of Washington, preliminary to the move home. The Baltimore and Ohio Railroad took the men to Parkersburg, West Virginia, where they boarded the steamer *Nevada* for the river trip to Louisville, Kentucky, one of the field rendezvous sites. After two weeks, the paymaster arrived, and the troops received their pay. July 4 saw them participate in their final march in review, and after another two weeks, they were mustered out. After crossing the Ohio River, they proceeded by train to Madison, Wisconsin, arriving there on July 24, whereupon the unit deposited its regimental flags in the state capitol. The unit historian summed up the entire demobilization process, with all its various transportation modes and periods of waiting, in one word: "Finis!"[28]

Memoirs written many years after the war by Asa Beak Smith of Company C, 97th Ohio Infantry Regiment, described the demobilization experience of this unit. At the time of Lincoln's assassination, the regiment was at Blue Springs, in eastern Tennessee. Next they moved to Nashville, where the troops were mustered out. On June 10, the unit moved on by train to Louisville. Then a steamboat conveyed the regiment to Cincinnati, where the men were loaded on trains and taken to Columbus. Paid off and disbanded on June 15, the men were home by June 19.[29] Though the entire process must have seemed interminable to the men of the unit, it actually moved relatively swiftly.

Not all troop transfers took place with the advantages of a voyage on the inland waterways or the open seas. A significant force of cavalry transferred from the Potomac River to the Arkansas River, and then on to the western plains. While some short segments of the journey utilized riverboats, most of the trip was by rail. These and other redeployments were carried out while demobilization was going on.[30]

Some redeployment occurred without long, involved, and tiring traveling. The 57th Massachusetts Volunteers, after taking part in the Grand Review, remained on guard duty for three months in Tennallytown, Maryland, near the Chain Bridge over the Potomac River. Tennallytown, today part of Washington itself, was only a few miles from the center of the capital. Men from this regiment performed provost duty in and around Washington, patrolling the streets, bars, theaters, amusement places, and even "brothels and bawdy houses." When not on provost duty, they had their normal camp routine in a setting that was "almost idyllic," but it included drill and dress parades in full dress uniform, despite the summer weather. The camp had plentiful water, and the soldiers could wash and shave daily, an unaccustomed luxury. Even though the men obtained new uniforms, they received few passes to Washington, so the troops were not often able to display their new finery in public. After the excitement and pageantry of the Grand Review, however, things military quickly lost their appeal. The troops felt they had completed the mission for which they had volunteered, and they just wanted to go home.[31]

In prewar times, no doubt any one troop transfer would have required the best thinking and planning of all available personnel; now, with the experiences of war as a guide and pattern, many such troop movements proceeded simultaneously, and in widely separated parts of the country, with relative ease and a minimum of confusion.

One soldier in the 1st Pennsylvania Cavalry Regiment pursued an especially arduous path toward discharge. Aaron E. Bachman had been captured by the Confederates, but escaped just prior to the end of hostilities, making his way to a Federal outpost and eventually to Nashville. Bachman's enlistment had expired ten months earlier, while he was a prisoner of war, but he still had to go through the pipeline. After receiving a new uniform, the process sent him on to Louisville, Kentucky. He crossed the Ohio River at Jeffersonville, Indiana, where he began a lengthy train trip. Traveling by way of Indianapolis to Pittsburgh, he finally arrived in Harrisburg after a grueling trip, the journey from Pittsburgh to Harrisburg alone requiring twenty-four hours. Since he had entered service at Reading, he had to go to Philadelphia for final processing. Back on the train, Bachman made his way through his home territory to learn that he could not complete the separation process without certain "description lists," which would have to come from Washington. Bachman spent the next week in a transient camp outside of Philadelphia, but to his surprise and delight, the necessary papers came through quickly, and he was finally discharged and paid.[32]

Members of the 73rd Illinois Infantry Regiment had their own troubles with army red tape. During almost two months in Nashville, unit paperwork was both the main objective and obstacle. According to the regimental historian, "it was found difficult to make out the history of each man, as required." Early in June 1865, with the agonizing prospect that the work might have to be redone, some muster-out rolls were submitted to higher authorities so that they could be checked against the requirements. "Eight rolls [forms] were required for each company, and eight rolls for each officer." On June 7, the rolls were completed, and the unit was ready to be mustered out. Four days later, the regiment was on its way to Chicago, arriving at Camp Butler, Illinois, on June 15. To the relief of all concerned, the rolls passed inspection as correct; the men signed both muster rolls and payrolls, but it was not until June 24 that the regiment was finally paid off.[33]

Part of the paperwork problem was due to the unavailability of experienced and skilled clerks needed to complete the necessary rolls and other records. On May 28, Robert Tilney, chief clerk in the V Corps' adjutant general's section, noted that "clerks are getting very scarce here now; so many have gone home . . . clerks are decidedly at a premium." When Tilney's discharge came due, at the request of the colonel in charge of the section, he consented to remain on duty. By June 21, only ten regiments remained in the entire corps. Tilney stayed at headquarters until the middle of August, when he rejoined his regiment at Hart's Island, outside of New York City, just off City Island, where he was mustered out on August 21.[34]

Lucius C. Wox of Company I, 17th Pennsylvania Cavalry Regiment, found himself in Pleasant Valley, Maryland, a few weeks after the surrender of the Army of Northern Virginia. He had been detailed to work in the unit bakery, so his duties could not have been too arduous, though the hours may have been awkward. At the end of April, his unit had been transferred to Chapel Point, Maryland, about thirty miles below the nation's capital. Wox wrote to a lady friend:

> It is reported that we will all be discharged here soon. I can't keep still long enough to eat my dinner—indeed. I am afraid some of us will get nearly crazy if our officers don't sober up a little and send us home. . . . [I] intend to stay with my regiment till it is discharged.[35]

The quartermaster general had given specific, precise instructions, in standard military prose, concerning the safety and comfort of the men traveling by railroad. The reality, however, was not always so comfortable.

When the 73rd Illinois Infantry Regiment traveled from Nashville to Chicago, the soldiers rode on bare wooden seats. Such discomfort would have seemed minor to the men of the 11th New Jersey Infantry Regiment, who rode in boxcars on their trip home from Washington. The boxcars were "stifling," so "all who could climbed on top." But no doubt the soldiers of the 2nd Minnesota Infantry Regiment would have been more than happy to trade places with either of these regiments. These men were loaded on open coal cars, with rough board benches for seats. Completely exposed to the rain, which fell upon them in torrents, the men quickly learned that the coal cars were watertight. William Bircher, a drummer boy in the regiment, wrote that "this was one of the rare cases where we traveled by land and water at the same time." The car had sides about two feet high, and soon each car contained about six inches of dirty, black water, in which the men's feet were continuously immersed. As the train ascended a grade, the water sloshed back with a rush and out over the end of the car. On the descent, the water reversed its course. By the time the train reached Cumberland, Maryland, the men had had enough. They "procured axes and knocked out a few boards from the bottom of the cars; after which [they] had a little more comfort."[36]

After being mustered out in Mobile, Alabama, the 14th Wisconsin Infantry Regiment traveled by a variety of means to Madison, Wisconsin, the state rendezvous point. First, from Dauphin Island, a side-wheeler took the men via Mississippi Sound, through the Rigolets, and across Lake Ponchartrain. Then, by means of a paddle-wheel steamer, the regiment made its way up the Mississippi River. At Cairo, Illinois, they transferred into "box and cattle cars that hadn't been very well cleaned out and had no straw or hay for bedding." The cars were so crowded that "all had to lay on the same side." Despite these conditions, as Pvt. Elisha Stockwell expressed it, "there was but little fault found for we were going home." The men arrived at Freeport, Illinois, after spending two days and nights on a sidetrack without an engine; the 375-mile trip from Cairo was finally over. From Beloit, Wisconsin, the 14th Wisconsin continued in "clean new box-cars" to Madison, where "in a few days we were paid off and given our discharge."[37]

All War Department directives and instructions for the entire demobilization procedure emphasized speed, but it appears that this concern dissipated by the time it reached the railroad officials and engineers responsible for routing and operating the trains. For Pvt. Theodore Gerrish and the rest of the 20th Maine Infantry Regiment, the train trip from Washington to Philadelphia required eighteen hours. But the soldiers of this regiment faced worse vexations. After passing through New York City and Boston, the men reached Portland, Maine, on June 8, 1865, late in the afternoon. The weary soldiers consumed a feast in the city hall, and then moved into some old barracks. Insultingly, the fenced camp had members of the Invalid Corps as guards. No passes were given out, and the diet was a familiar one—field rations of coffee and hardtack. Seething with anger, the men of this brave, battle-hardened regiment pelted the camp commander with hardtack and overpowered the guards, then broke up the gates and burned them. But the government won in the end, and the regiment's discharge was delayed. It was "several weeks before we received pay and took our departure." Nevertheless, it is likely that the soldiers of the 20th Maine thought their response to such unwarranted treatment was worth the delay.[38]

Camp Chase, Ohio, outside Columbus, was the scene of another disturbance. Troops of the 94th Ohio Infantry Regiment, having moved by stages from Wilmington, North Carolina, "a rather nice place," made their way to the Washington area and participated in the Grand Review. On June 6, 1865, the regiment left Washington by train for Camp Chase. A "splendid" dinner was provided by the citizens, and after the customary speeches, the men moved out to Camp Chase. Aaron S. Turner of Company G describes the men waiting patiently for their "eagles and greenbacks." He went on to note in his diary: "While . . . at Washington . . . we was allowed to go whear we pleased. Now when are in a maner at home we are put as one might say in a bulpen underguard. Won't stand it mabe." Apparently the troops did not stand it, as Turner's entry for the next day, June 11, states that "the boys made an attack on Camp Chase last night tore down some of the fence and made a raid in the sutler's shop. Signed the payroll this evening. May get our discharge and pay tomorrow." Actually, the men were paid off June 14. As Turner wrote in his diary: "Got my eagle. Struck out for home immediately. Arrived at home about dark. So ends the chapter. I am a citizen now. I think I feel a change."[39]

It took two months from the day the men heard of Lee's surrender for the 94th Ohio to be mustererd out and discharged. Road marches, canal barges, steamships, and railroad all were used to move these men from the Atlantic coast of North Carolina to the Columbus, Ohio, area. All in all, their demobilization went rather well.

Almost twenty years after the war, Colonel Townsend, the assistant adjutant general, summed up the demobilization procedure in his memoirs:

[The soldiers were] transported to fifty depots near their homes; they were mustered out of service . . . before they left the field;

final muster rolls were boxed and transported with them. At the depots paymasters awaited them, and having been transported and subsisted up to the last moment, they were paid in full, and discharged almost at their very homes.

The historian of the 2nd Minnesota Infantry Regiment told it a bit differently. There were no paymasters waiting for this regiment as the men departed the train. Actually, these soldiers "were obliged to wait several days for our final payment." This statement was a bit generous, as the regiment arrived at Fort Snelling, Minnesota, on June 15, 1865, and final payment was not made until July 20, five weeks later. The troops of the 73rd Illinois Infantry Regiment were more fortunate. They arrived at Camp Butler, Illinois, on June 15 and were paid June 24.[40]

Stephen H. Smith, a member of the 178th New York Infantry regiment, was at Mobile at the time of its surrender. The unit moved to Grunville, Alabama, by road marches. It was not until April 19 that the unit received official notification of Lee's surrender. At this news, "every man fired off his musket." The pay history for this unit was spotty. The last day of April, the regiment was mustered for six months' pay. Late in August, the men went to Greenville, Alabama, and on the last day of the month, they were mustered for another six months' pay. Late in October, they received pay for four months; this payment brought them up to July 1. At the end of October, they received pay for the final four months. Thus, over a period of six months, the regiment received pay for twenty months.[41]

Sometimes soldiers did more than just wait impatiently for their final pay. When the 11th New Jersey Regiment arrived in camp near Trenton, the state rendezvous point, they hoped and expected to receive their pay promptly, in accord with Colonel Townsend's blithe description of the process. After a week, which the anxious and irritable men termed "a long delay," the soldiers were finally paid off. The day before, however, the men began to take action:

> Nearly two hundred men of the Eleventh and 12th New Jersey Infantry Regiments formed in lines and marched to the State House to ascertain just when they were to be paid. Being assured that it would not be later than the next afternoon, they quietly marched back to camp.

Peaceful demonstrations in the presence of state officials seemed to achieve results, even in 1865. To be sure, the delay was only a week, a much shorter time than many units waited, but the charged-up enthusiasm and exuberance involved in the entire demobilization process were so pervasive that, in its final stages, any delay, even a week, seemed intolerable.[42]

After the 140th New York Volunteer Infantry Regiment had gone through the preliminary steps of demobilization, "cleaning up" after the surrender by collecting surrendered Confederate property and shipping it to Washington, guarding railroad lines, marching toward Washington with a pause in Petersburg for a review by Gouverneur K. Warren, the ex-commanding general of the V Corps, and yet another review in Richmond in which the entire Army of the Potomac participated, it finally reached its goal of Washington. Even after the Grand Review, the regiment still was without its pay. Early in June, the unpaid unit reached its enlistment site, Rochester, New York. Heartened by word that the paymaster would be available "tomorrow," the regiment paraded in Rochester and partook of a "substantial repast." But the next day, there was no paymaster. A week later, on June 13, 1865, the troops were finally paid, and the unit was officially disbanded.[43]

The delay in pay was no respecter of rank, as the letters of Maj. George Shuman of the 9th Pennsylvania Cavalry Regiment reveal. Written after Appomattox, the letters have common threads, one of which was his pay—or, rather, the lack thereof. Two weeks after the surrender, he wrote from Durham Station, North Carolina, that he had "near eight months pay due which will amount to over $1,000. I suppose we will be paid some soon." Late in May 1865, Shuman informed his wife that "our living is pretty poor now since hostilities have ceased. We have no money, consequently we must live on government rations and that goes pretty hard after the way we had been living." A letter of June 12 sounded a bit more desperate: "I think it is a shame that we are not paid as some men's families have to go to the Poor House for the want of the necessaries of life." Writing home a few days later, the major complained that "the Government now owes me near $1,400 and I would like to have some and I suppose you need some." A June 17 letter to his wife echoed a forlorn note: "No pay master yet and I guess poor prospects of any for a while." But two weeks later, a July 4 letter contained the good news that "the pay master is reported to be here tomorrow."[44] That was the last reference to his back pay, so it is fair to assume that the regiment was indeed paid off on July 5.

The complaints of Major Shuman were echoed in a letter, quite likely written by an officer, to the editor of the *New York Times*. From Norfolk, Virginia, dated June 20, 1865, the writer reported that "the troops here have not been paid since March 1 . . . [and] then only up to January 1." He further stated that the soldiers' "families are absolutely suffering for the very necessaries of life." The letter writer asked the editor to speak out on behalf of the troops, urging that "one word from you will accomplish more than a dozen communications through the slow and tortuous official channels."

In reporting the arrival of the 150th New York Infantry Regiment, a unit from Duchess County, the *New York Times* noted the forthcoming presence of the paymaster. "The paymaster, who has not seen them for seventeen months, will . . . make his welcome and final visit in Poughkeepsie."[45]

One of the most significant factors in the effectiveness of any army unit, be it a squad or a corps, is the morale of the individuals who make up that unit. This intangible factor is so important that armies throughout history have always been aware of its crucial value. Morale is not something that lends itself to empirical measurement; often its worth is only recognized and appreciated when it is missing, or at least noticeably reduced. Moreover, the morale or *esprit de corps* of a unit may be evaluated in garrison as well as in combat, and so it is possible to gauge the morale of units and soldiers during demobilization. Perhaps the postcombat experience presents the best opportunity to measure a unit's morale, since the dangers of warfare have passed, and the units are awaiting separation from service.

In his history of the 1st Brigade of New Jersey Volunteers, originally Gen. Philip Kearny's brigade, later assigned to the 1st Division, VI Corps, Camille Baquet accurately summed up the emotional condition of the men awaiting mustering out and discharge with the phrase "restlessness and discontent," a description by no means unique to this unit.

Daniel Faust, of Company G, 95th Pennsylvania Infantry Regiment, wrote home from Burkeville Junction, Virginia, in the middle of May:

> I scarcely know what to write for I expect to get home soon. . . .
> We have been expecting to go to Washington long before this but
> it takes them a long time to get us started. We are the last troops
> out here in the field. We always have had to do all the dirty work
> and I think they mean to keep us doing it to the last end.

Under such circumstances, keeping soldiers busy and occupied with parades, reviews, inspections, and other miltary activities was the order of the day. Men of the 195th Pennsylvania Infantry Regiment, wrote Bentley Kutz in a letter home dated May 4, 1865, were "on parade with white gloves which looks very well, only I think it is too much of the good thing for soldiers in the field."[46]

Daniel Sterling, a soldier of the 1st Michigan Engineers and Mechanics Regiment, wrote on June 21, 1865, from a camp near Louisville, Kentucky, that the "future [is] veiled in uncertainty as yet. Some think . . . we shall be home in a month, others that we shall have to stay till fall. . . . Write often—tell me how the people feel about the soldiers being kept so long." Apparently, Sterling felt his morale needed a boost from the home front. Three months later, on September 17, he wrote from Nashville:

We as a regiment are making some progress toward coming home. We have received orders to make out muster out rools ameidotly [immediately]. We have been at work on them for several days back and think we shall finish the rools by Tuesday or Wednesday night. Then it will take one or two days to inspect the rools and one day to muster-out which will bring it to Friday or Saturday, so we think we shall start for home by Saturday or Sunday next, and you may expect to hear from us next week in Detroit or Jackson. . . . As soon as I can ascertain at which place we shall rendevous I will let you know.[47]

James Williams of Company A, 23rd Indiana Infantry Regiment, wrote to his wife, from Raleigh, North Carolina, on April 27, 1865: "The wore [war] is over and we are agoing home. . . . I want to be own bos again." Another expression of that ever-present desire of the citizen-soldier to return to civilian life appears in a letter written early in September 1865 by William H. H. Gripman of the 1st Minnesota Heavy Artillery Regiment, from Chattanooga:

We expect to be . . . mustered out either this or next week. A regt . . . arrived night before last to relieve us and we expect our orders every hour. There is no hoax about this. Our officers say we will be on our way in a week. We think we will be home about the

25th of this month. Oh, what a happy hour it will [be] for me
when we pick up our knapsacks for the last time in Chatt[anooga]
and happier yet when I meet those I love most on earth.[48]

Unfortunately, an element of racism lowered the morale of the 47th
Pennsylvania Infantry Regiment, stationed in Charleston, South Carolina.
After spending six weeks in Alexandria and two months on garrison duty
in Savannah and Charleston, the regimental historian stated that the men
were "discontented and unhealthy; unpleasantly situated and harder worked
than . . . ever. . . . There are none but colored troops around us, colored
officers among them."[49] This observation confirms the fact that as Northern white volunteers were mustered out, the percentage of black soldiers on
duty in the South increased.

Maj. George Shuman of the 9th Pennsylvania Cavalry Regiment, he
who complained so bitterly about his back pay, also commented on the
demobilization program in general and, particularly, as it affected him and
his unit. In a letter of May 24, 1865, Shuman wrote, "I think the war is
over and we have as good a right to be mustered out as the rest of his [Sher-
man's] army, though I don't think we will be kept here after the civil law is
restored again." On June 1, 1865, he expanded on this line of thought: "As
the government requires the services of soldiers for sometime yet, they have
concluded to keep veterans. We have mustered out all our one-year men
whose time would expire before October." He went on to say:

> I do not think we are used fair after being with [Maj. Gen. William
> T.] Sherman so long and to be left behind now and kept in service
> is not fair, but I suppose the Government knows what it is doing. I
> hope they won't keep us much longer. I think the odium against
> Sherman is wearing off as I don't see half so much fuss in the
> papers against him as there was sometime ago.[50]

Five days later, Shuman struck the same note of dissatisfaction: "I cannot
tell you anything about when we will be relieved and sent home. It is
hardly fair that we that have been in so long should be kept till the last."[51]

Even the chaplains were not immune to feelings of pessimism and frustration. A chaplain of the 86th New York Infantry Regiment, Henry
Rinker, was an experienced soldier, having previously served as a private in
the 11th New Jersey Infantry Regiment. "How long we shall be retained

in service," he wrote home on June 17, 1865, "of course, we cannot tell. There is no prospect now of a very speedy discharge. . . . It seems to be the impression that this regiment will not be discharged till fall, and perhaps not then."[52] It could not have been easy for this man to bolster the morale of others when his own was so low.

Hospital chaplain Lyman Daniel Ames made some penetrating observations concerning the morale of the troops. While at Louisville, Kentucky, waiting for the final rolls to be prepared so that Ohio troops could return to their homes, Ames wrote in his diary: "Men [are] demoralized . . . suspense is becoming painful. Affects the moral tone of the men. . . . The mood of the men is not good. They feel sour from disappointment."[53]

A member of the 17th Pennsylvania Cavalry Regiment, Peter Boyer, wrote to his father from Camp Remount, near Pleasant Valley, Maryland, in the middle of May 1865:

> I am very much disapointed about staying out hear so long. If there were any fighting, I wouldn't think of going home, but now the battles are fought and the victorys won, and now they keep us still out hear, just for nothing and make us drill every day. . . . We have always done our duty, and every fight we was in we done our share and never was at home once. . . . Now they don't care for the poor soldier when he gets home or if he gets home at all. . . . I don't know when they will do us that favor to muster us out and pay us off, but I heard last night that we wouldn't be discharged until October.[54]

Feelings ran high among the troops in response to delays. Another Pennsylvania soldier, William H. Martin of Company A, 18th Pennsylvania Cavalry Regiment, wrote to his wife on June 25, 1865: "We have been very badly treated and worse than all, neglected by our officers. Ever since our arrival at this camp [Cumberland, Maryland], we were fed on half rations till the men's patience were entirely exhausted." Much to his relief, two weeks later, he was able to write: "I am coming home!"[55]

In contrast to Martin's experiences at Cumberland, George B. Jennys, a clerk for the brigade surgeon at Camp Stoneman near Washington, D.C., sent word to his parents that "we get plenty of vegetables and any quantity of fruit, and with good rations, we live first-rate." Six weeks later, he wrote from Camp Chase outside of Columbus, Ohio: "We have in every respect better than I ever got before in the army, and if we only had a little excitement occasionally, I would be perfectly satisfied, but everything is getting distasteful to us in camp."[56] No doubt the combat veterans would have had some trenchant comments to make about the availability of fine rations for medical personnel. Similarly, the same veterans probably would have felt more than satisfied with the quantity and quality of "excitement" they had already experienced. After what they had seen and gone through, additional excitement was likely the last thing they wanted.

Excitement during demobilization did occur, albeit in quite a different form than that envisioned by George Jennys. Men in the 109th Pennsylvania Volunteer Infantry Regiment, on occupation duty in Savannah, Georgia, traveled by ship to Wilmington, North Carolina, and from there started for Raleigh, North Carolina, by road marches. On April 28, 1865, they returned to their previous camp at Goldsboro and there began to prepare the company accounts, issue rations, and, in general, get ready for a road march that would ultimately end in Washington, D.C. "Steady marches and long halts, too long where [they] had to sit in the hot sun," brought the unit closer to Richmond. Eight days into the journey, Sgt. Fergus Elliot recorded that three soldiers of the 2nd Brigade had suffered unusual non-combat casualties:

> [One soldier] was bitten by a moccasin snake and died three minutes after . . . another was bitten by a black racer, [and still] another while lying in the woods was bitten by a spider, the species called the "Chantillope" and was cramped all through his body but at evening was not dead, though expecting to die.

The troops in this unit marched in review in Richmond, "with bands playing, flags flying and the boys in the best of spirits. It was a splendid sight. . . . It was a pretty sight." From Richmond, the men moved on foot through the swampy areas common to that part of Virginia, ever alert to the "snakes and all kinds of poisnious reptiles [that] abound in the woods making it almost unsafe for one to rest for a few minutes." Passing through the battlefields of Spotsylvania Court House and Chancellorsville, men gazed upon "many unburied skeletons" as they gathered relics and trophies. Plagued by a shortage of potable drinking water, they finally arrived at Fairfax Court House, and from here they made ready to participate in the Grand Review in Washington.[57]

Pvt. Ernest H. Jacob of Company K, 8th New York Heavy Artillery, wrote in his pocket diary on May 15, 1865, while in camp five miles from Washington, "I think we will stay here for some time till after the review at any rate." The unit did participate in the review, leaving camp at 7 A.M. and passing in review at 8 P.M. That extended day was just the first in a long series of typical army experiences. There are many entries in the diary saying, "not much of any a count going on," "nothing of importance going on," "nothing new today," and so on. Finally, in September, after several months of delay, the unit was sent to Hart's Island, outside New York City, and on October 9, 1865, the veteran soldiers once again became civilians. It had been, indeed, "some time" before the unit was disbanded and personnel discharged.[58]

Another diary, maintained by Stephen P. Chase of Company H, 86th New York Infantry Regiment, recounts in a cryptic manner the unit's progress from Petersburg to Farmville and then back to Burksville, Richmond, Manchester, Fredericksburg, Alexandria, Washington, and the Grand Review. A month later, the homeward journey resumed. Through Baltimore by train and on to Elmira, New York, the regiment made its way, and on July 4, 1865, the soldiers were discharged. Interspersed with the litany of places are several comments that reveal Chase's state of mind: "My mind has been on home more of late than it has been since I was a soldier," "very much down," "downspirited, discontented; never felt more anxious to go home." These comments occur during the first month after the Appomattox surrender. In the next month, he wrote: "I am anxious to get out of service," "I am not feeling very well in mind. My mind is on home." His June 27, 1865, entry reveals a lot in just a few words: "Mustered out. I feel better." The next day, on the way to Elmira, he expresses a complete change of spirits: "I am feeling very well."[59] On that positive note, he ended his comments on his state of mind.

In a June 4, 1865, editorial, the *New York Times* praised the voluntary efforts of the Northern civilians, even attributing to them "the great achievements of this war."[60] Actually, the editor was alluding primarily to the volunteer soldiers who fought during the war, but the sentiments applied to the many civilians on the home front as well. The civilian efforts in behalf of demobilization were extensive, reaching to nearly every city and hamlet. One contribution was in the form of "bounteous repasts," "substantial dinners," and "bountiful collations," served to the troops as they made their way homeward.[61] Such attention paid to local troops upon arrival in their home areas is readily understandable, but such feasts were not restricted to local sons.

Both Philadelphia and New York City were generous in their reception and treatment of transient troops, and most homeward-bound soldiers received heroes' welcomes in all major cities and at train junctions. When the 20th Maine reached Philadelphia after its long ride from Washington, the local citizens enthusiastically received the soldiers and treated them handsomely. "A fine dinner" prepared the troops for the remainder of the journey to New York. There, after a brief respite at the Battery, they marched down Broadway to the steamer that would take them to Boston. "We were never received anywhere with greater enthusiasm than in the city of New York," said one soldier. According to the historian of the 11th New Jersey Infantry Regiment, "No city in the Union did more—if as much—for the soldier than did the city of Brotherly Love." Upon arriving there at 2 A.M., the troops were provided breakfast by the local civilians.[62]

But not every unit was as fortunate, although the coffee, pork, and beans provided to the men of the 2nd Minnesota Infantry Regiment in Cumberland, Maryland, still must have been quite welcome, especially in view of the inclement weather. The troops of five regiments bound for New England, the 7th Rhode Island, the 35th and 33rd Massachusetts, and the 9th and 18th New Hampshire, had to be content with more familiar fare, since they "were provided with rations at the Battery Barracks and took cooked rations with them."[63]

One regiment received a cooler reception in their own home state. When the men of the 105th Illinois Infantry Regiment passed through the country on their way from Washington to Chicago, they were well treated all along the route. The troops were "singing, cheering and yelling . . . happy and noisy as children." Their journey took them through Baltimore and Pittsburgh and other large towns and "at every city we were made welcome and great measures were taken to feed us." Regardless of the hour, day or night, when the train stopped, the men "were greeted by bands of music and by processions of patriotic men, women, boys and girls, and escorted to some large hall where everything good to eat had been provided for [them]." Their train and engine, practically completely covered by banners, finally reached Chicago. Here, not only was there no repast or feast waiting for them, but there was no housing either. Without supper the night of their arrival or breakfast the next morning, the hungry soldiers marched across the city to a temporary campsite, where they found "some rations." But the crackers, probably hardtack, were "alive with worms and the meat was so maggotty that we could not eat it," wrote Robert Hale Strong. Regimental officers eased the situation somewhat by buying dinner for the troops, but their anger had already been aroused. Indeed, the men threatened to hang the quartermaster if he did not come up with some "full, clean rations." Meanwhile, the existing potential for violence was augmented by alcohol when soldiers of the 105th, together with men from other regiments, began drinking in a "Dutch [likely German] beer garden." The combination of beer, empty stomachs, homesickness, anger over being so mistreated in their native state, and impatience for quick demobilization led to a "two-hour battle, using fists, chairs, and clubs." During the melee, the soldiers overpowered the police who had been sent to quash the disturbance and took their clubs. Nevertheless, order was finally restored, and the unit was discharged at Chicago on June 13, 1865.[64]

The men of the 22nd Iowa Regiment also found their reception at their state rendezvous point, in Davenport, Iowa, something less than enthusiastic. Hailed as conquering heroes all along the way, they traveled from Savannah, Georgia, by ship to Baltimore, then by train across the country. But when they arrived at Davenport, according to one soldier, they were "very coldly treated." The reason for this citizen indifference is unknown. The date was July 31; it is unlikely that the local population could have been jaded and bored at this early date by so many troops passing through. And after all, this was the troops' home state.[65] Whatever the explanation, there definitely were some negative aspects to an otherwise successful and publicly supported demobilization.

A particularly striking example of civilian support and assistance in demobilization, especially in facilitating the transportation of returning veterans through town, was the Strawberry Fund of New York City. Col. Vincent Colyer of the Soldiers' Rest, sometimes identified as the State Depot, distributed fresh meat, ice, vegetables, and fruit, especially strawberries, to the campaigners. Although the program began in a modest way, it grew to be quite a large operation. On one occasion, Colonel Colyer distributed about "500 baskets of the delicious fruit" (strawberries); another afternoon, "three thousand baskets of strawberries were sent . . . to the troops on Hart's Island," one of the rendezvous points. On June 19, in addition to fruit, "2,000 heads of salad, 1,000 heads of cabbages, and five crates of turnips" were furnished to the soldiers on Hart's Island. The hungry troops, weary of army fare, consumed these treats eagerly and enthusiastically. As

the word spread, market men and produce dealers donated fruit and vegetables, and interested and generous civilians contributed funds. The benevo-
lent work went on as long as returning soldiers made their way through the
city. Colonel Colyer went out to troopships lying in the harbor, distributing the tasty foodstuffs, as well as to the various rendezvous camps near the
city. No doubt many grateful veterans remembered the colonel and New
York City's Strawberry Fund to the end of their days.[66]

One of the officers of the 115th New York Volunteer Infantry, 1st Lt.
Nicholas J. DeGraff, the commanding officer of Company D, recorded in
his diary that the men were served with "a good dinner" at the State
Armory of the National Guard in New York City. He added that "the
greatest enthusiasm prevail[ed]." This stop was one of the last on a journey
that began in Raleigh, North Carolina, and finally ended in Albany, New
York, on June 27, 1865. Following a five-day delay for more paperwork, all
the troops were paid in full and mustered out of state service. As Lieutenant
DeGraff wrote, "For us the Civil War was at an end and all were glad to
return to the rewards of peace." By road marches, train travel, and a Hudson River steamer, this unit reached home strengthened and encouraged by
the hospitality shown them in New York City.[67]

Thus, with a wide variety of experiences, the Union veterans of so
many battles, campaigns, and seemingly endless days of monotonous service
gradually made their way home to their eagerly awaiting families.

CHAPTER EIGHT

Detour via
the Texas Border

*The big war not yet completely done, and
another, like a brush fire, threatened
To erupt along the Rio Grande, spurred on by
misplaced visions of grandeur.*

All during the war, along with the very real hazard of foreign recognition of the Confederacy, the saber-rattling of Napoleon III in Mexico with his puppet "empire" created the distinct possibility of Union military action to seal the border, as well as to prevent the French from gaining a permanent foothold in the hemisphere, which would be a definite violation of the Monroe Doctrine. Initially, with its army totally involved with the Rebellion at home, there was not much the Union could do except voice strong protests. In 1863, the French sent troops to Mexico, and in 1864, Archduke Maximilian of Austria arrived on the scene to assume the dubious position of emperor. Despite an ill-fated campaign to reach Texas via the Red River in Arkansas, the Federal government effectively postponed any overt military action until the cessation of most of the hostilities with the Confederacy. At that point, the Federal government speedily dispatched an effective force to Texas. This transfer of manpower created a detour for many units during the demobilization process, and the possibility of transfer to the Texas-Mexico border was rumored among many units, as evidenced in letters and diaries.

Lt. William N. Ashley, a member of the 2nd Provisional New York Cavalry, in a letter to his uncle, wrote from Clouds, Virginia:

I haven't the slightest idea what our duties are to be in our new
field of action. We are ordered to report to Major General [John
A.] Logan. There is a rumor floating around that our final destination will be Mexico but I can't hardly swallow that.[1]

In light of the fact that Gen. Philip Sheridan went to the Mexican border
immediately after most of the surrenders and before the Grand Review,
perhaps it was more of a possibility than Lieutenant Ashley realized.

Members of the 59th Illinois Infantry Regiment were in Georgia at
war's end, at Warm Springs, where the most popular rumor had everyone
going home soon. Instead, the regiment movd to Texas via New Orleans.
The Illinois unit took an inordinately circuitous route, going down (essentially north) the Tennessee River to the Ohio River, then to Cairo, Illinois,
and then down the Mississippi River to New Orleans, and so on to Texas
by ocean transport. Compared with rail travel of the day, travel by water was
cheaper for the government and more comfortable for the men, although
more time-consuming. To have come so close to home at Cairo en route
must not have been easy. The men were temporarily stationed as "a sort of
occupation force" in Texas, where they spent most of their time hunting
small game, alligators, and deer; putting on entertainment; and practicing
signals, along with some drill and guard duty. The regiment finally departed
for Illinois on Christmas Eve, 1865, first by ship to Vicksburg, Mississippi,
and then by steamer to Cairo, Illinois, where the troops then transferred to
the railroad. Despite an engine explosion en route, the men finally arrived
at Camp Butler early in January 1866. At long last, on January 9, 1866, they
signed the rolls, and four days later, the regiment was paid off.[2]

Members of the 2nd Rhode Island Infantry Regiment had also heard
the rumors of a possible detour along the Mexican border, as letters of
Charles E. Perkins to his sister testify. On May 11, 1865, he wrote:

We are camped on the rail road between Burks Station and Petersburg but do not expect to stay here long but whare we shall go no
one seams to know but I hope we will go home but I am afraid
thay will ceep a great part of us. Thay are agoin to discharge all the
disabled soldiers and all that thair time expires before the first of
July and that is why I think thay will ceep the rest of us. They will
ceep the most of us until after the trouble is settled in Texas. I see
by the papers thay think a great many of the rebels will go thair and

try and do all thay can and if thay do try anything of that cind we old soldiers will be the ones that will be sent after them but you can bet I will try to git out of the army as soon as posable for I think I have don about my part and would like to come home once more and see how it would seam to be a free man once more.

Five weeks later, in a camp near Washington, D.C., Perkins apparently had determined that his unit would not be transferred to Texas, but he complained about the continued absence of the paymaster. "If he ever does come it will be a good pile for thay owe me nearly 6 months pay now."[3] Short of gambling and the purchase of sundry articles, there does not seem to have been much practical use for the cash. Apparently it was simply the desire to have in one's pocket the funds owed that underlined the soldiers' constant complaints of delayed pay.

Army life in Texas was not all recreation and minor military duties, as the men of the 48th Ohio Infantry Battalion, a provisional unit constituted from three veteran regiments, could attest. So irate did they become over the perceived inefficiency of the mustering-out process that a mutiny resulted. The War Department's plan was to replace volunteer units with regular soldiers as they became available, but there were inevitable delays in the arrival of the regulars. In addition, there was a conflict between the civilian government of Texas and the Federal military authorities. Aware of the need for security, the governor of Texas felt that demobilization was proceeding too quickly. Gen. Philip Sheridan, however, as commanding officer of the district, wanted to alleviate unrest among the volunteer soldiers by discharging them as quickly as possible.

When a black cavalry brigade of the XXV Corps received orders to go to the Gulf area, they also mutinied. The 4th United States Cavalry Regiment, a Regular Army unit, transferred to San Antonio to replace the volunteers in Gen. Wesley Merritt's command. The first task of the 4th U.S. Cavalry was to suppress the mutiny by insurgent volunteers demanding to be discharged. In Galveston, Texas, the citizens much preferred black troops to the soldiers of the all-white 17th United States Infantry Regiment, who had reputations of drunkenness, disorderly conduct, fighting among themselves, and even fomenting a small race riot. Partly because of these incidents of unrest and impatience, volunteer troops remained on duty in Texas longer than did their counterparts in the rest of the South. Of the seventy-three volunteer regiments of all branches of service that were mustered out in Texas by the end of 1865, more than half, forty, went through the system between November 1 and December 31. Obviously, the demobilization process proceeded at a slower pace in Texas.[4]

Coinciding with demobilization of the volunteer units, yet another military activity, redeployment of regular troops, was a constant occurrence. A major transfer involving 25,000 soldiers took place in May 1865, when the XXV Corps moved from the James River in Virginia to the Rio Grande area of Texas as part of the protection required to offset the potentially volatile situation in Mexico. Simultaneously, 7,000 men transferred to Savannah from the Potomac River area. The latter movement was part of the overall plan for maintaining a military force in the territory of the late Confederacy. The volume and magnitude of such moves, no less than those of the demobilization program, are obvious when one realizes that the twelve-day voyage of the XXV Corps from City Point, Virginia, required fifty-seven ocean steamers. Chartered steamers were more economical than railroads and obviously quicker than road marches.

The 26th Ohio Infantry Regiment, one of the regiments in the IV Corps, was another outfit that saw service in Texas before being mustered out and finally discharged. Early in May 1865, the unit was at Camp Harker, near Nashville. According to Henry Shedd, a member of the regiment, the troops had "easy times and plenty to eat"; they even received what Shedd termed "sanitary supplies."

By June 10, rumors about Texas began. On June 27, the journey began: from Nashville by train to Johnsonville on the Tennessee River, then down (north on) that river by steamboat to Paducah, Kentucky. The unit then traveled on the Ohio River to Cairo, Illinois, and on the Mississippi River to New Orleans. Up to this point, the transfer of troops was fairly routine, although "the soldier's fare was so poor—hard crackers and raw meat." Unfortunately, the only drinking water available was that which the river provided, and it was "very poor . . . warm and muddy."

For the next month, the 26th Ohio was in camp five miles below New Orleans, among alligators, magnolias, figs, oranges, and the ever-present dirty river water. It was then on to Texas by the end of July, where the regiment initially bivouacked on the prairie in a location with plentiful shade and water. Unfortunately for Shedd and many others, the clean water came too late; he wrote that he had diarrhea, that many soldiers were sick with the same complaint, and that some were dying every day.

After a move near Matagordo Bay, and despite the improvement in food, as Shedd described the "flour, beef and beans," supplemented by fresh oysters from the bay, he was still sick. His weight had dropped from 160 to 140 pounds. In the third week of October 1865, the homeward journey began, first by steamboat to Galveston, and then via another steamer to New Orleans, which they reached on November 4. The trip up the Mississippi River took six days; at Cairo, the men switched to the railroad, arriving at Columbus, Ohio, November 12. Shedd finally made it home on November 16, "sick with army diarrhea" and still wondering why the IV Corps had been sent to Texas. Sixteen months later, Shedd was dead from his wasting disease, yet another casualty of the war.[5]

The threat to national security along the Texas border lessened as diplomatic pressure, together with the very real presence of a powerful army of U.S. forces, gave the French second thoughts about their support for the "empire." As their support waned, the forces of Benito Juárez became more successful; ultimately, the "empire" collapsed, and Emperor Maximilian suffered the ultimate penalty, execution. As a result, no longer was there a realistic possibility of military action in the area. For the most part, the troops that had been detoured to the Texas border could now return to the demobilization pipeline and the established system. The troops in these units, as a result of their delayed processing, had the advantage of entering a system that was functioning well, with the initial hurdles and obstacles long removed.

CHAPTER NINE

Confederate Demobilization: The Reality

Disbanded soldiers, tramping toward the West
In faded army blouses, singing strange songs.
Heroes and chicken thieves, true men and liars,
Some with old wounds that galled them in the rains
And some who sold the wounds they never had
Seven times over in each new saloon.
—Stephen Vincent Benét

By the time demobilization was necessary, the Confederacy had no organized programs of any kind, let alone demobilization. This is not to say, however, that the journeys of the homeward-bound Confederates were uneventful. In some respects, the men in gray had perhaps even more interesting experiences than did their erstwhile opponents in blue.

In a very real sense, the paperwork concerning the demobilization of the Confederate armies started and, for all practical purposes, ended in a period of two days at Appomattox Court House. An unnumbered Special Order from Confederate Headquarters, dated April 9, 1865, read as follows:

Lieut. Genl. J. Longstreet, Major General J. B. Gordon and Brig. Genl W. N. Pendleton are hereby designated to carry into effect the stipulations this day entered into between Lieut. Genl. U. S. Grant, Comdg. Armies of the United States and Genl. R. E. Lee, Comdg. Armies of the Confederate States, in which Genl. Lee surrendered to Genl. Grant the Army of Northern Virginia.

By command of General R. E. Lee.[1]

This order is especially interesting in that it is headed "Armies of the Confederate States," and yet it pertains to the surrender of only one of those armies, the Army of Northern Virginia. The following day, a matching Special Order was issued, also without a number, by Headquarters, Armies of the United States:

> All officers and men of the Confederate service paroled at Appomattox C. H., Va., who to reach their homes are compelled to pass through the lines of the Union armies, will be allowed to do so and to pass free on all Government transportation and Military rail-roads.
> By Command of Lt. Genl. Grant.

This order was countersigned, "By command of Genl. R. E. Lee," making it official for the Confederate troops.[2]

Perhaps never before or since has so little paperwork generated such a tremendous upheaval and such a monumental movement of troops. One of Jeb Stuart's cavalrymen described rather graphically the transformation that resulted from these two documents: "Suddenly they were free—free from starvation, free from restless nights of trying to sleep under blankets of rain and snow, free from death itself, free to go home, and free to start rebuilding for the future."[3]

In a postwar memoir, William Forbes II, a member of Captain Croft's Flying Artillery Battery from Columbus, Georgia, described the events that occurred almost exactly a month later and several hundred miles away from Appomattox Court House, in Citronelle, Alabama, following Gen. Richard Taylor's surrender to Gen. E. R. S. Canby: "Now, two hundred miles from home, one more march began; one that would lead weary men down dusty roads to more hardships and the leavings of a conquering army."[4]

Lt. Gen. James Longstreet described the Appomattox surrender scene, writing that the Army of Northern Virginia "deployed into line, stacked their arms, folded their colors, and walked empty-handed to find their distant, blighted homes," carrying with them only their "rage, anguish at failure and defeat, bewilderment and helplessness, uncertainty as to who they were, [their] rights, position and property, [as well as doubts concerning] any hope for the future."[5]

Some of these defeated veterans did possess material resources, however. Included in the surrender terms for the Army of Tennessee was the provision that "each returning body of soldiers might hold a number of rifles, equal to one-seventh of their numerical strength, for protection and hunting on the way."[6] When Gen. Nathan Bedford Forrest surrendered, as a part of the troops included in Taylor's submission to Canby, the chief of artillery, John Watson Morton, told his men, "You have your paroles in your pockets; and if everyone does not ride home on a good horse, it will be no fault of mine."[7] This was an allusion to the provision generally included in all the surrender agreements that men who possessed horses and mules might keep the animals.

One articulate artilleryman, whose memoirs have been widely quoted, used his wits to ease his journey home. Edward A. Moore, a member of the Rockbridge Artillery, did not rate a horse, as he was a cannoneer. At Appomattox, he prevailed upon a Lexington neighbor and former teacher, Gen. William N. Pendleton, chief of artillery for the army, to appoint him to the position of courier. This particular assignment required a horse, and so Moore rode home and then, after fattening the animal, was able to sell him for "a good price, and was thus enabled to return to Washington College and serve again under General Lee."[8]

Many are the references to the worn-out condition of the men, their uniforms, their shoes, and their wallets. An Englishman, Francis Lowley, observed the surrender at Appomattox:

By the evening of the 12th the paroles were . . . distributed, and the disbanded men began to scatter through the country. Hardly one of them had a farthing of money. Some of them had from 1,500 to 2,000 miles to travel over a country of which the scanty railroads were utterly annihilated.[9]

Another observer of the Appomattox scene described the condition of the men of the 26th North Carolina Regiment and their fellow soldiers: "Thousands were penniless. Many had hundreds of miles to travel without money or means of transportation."[10]

Even though General Grant's order permitted use of government transportation, the ruined condition of most of the Southern railroads effectively blocked their use for demobilization or any other purpose. The veterans of the Army of Tennessee were in similar straits, as the following, in part based upon St. Paul's Epistle to Timothy, indicates:

On foot, or astride the bony army horses, or piled in the patched-up, creaking army wagons, they started home over the mountains [from Durham Station, North Carolina]. They had fought a good fight, they had finished their course, they had kept the faith . . . most of them were barefoot, in rags, and destitute of any personal property.[11]

Still another spectator of the surrender at Appomattox Court House described the Confederate soldiers in graphic terms:

As a rule they were tall, thin, spare men, with long hair and beard of a tawney red color. They were all clad in the uniform of Southern gray; nearly all were ragged and dirty, while their broad-brimmed, slouching gray hats gave them anything but a soldierly appearance.[12]

Although the observer does not mention it, there seems to be an implicit wonder that these men could be the savage opponents of so many bloody battlefields. After the surrender ceremony, according to a Union soldier, "the southern soldiers returned to their bivouac areas, either to be paroled or to gather their few belongings . . . then start for home, without a cent . . . ragged and lousey." A veteran of the 30th North Carolina Regiment described how they "were turned out into the world[,] most of us without any money, with one weather-beaten suit of cloths, and nothing to eat, entirely on the mercy of somebody else."[13]

One predominant characteristic of the relationship between the victorious Yankees and the defeated Rebels, which appears again and again in diaries and memoirs, is the kind and charitable assistance rendered the defeated soldiers by their conquerers. Many of the Confederate officers renewed friendships with their prewar army comrades and their West Point classmates. Gen. Edward Porter Alexander related how a classmate, Union lieutenant colonel Edward R. Warner, offered to advance him "two or three hundred dollars." Alexander had already borrowed some funds from another acquaintance, but he considered Warner's offer a gracious gesture. At Appomattox, General Grant ordered sufficient rations to be distributed to the Confederates, and thus the Confederate veterans had something more substantial to eat than the parched corn that, together with some scrounged fruit, had been the mainstay of their diet for too long. Col. Asbury Coward of the 5th Regiment, South Carolina Volunteers, sincerely appreciated the "bread, cheese and a cup of real coffee."[14]

"Courtesy, consideration, and good will"—these words, or ones similar in meaning, abound in the recollections of individual Confederates at the time of their capture or surrender. At Waynesboro, Virginia, Pvt. Henry Robinson Berkeley, a member of the Hanover Artillery, had become a prisoner early in March 1865, when Gen. Jubal Early's force was defeated at the conclusion of the second Valley Campaign. Berkeley recalled that "the Yankee guards . . . [were] still kind and considerate, taken as a whole. A few . . . [were] sometimes cross and ugly." William R. Talley, a cannoneer in the Confederate artillery for most of the war, surrendered at Greensboro, North Carolina, on April 20, 1865. He too remarked that "the Yankees were very kind to us." The Union soldiers loaned the paroled Confederates three wagons and teams for their baggage and cooking utensils. The only condition for the loan was that the men return the wagons and teams to the U.S. Army when they reached Perry, Georgia. Men of the 3rd Texas Cavalry, part of Gen. Richard Taylor's army that surrendered to General Canby in Alabama, were "pleasantly surprised by the kindness and generosity of their erstwhile enemies."[15]

Kindness and generosity, and even offers of funds, were not limited to general officers who had known each other in happier days. A private in the 14th North Carolina Infantry Regiment mentioned Yankee offers of money to the Confederates. He pointedly said that "they did not know the hospitality of Dixie. That wherever we went on our long road . . . food would be freely given . . . to assist a veteran of Lee's army."[16]

For the most part, this veteran's observation was confirmed by fact. "The local inhabitants shared their homes and food with the returning soldiers." In a typical example of Southern hospitality, two soldiers were headed for Richmond on foot, with nothing to eat and no money with which to buy any food. On the second day of their journey, they reached a house where the housewife made them welcome and fed them hoe-cake, cornbread, bacon, and buttermilk.[17]

Soldiers from North and South Carolina were pleasantly surprised to be cheered by the men of the Union V Corps; they wished each other speedy and safe return trips to their homes. One Confederate, a native of Farmville, Virginia, on his way home from Lynchburg, "met a Federal soldier. . . . We met face to face, shook hands cordially, and by common consent sat down . . . and began discussing the situation and outlook generally. . . . The manly way with which he met me . . . was a great gratification to me." A member of the 45th Pennsylvania Infantry Regiment related how "we got to be quite chummy with the Confederate paroled prisoners." Money was exchanged by men from both sides at a rate of $100 Confederate for $1 U.S.[18]

Kindness and consideration were evidenced in other ways. A cavalry escort from Company F, 4th Massachusetts Cavalry, under the command of 2nd Lt. Samuel C. Lovell, was detailed to conduct General Lee and his staff along the road to Richmond. After some twelve miles along a road "strewn with dead mules and wreckage," General Lee shook hands with Lieutenant Lovell and wished him a safe homeward journey, and the commanding general's party continued on its way. Sgt. William B. Arnold, who occupied the position of honor in the escort, the right guard, described General Lee's breakfast that eventful morning as "hard tack, fried pork and black coffee." "A splendid looking soldier," General Lee was neatly dressed in his gray uniform. After receiving farewells from his corps and division commanders, General Lee started through the Rebel lines. His passage was marked by ovations and the Rebel yell from the men of the Army of Northern Virginia, a sort of a final salute to their commander. Their duty to General Lee completed, the men of the escort returned to their unit at Appomattox.[19]

Not every Confederate's journey started out as conveniently as did General Lee's, as Gen. John B. Gordon related in his memoirs. After receiving what he termed a "cordial farewell from Union soldiers," he and thousands of other men began their long journey home. En route to Georgia, his first stop was at Petersburg, where his wife was recovering from an illness. He and his wife and child, together with an aide and his family, began their "arduous trip homeward, over broken railroads and in . . . dilapidated conveyances."[20]

Some of the return travels were long indeed. A sergeant from Texas, Valerius C. Giles, had been away from home for four years and five months. Slowly and "painfully," he then spent three months on his way home. Upon his arrival, he stated: "It is finished. I have worn my last gray jacket. I have fired my last shot for Dixie."[21]

A much longer journey was made by Gen. John C. Breckinridge, the last Confederate secretary of war, a former Kentucky legislator, congressman, senator, vice president of the United States under President James Buchanan, and presidential candidate in the crucial 1860 election. His travels were as remarkable as his prewar political career. Realizing that his wartime experiences as general and as secretary of war in Davis's cabinet made him a special target for possible retaliation, Breckinridge started out for Florida and the rivers and waterways of that state, on his way to freedom. Using a small boat, together with two military aides and a servant, he gradually made his way by sailing and rowing. Once the men placed the boat on a wagon drawn by oxen in order to proceed to the Indian River, a distance of twenty-eight miles. "Through Florida we received nothing but kindness," said Breckinridge, although the driver of the wagon was "the only person in Florida who dealt closely with us." In order to avoid Federal outposts and blockaded inlets, the men hauled the boat across a sandy strip of land and thus were soon afloat on the Atlantic Ocean. On their way to the Bahama Islands, the crew of a U.S. vessel nearly captured them, but they posed as local fishermen and hunters, and so escaped capture. Adverse winds foiled their attempts to reach the Bahamas, and so they decided to go to Cuba.

After procuring some food from some Seminole Indians, the men traded their boat, together with a $20 gold piece, for a more seaworthy vessel. With this added advantage, they started out for Cuba. After working their way southward along the Florida coast, they began the most hazardous part of the journey. Steering by the stars and a small pocket compass, a three-day trip brought the party to the harbor of Cardenas, Cuba, on June 11, 1865. From this point, they proceeded to Havana. July 28 found Breckinridge in London, England. Before returning to the United States in March 1869, Breckinridge traveled through Switzerland, down the Danube River, reaching Turkey, then Greece, Egypt, Palestine, Italy, and back to England. His next stop was Toronto, Canada, where he settled for a time, until finally he was permitted to return to Kentucky. His return home was possibly the longest in both time and distance; the fact that he was amply provided with funds, an advantage enjoyed by few Confederates in 1865, made such a trip possible.[22]

In a postwar memoir written and published very soon after the close of hostilities, Gen. Jubal A. Early described how he had started to join Gen. Kirby Smith in the Trans-Mississippi Department, following his own relief from command at the end of March 1865. Before he was able to reach Smith's army, General Early learned of its surrender and headed to Mexico:

> After a long, weary, and dangerous ride from Virginia, through the states of North Carolina, South Carolina, Georgia, Alabama, Mississippi, Arkansas and Texas, I finally succeeded in leaving the country; a voluntary exile rather than submit to the rule of our enemies.

Aided by a disguise, he finally reached Mexico, but after a few years there, he returned to Virginia and his law practice in Lynchburg.[23]

Gen. Pierre Gustave Toutant Beauregard's trip home to New Orleans was relatively mild and not too demanding physically. He and his party, consisting of his staff and some officers from Louisiana, went south from Greensboro, North Carolina, after Johnston's surrender to Sherman, traveling part of the way in army wagons. At times, they were able to trade army provisions for food. As they passed through South Carolina, officers from that state left the party to go home. Beauregard visited with the governor at Edgefield, South Carolina, and then made his way to Augusta, Georgia, thence on to Mobile, Alabama, where he was able to book passage on a U.S. naval transport. He arrived in New Orleans on May 21.[24]

Not every general in the conquered Confederate military had access to funds that would ease the transition from the fields of surrender to their homes or other destinations. Gen. Richard Taylor is a case in point. An extremely wealthy man prior to the war, at war's end he was completely out of funds. "I was without a penny," he wrote in his account of his post-surrender travels. He had surrendered to General Canby at Citronelle, Alabama, about forty miles north of Mobile. Together with a few staff officers, he remained at Meridian "until the last man departed"; then he went to Mobile. Granted transportation with General Canby, he and his servant, together with two horses, went to New Orleans. His vast estate had been confiscated and sold, and his investment in slaves had disappeared. At this point, he sold the horses and thus obtained funds sufficient to move his wife and children from the Red River to New Orleans. Taylor praised General Canby as being "just, upright, and honourable," another instance of smooth cooperation between quondam foes.[25]

Gen. Joseph Wheeler had some unusual experiences before he finally arrived home. One of the Confederates who absented himself from the formal surrender at Durham Station, North Carolina, Wheeler, together with a few of his men of the cavalry corps, started out from Washington, Georgia. On the way, others joined, and finally Wheeler was forced to dismiss many of the soldiers "because they made a company too large to escape observation and too small to defend themselves." There was still a sense of fight in this feisty general, a trait that would become manifest in the Spanish-American War, when Wheeler donned the blue uniform of the U.S. Army. General Wheeler and his party were betrayed by a black man and thus were captured in broad daylight in their bivouac area. Arrested and sent to Fort Delaware, on Pea Patch Island in the Delaware River, he remained in solitary confinement but was released after some months on orders of the secretary of war. In what some historians have termed "the last battle of the war," on his way home, General Wheeler was taken sick in Nashville. Two Union officers who had just been discharged from service assaulted him in his hotel room. Wheeler successfully fought off the two attackers, finally making his way home, and thus lived to fight another day, in another war.[26]

Even generals experienced a downside in connection with Southern hospitality, which apparently had some limits. Gen. William Mahone and his party of six officers and men were on their way from Appomattox to Charlotte Court House. They were cold, hungry, and tired when they came upon a beautifully appointed country home that seemed to be surrounded by flocks of sheep and lambs, turkeys, chickens, and even pigs. This sight was indeed welcome to their eyes, and they had every expectation of at least an opportunity to sleep and eat, perhaps even feast. General Mahone sent one of the party forward to request hospitality of the owner, even to the extent of paying in gold, if necessary. The major returned with word that the owner, a woman, did not want any soldiers about the place, they could not stay there, and they should move on. The general sent the major back with the information that this was not just any group of soldiers, but rather Gen. William Mahone and his staff. The answer was the same; not only did the owner not want any soldiers there, she informed the major that she had never heard of General Mahone, much less the major. The men had the fleeting temptation to stay on the property anyway and to help themselves to fodder and food. But Mahone felt that such action would create a bad example, so the group continued on their way to Charlotte Court House, about four miles farther along the road. As the major asked rhetorically, "What is fame?"[27]

A correspondent of the *New York Tribune,* observing the paroled and surrendered Confederate soldiers, remarked:

[I was] daily touched to the heart by seeing these poor homesick boys and exhausted men wandering about in threadbare uniforms, with scanty outfits of slender haversack and blanket roll hung over their shoulders, seeking the nearest route home; they have a careworn and anxious look, a played-out manner.

A young lad in a small town in North Carolina described the sight as "a sad procession; some were halt and lame, and some with one arm or one eye."[28] Yet these men, careworn, anxious-looking, and wounded as they may have been, were on their way home, and nothing was going to prevent them from making their way, however long and circuitous, to that goal.

On his way back to Texas, a soldier saw a sight in Greenville, Tennessee, that he considered especially significant. In his diary entry for May 19, 1865, he described the sight of black children going to school, saying, "I was never more surprised in my life." He asked a twelve-year-old girl questions about grammar, geography, and arithmetic, based on her fourth reader, "which she answered very readily and correctly." With great foresight, he wrote that in the future, black and white will be in professions, farmers, and merchants, and that "the smartest man will succeed without regard for color. The smartest man will win—in every department of life." White children "will have to contend for the honors of life against the negro in the future."[29]

Without the fanfare and martial splendor of 1861, the scene in the late Confederacy in 1865 was quiet and subdued as, "singly and in small groups, the army . . . dissolved into history and myth."[30]

CHAPTER TEN

Repatriation of Prisoners of War

The triple stockade of Andersonville the damned,
Where men corrupted like flies in their own dung
And the gangrened sick were black with smoke and their filth.
There were thirty thousand Federal soldiers there
Before the end of the war.
—Stephen Vincent Benét

Because of their special conditions and circumstances, the demobilization of two categories of service personnel—prisoners of war and hospital patients—was of a different variety. Each side had many thousands of prisoners, and each army's hospitals held large numbers of wounded and ill soldiers. Even the structured demobilization plan of the North could not handle these two categories of men.

The best known of the Southern prisoner-of-war camps holding Union soldiers was Camp Sumter, in west-central Georgia, better known as the Andersonville Prison, although this was not the only prison in the South. Andersonville also was not the only prison in which foul and death-threatening conditions existed. The North also had several substandard Civil War prisons, including Elmira Prison, in New York State; Point Lookout, Maryland; and Johnson's Island, in Lake Erie. Present-day historians do not hesitate to describe many such prisons, both North and South, as "concentration camps" or "death camps." Some of the harsh conditions were due to the universal belief that the war would be over in a short time, with no need for provisions for prisoners; revenge for treatment of the opposite side's prisoners; cessation by the Union of the parole and exchange policy for captured soldiers; and in the South, the Union naval blockade, which resulted in a dearth of needed medicines, as well as poor transportation facilities, which prevented distribution of food and supplies for prisoners.

Andersonville Prison, Georgia, showing overcrowded conditions

Early in August 1864, S. P. Moore, surgeon general of the Confederate Army, asked Joseph Jones, a surgeon in the Provisional Army of the Confederacy and also professor of medical chemistry at the Medical College of Georgia, to make an in-depth study of conditions at Camp Sumter. This report, which is extremely detailed and remained unfinished at the time of Gen. Joseph Johnston's surrender on April 26, 1865, was never submitted to the surgeon general. The report reveals graphic descriptions of the camp, its operations, the diseases that caused so many deaths among the Union prisoners, as well as some poignant opinions and comments by Dr. Jones. His description of the physical condition of prisoners portrayed a grim picture:

> The haggard, distressed countenances of these miserable, complaining, dejected, living skeletons, crying for medical aid and food, and cursing their Government for its refusal to exchange prisoners, and the ghastly corpses, with their glazed eye-balls staring up into vacant space, with the flies swarming down their open and grinning mouths, and over their ragged clothes, infested with numerous lice, as they lay amongst the sick and dying, formed a picture of helpless,

hopeless misery, which it would be impossible to portray by words or by the brush. A feeling of disappointment, and even of resentment, on account of the action of the United States Government upon the subject of the exchange of prisoners appeared to be widespread, and the appparent hopeless nature of the negotiations for the general exchange of prisoners appeared to be a cause of universal regret and of deep and injurious despondency. I heard some of the prisoners go so far as to exonerate the Confederate Government from any charge of intentionally subjecting them to protracted confinement, with its necessary and unavoidable sufferings, in a country cut off from all intercourse with foreign nations, and sorely pressed on all sides, whilst on the other hand they charged their prolonged captivity upon their own Government, which was attempting to make the negro equal to the white man.[1]

Another section of this report accurately sums up the many problems the Confederacy faced in relation to its ability to maintain such a prison in anything remotely resembling satisfactory conditions:

As long as the Confederate Government is compelled to hold these prisoners as hostages for the safe exchange of the captive men of its own armies, it is difficult to see how the sufferings of such an immense army of prisoners, equal in numbers at least to one-fourth of the Confederate forces actively engaged in the field, can to any extent be mitigated in a purely agricultural country, sparsely settled, with imperfect lines of communication, with an inflated and almost worthless currency, with no commerce, with few or no manufactories of importance, cut off from all communication with the surrounding world, and deprived of even the necessary medicines, which have been declared "contraband of war" by the hostile government. With torn and bleeding borders, with constantly diminishing powers of subsistence and resistance, with its entire fighting population in arms, with a constant retreat of the armies and population upon the central portions of the country, and with corresponding demands upon the supplies of the overcrowded interior, and with corresponding increase of travel upon the dilapidated railroads, the maintenance of the prisoners becomes every day more difficult and onerous.[2]

Following the April 9 surrender of the Army of Northern Virginia, "arrangements were made to formally release the remaining prisoners of war of both sides." At Camp Ford, Texas, when the news of the surrender reached the camp, the guards took off for their own homes, leaving the Union prisoners to fend for themselves. "At nearly . . . [all] other locations, . . . the POWs were held anywhere from several more weeks to several more months." Part of the delay in returning Confederate prisoners to the South was due to the concern that the U.S. government had in locating and arresting prison commandants and officers of Southern camps and prisons. Likewise, the return to the North of Union prisoners held in the South received greater priority. As a consequence of these objectives, there were more than 64,000 Confederate prisoners in twenty-two prison facilities in the North. The problem was far from inconsequential.[3]

By the end of May 1865, there were still 48,000 POWs held in the North, with almost 19,000 of this total in Point Lookout, Maryland, alone. The assassination of President Lincoln temporarily halted the return of Southern prisoners to their homes, but by late April, the process had resumed.

Even though the discharge of prisoners was again under way, General Order No. 109 was issued by the U.S. War Department on June 6, 1865, to formalize the procedure for discharge. All enlisted men in both the Confederate Army and Navy, including petty officers, merely had to take the oath of allegiance in order to obtain discharges. Officers—captain and below in the army, and lieutenants and below in the navy—obtained discharges, unless a man had held a commission in the U.S. Army or Navy at the beginning of hostilities. Upon the completion of such discharges, higher-ranking officers would receive treatment according to regulations that were to be issued at a later date. The usual regulations granting priority to men who had been longest in prison and who had to travel to remote points in the country applied. Likewise, transportation by rail or steamboat was authorized by this order, although such transportation had already been provided to many thousands of paroled prisoners.[4]

During the next two months, thousands of Confederates made their homeward treks; by the end of July, only 2,500 POWs remained in Northern camps, 1,000 of whom were held in New York's Elmira Prison.[5]

Generally, Confederate POWs in camps and prisons in the East received rail transportation to Richmond or other major points in the South. Prisoners in the Midwest, however, were not so fortunate; despite the provision for transportation in the general order, many of them were simply released and had to find their own way home. Weak from poor nutrition, scantily clad, and often partially disabled by war wounds, the men moved slowly by foot through the countryside.

Fort Lafayette, which was located on a small island in the harbor of New York City and now exists only in the fill used to support one of the towers of the Verrazano-Narrows Bridge, was the last major Union prison to hold Confederate prisoners of war. By the end of October 1865, only forty prisoners remained at the fort; most of the military prisoners were released the following month, and by year's end, the prison held only four men, who were political prisoners.[6]

Despite all the delays, inconveniences, and limitations, these freed ex-prisoners were the lucky ones: They were alive! Some 56,000 prisoners, both Union and Confederate, did not survive their incarceration. These men found their final resting places far from their homes, often in unmarked graves.

For the men who were still alive in Andersonville at the end of the war, arrangements were made to return them as quickly as possible to their homes in the North. Prisoners were shipped out of Andersonville by railroad and riverboat. Large groups of soldiers, one of 900, and two contingents of 1,500 men each, traveled to Vicksburg, Mississippi, to the parole camp located there. The last group returned to Andersonville, presumably for exchange via Savannah rather than Vicksburg. Three trains, each with more than 3,000 prisoners, started for Savannah by way of Macon, Georgia. Thanks to the threatening Union cavalry raids, the trains had to detour to Florida via Thomasville, Georgia. The parole and exchange took place at Baldwin, Florida, just west of Jacksonville. The authorities abandoned the prison compound at Andersonville by May 4, 1865.[7]

Several disasters ocurred in transporting the men, each representing a tragic loss of life. The worst of these was the April 27, 1865, *Sultana* disaster, which has been called "the worst maritime disaster in American history."[8]

At the end of the hostilities, the prisoners from Andersonville in Georgia, as well as captured Federal soldiers held in Cahaba Prison, some ten miles south of Selma, Alabama, on the Alabama River, were moved from their prison sites to a neutral exchange camp, Camp Fisk, set up near Vicksburg, Mississippi. In this installation, the men were to prepare physically for their journey home and receive proper uniforms. Many of these returning soldiers had not only suffered greatly while in the Confederate prisons, but they also endured some arduous traveling en route to Camp Fisk. Including both rail and river travel, as well as road marches, the trip to the camp was not without dangers and difficulties; there were at least three derailments and two train wrecks, resulting in injuries to some of the recently freed men.[9] From Camp Fisk prisoners of war were sent home on a daily basis, in both large and small groups, supposedly not exceeding one thousand men, depending upon the availability of suitable vessels.

Launched in January 1863, the *Sultana,* a luxuriously appointed vessel furnished with the latest safety equipment, had just passed its periodic safety inspection and received a certificate of approval.[10] The steamboat departed from New Orleans on April 21, 1865, yet due to a boiler problem, it took two days to reach Vicksburg. Here it should be noted that the *Sultana* was equipped with tubular boilers, rather than conventional boilers, a fact of some importance in the unfolding events. At Vicksburg a local mechanic, under direction of the vessel's chief engineer, made hasty, patchwork repairs to the boiler so that the ship could proceed without delay to St. Louis. Meanwhile, three trainloads of paroled prisoners were transferred from Camp Fisk to Vicksburg, ready to board the first available vessel for the first leg of their journey to Camp Chase, Ohio, where they would undergo their final processing.

It was at this point that incompetent officials took over, with individuals, who had never seen the boat, ordering and controlling the loading process. A more accurate term would be overloading; one crew member, the First Clerk, told Sgt. Alexander C. Brown of the 2nd Ohio Infantry that there were "more people on the Sultana than were ever carried in one boat on the Mississippi River." The best estimate of the total number loaded on the boat is 2,400 soldiers, 100 civilian passengers, and 80 crew members, not to mention freight and animals. The legal capacity of the *Sultana,* however, was 376 passengers and crew.[11]

The situation was somewhat complicated by the fact that the requisite rolls had already been made out; to change the loading schedule at this point would have required much additional clerical work. During the loading phase both the ship's captain and Maj. W. H. Fidler, who was in charge of the returnees, complained about the obvious overloading, which made the hurricane deck sag due to excessive weight. In order to ease the problem, some of the men were redistributed to other parts of the vessel. A photograph taken during a short layover at Helena, Arkansas, shows the great crowd of people on board. Also, at this time, the river was at an exceptionally severe flood stage due to melting snow and ice upstream and heavy rains.[12]

Upon arrival at Memphis on April 26, tons of freight that had been on the lower decks was offloaded, and with the weight of so many men on the cabin and hurricane decks, the ship became top-heavy. Thus imbalanced, the *Sultana* left Memphis just before midnight.[13]

At about 2 A.M. on April 27, three of the ship's four boilers, including the one with the patchwork repairs, exploded. Overcrowding, flooding, and a strong current meant that the vessel had to run under increased pressure. This additional strain was too much for all the boilers, not just the one with patchwork repairs. Also, the river's muddy waters had caused clogging in the boilers' tubes, a disadvantage of this particular type of boiler. Add to all this the top-heaviness of the boat, and it is easy to see how the disaster occurred.

The explosion killed hundreds of soldiers, and hundreds more were hurled into the river. Many were unable to swim and thus drowned. When the cabin deck gave way, hundreds more slid down into the shattered furnace. In the cold water, surviving soldiers and passengers fought over pieces of floating wreckage, some clinging to dead horses and mules for warmth, with many suffering from exposure. An Arkansas man with a raft managed to rescue thirty-seven men from the wreckage.[14] About seven hours after the initial explosion, the *Sultana* finally sank. The exact number of deaths is not known, but the best estimates place it between 1,700 and 1,750.

In the early 1980s Jerry Potter located the remains of the vessel beneath the surface of an Arkansas bean field. Thanks to the ever-changing river course and the use of a magnetometer, the *Sultana's* location is now known. No excavation has been done, however, due to the high cost of such work and the likelihood that nothing remains except some charred timbers and pieces of metal.[15]

Soon after the *Sultana* disaster, the quartermaster general called for the "strictest attention" to details so that only perfectly safe transports were employed, and these should not be "overloaded." "Extreme caution" was to be used at all times. Even so, on June 9, 1865, a steamer on the Red River, loaded with 1,200 paroled Rebel prisoners, sank in three minutes after hitting a snag below Shreveport, Louisiana. The initial report was that approximately 200 soldiers lost their lives, but an eyewitness account a few days later stated that "the loss of life has been greatly exaggerated, that only fifteen or twenty whites and perhaps fifty Negroes were lost, instead of two hundred, as reported." (This report reflects the racial discrimination typical of that era, even in the face of tragedy.) In another accident, a steamer loaded with troops collided with a monitor near Cairo, Illinois, on June 19, 1865. This steamer also sank, but the loss was confined to "a number of horses and much government freight."[16]

For Union prisoners remaining in Southern prison camps during the last few months of the war, the situation was one of total confusion, much of which resulted from the ubiquitous presence, both real and rumored, of Gen. William T. Sherman's Army of the Tennessee. Communication was slow and often inaccurate, leaving the Confederate officials in the dark as to the best path to follow in their attempts to maintain the prisoners and avoid confrontation with Sherman. One historian described the confusion:

> The Confederates were in a quandary. By mid- to late December [1864,] they had POWs going in every direction and were never certain where they were at any one time . . . others seemed to be traveling in circles, surrounded by [guards] along the railroad . . . during the night and heading out to some other destination each morning.

One Union POW remarked, "The Rebels were terribly puzzled what to do with us."[17]

There was confusion on both sides in the days immediately following the major surrender at Appomattox, and even before the surrender of Gen. Joseph E. Johnston's force at Durham Station, North Carolina, as correspondence reveals. On April 19, 1865, Gen. Bradley T. Johnson received a rather frantic request from the officer in command at Greensboro, North Carolina: "Is any one at Salisbury in charge of Federal prisoners? I have 200 at my headquarters that I wish to dispose of. Please answer at once." The next day, from Little Rock, Arkansas, Maj. Gen. Joseph J. Reynolds sent a message to Maj. Gen. Henry W. Halleck in Washington to inform him that there were about 100 POWs in the Department of Arkansas who had applied for parole, believing the Rebel cause hopeless. He asked, "What shall be done with them?" At almost the same time, on April 22, 1865, the Union commissary general of prisoners informed the commissioner for exchange that "it is important to release the numerous prisoners waiting at parole camps."[18] Although this was fine in theory, the reality failed to measure up to it.

Libby Prison, Richmond, Virginia, used for commissioned prisoners

Maj. Thomas J. Halsey, 11th New Jersey Volunteer Infantry Regiment, captured at Petersburg in June 1864, first went to Libby Prison in Richmond, then to Macon, Georgia; Charleston, South Carolina; and ultimately to Columbia, South Carolina. Exchanged at Northeast Ferry, North Carolina, he rejoined his regiment at Appomattox in May 1865. One revealing letter, dated February 10, 1865, said that the prisoners had had no meat since October 4 of the previous fall. Despite the short rations, he was optimistic about the prisoner exchange process. His optimism was well placed, although its fulfillment did take some time. Early in June 1865, he wrote that they "expected to be mustered out tomorrow and leave for Trenton."[19] This was one soldier who maintained his morale at a high level, despite the poor food and his status as prisoner, along with all the usual characteristics of army life.

The lack of a structured Confederate demobilization program carried over to the treatment of Union prisoners of war. One such soldier, Corp. James Benedict, a member of the 140th New York Volunteers, captured at Bethesda Church at the time of the attack at Cold Harbor, Virginia, in June 1864, regained his freedom in a most informal fashion. After incarceration

Camp Douglas, south of Chicago, used for Confederate POWs

in Belle Isle prison at Richmond and at Andersonville, Georgia, Benedict was transferred to Jacksonville, Florida. On April 9, he was "one of a large number who were turned loose in Florida to find [Federal] lines best they could." Somehow he made his way North and arrived in Rochester, New York, in advance of the regiment.[20] No doubt this man's story was one of the most unusual accounts of service experiences.

For the most part, aside from the Red River incident, the returning Confederate prisoners of war did not experience tragic accidents or catastrophes, although they often had to follow rather involved and roundabout routes in order to reach their homes, with circumstances forcing them to use any form of transportation that presented itself. The fact that some of the Northern prisons and prisoner-of-war camps were relatively close to the South did not make much difference in the travel the men had to undergo.

On the way, they underwent a broad spectrum of receptions from the local civilians. Confederate veterans from heavily pro-Union areas in some instances encountered kindness, but often they detoured to avoid the pro-Union sectors, and sometimes they even went into unfamiliar areas because of the pro-Union sentiments.

In Rock Island, Illinois, a physician's wife provided food for the prisoners released from Camp Douglas, near Chicago, who were waiting for riverboats. Men from Johnson's Island received two days' rations from a kind citizen in Ohio. Women in Louisville, Kentucky, were also hospitably inclined toward prisoners, according to postwar memoirs.

All was not kindness and concern, however. Women in Cincinnati had given R. A. Bryant and his companions some food, but a Union captain "kicked the baskets in the river, cussed the women and left [the men] hungry." When John Hickman arrived in Louisville, he was arrested, taken to the local Union headquarters, and had the "brass buttons cut from [his] uniform."[21]

One Confederate soldier in Wilmington, North Carolina, apparently had had more than enough of the war when he wrote on July 20, 1863: "I want the Yankees to take me prisoner and parole me and let me go home."[22] Whether or not his wish was fulfilled we do not know, but it is safe to say that his request was an unusual one.

One Texas soldier, Charles A. Leuschner, who was hardly more than a lad, was captured at Spring Hill, Tennessee, in November 1864. He finally arrived at Camp Douglas, Illinois, early in December, after a combination of train trips and road marches. On May 1, 1865, well after the surrenders at Appomattox and Durham Station, he and the men with him learned that 500 Confederates were eligible for exchange and that he was one of the lucky ones. By railroad from Chicago to Cairo, Illinois, and then by means of river steamer, the group moved to New Orleans. The trip proceeded rapidly; they had started from camp on May 4, and on May 10, they arrived in New Orleans, after having passed through Columbus, Kentucky; Memphis, Tennessee; Helena, Arkansas; Vicksburg, Mississippi; and Baton Rouge, Louisiana. At this point, they entered a prison under the guard of black soldiers, who, according to Leuschner, treated them better than had the white soldiers at Camp Douglas. Two weeks later, they traveled back up the Mississippi River to the mouth of the Red River, where they were exchanged and transferred to their own boat, presumably one especially set aside for their use. They started up the Red River on May 27, 1865, and arrived at Shreveport, Louisiana, the next day. Here they began a road march, and thus this small group of seven men entered Panola County, Texas, southwest of Shreveport. One man in the party retained a gun and carried a cartridge box, presumably because of the danger of Jayhawkers in the area. Begging food from the local residents, they always had enough to eat.

Their journey by foot meant a march of 250 miles, which they completed in good time, having started June 2 and arriving at Navasota, Texas, about 75 air miles from Houston, on June 12. Here, much to their surprise, they met other veterans of their unit, Company B, Lone Star Rifles, 6th Texas Infantry Regiment. These men had traveled from Greenville, Tennessee, to Nashville by train, and then by steamer to New Orleans and by ship to Galveston. On June 15, the reunited group marched on to Columbus, Texas, another 75 or so miles, where the local inhabitants provided them with "a fine supper." The next day, they arrived home in Victoria, thus ending a journey of a month and a half.[23]

One of Stonewall Jackson's foot cavalrymen, twenty-year-old Andrew Davidson Long of Company A, 5th Virginia Regiment of the Stonewall Brigade, wounded and captured at Spotsylvania Court House in May 1864 and processed through the Union evacuation system for the wounded, recuperated in Lincoln Hospital in Washington, D.C. By July, he had recovered enough to qualify for transfer to the prison camp at Elmira, New York, a few miles north of the Pennsylvania–New York border. He survived the winter and received a thirty-day parole dated March 24, 1865. Transferred by railroad to Baltimore, he then boarded a boat for Richmond, but he had to march the final three miles of the trip. Having in his possession some Yankee soap, Long was able to trade it for some Confederate chewing tobacco. He tried to arrange for transportation on the Virginia Central Railroad as far as Staunton, but he could not do it because the line was torn up. Neither could he use the canal to go to Lexington, as the locks had been damaged and were out of service. He was able to ride the railroad as far as Lynchburg; then he too resorted to the foot march. To walk the seventy-five miles from Lynchburg to Staunton was not much of a challenge to one of Jackson's veterans. Three days later, Long arrived in Staunton. Then he had only eleven miles to reach his home, where he arrived on March 29 to a belated birthday celebration. (He had turned twenty-one on March 9.) Even though he completed this journey just before the Appomattox surrender, his pattern of transportation provides a good view of the situation in that part of Virginia, which certainly did not improve in the short time that elapsed before the surrender. Aside from the three days spent on the road, the entire trip was made quite rapidly.[24]

Another example of early Confederate demobilization appeared in the memoirs of Henry Clay Mettem of the 1st Maryland Cavalry, C.S.A. Captured in West Virginia in August 1864, and after a trip via freight cars, he arrived at Camp Chase, a few miles from Columbus, Ohio. Even though he had participated in an unsuccessful tunnel escape, he obtained a parole for sixty days "unless sooner exchanged." On his way south, Mettem traveled by train to Baltimore and stayed overnight at Fort McHenry. He then went by steamer to Richmond, but the review of Adm. David Dixon Porter's fleet by President Abraham Lincoln, during the halcyon days of the first week of April, delayed him on the James River. Mettem finally reached Richmond and went on to Camp Lee, where he obtained a formal parole at last.

Mettem wanted to go back to Maryland to obtain some money with which to purchase some horses and then return to his unit. He was able to cross the Potomac River, and in St. Mary's County, he went to the house of a friend of his father's. His own home was in Pikesville, northwest of Baltimore, and Mettem decided to write to his father for funds while remaining in relative isolation. When his father replied, he informed his son that Lincoln had been assassinated and that Henry should stay where he was. Not wanting to endanger his friend for harboring a Confederate soldier, Mettem hid in the woods for about a month. News finally reached him of the surrenders, and he decided to try to make his way home. After borrowing some clean clothes, he went to Charlotte Hall and there was able to take a stage to Washington. Once there, he rode the Baltimore and Ohio Railroad to Baltimore, and then walked the few miles to his Pikesville home.[25]

Alfred R. Gibbons of the 1st Regiment of Georgia Cavalry, in Gen. Joseph Wheeler's Corps, was captured in July 1864, near Atlanta and thus was a prisoner at the time of Gen. Joseph E. Johnston's surrender. He had been a cadet at the Virginia Military Institute but had resigned and joined the army in December 1863. As a captured prisoner, he began his journey to Camp Chase, Ohio, but thanks to the inebriated state of the guards, he was able to jump from the train and thus make his escape. He decided at this point to try to make his way to Canada but was caught stealing some civilian clothes from a clothesline. Placed in the local jail and later sentenced to two years in the state penitentiary in Michigan City, Indiana, Gibbons consistently refused to take the oath of allegiance to the United States. "I never received a cent of pay and never had a furlough. I was never discharged and have never taken the oath of allegiance and never expect to," he wrote. At the end of August 1865, his father was able to pay him a visit. After a series of letters and petitions to the governor, Gibbons finally received his pardon. Together with his father, he traveled by train to Indianapolis, on to Chattanooga, and then into Georgia, arriving at Rome on a handcart, as it was Sunday and the trains were not operating. Gibbons is credited with being the last soldier from Floyd County to arrive home.[26]

Johnson's Island, in Lake Erie's Sandusky Bay, was another of the Northern prisons located in inaccessible spots for security reasons. Lake Erie may have been a reasonably pleasant spot a few weeks of the year, but for much of the time, it was one of the least desirable places in the Union, especially during winter. Winter in that clime was prolonged, to say the least. Many were the tales of poor shelter, limited clothing, and rations that barely sustained life. Despite all these hardships, prisoners were still in camp at the end of the hostilities, and these men were eagerly waiting to go home. One of them, James Cooper Nisbet of Company H, 21st Georgia Infantry Regiment, had become a prisoner at the July 1864 battle of Atlanta. By road march and train, he moved progressively from Atlanta to Marietta, Georgia, then on to Chattanooga, where the local jail became his temporary residence. From this point, he went on to the penitentiary in Nashville and then to Louisville, Kentucky. After traveling through Indiana and Ohio, he reached Sandusky, Ohio, and finally, Johnson's Island. Held there for more than three months after the surrenders, he obtained his release in September 1865. Knowing that his father had friends in New York City, he went there and received a gracious reception, turning down offers of money and business opportunities from his father's friends. On his way to his home in Georgia, he stopped over in Charlotte, North Carolina, where he visited the young lady whom he later married.[27]

Another prisoner of war at Johnson's Island was Lt. John H. Lewis, who had been in Huger's, R. H. Anderson's, and George Pickett's divisions of the Army of Northern Virginia. Captured at Gettysburg on July 3, 1863, he entered captivity at Johnson's Island via Baltimore and also Fort Delaware. Exchange of prisoners resumed in January 1865, but the process was very slow. By the time Lewis was in the pipeline, Richmond had fallen; thus he found himself back in Fort Delaware. On June 13, 1865, released and provided with transportation, he began the last leg of his already lengthy journey and arrived home two days later.[28]

Capt. F. M. Imboden wrote to his sister on May 18, 1865, from Johnson's Island about his prospects of getting home: "Don't know when I can hope to be with you again—possibly in a few weeks, tho' I hardly think so soon, as no policy has yet been announced towards us."[29]

Two winters on Johnson's Island were required of Thomas H. Malone, another one of Gen. Joseph Wheeler's cavalrymen. His prisoner-of-war status began at Shelbyville, Tennessee, late in June 1863. Within a month, he was at Johnson's Island, where he remained until early in 1865, after the resumption of exchanges. He and others who were eligible for exchange crossed the ice to the city of Sandusky, jumping from one floating ice cake to another. He took a train to Baltimore and a steamer to Fortress Monroe, then transferred to a "little steamboat" for the trip up the James River to the exchange point, presumably City Point. Once in Richmond, Malone received his back pay and was given a furlough permitting him to go home. He was, however, directed "to hold in readiness to join [his command] as soon as notice of exchange should be given . . . [but] such notice was never given. Indeed, the end came before the exchange was effected."

Like so many others before and after him, Malone experienced great difficulty in traveling south of Virginia, due to Federal raids and the destruction of railroads as part of Sherman's march through Georgia to the sea. He and two others, one a brother of the late Maj. John Pelham, headed for Montgomery, Alabama. They reached Danville, Virginia, by train, but here they had to make "a portage of several miles" to the next available operating section of railroad. Slowly they made their way through South Carolina and Georgia, alternately riding and walking. This phase of the journey required several days, as they carried their packs and bivouacked at night under the open sky. No food or supplies were available for purchase, but even if there had been something available, they had only Confederate money, which was practically worthless. Malone described the journey as consisting of "several hundred of us, marching as one body but each for himself." The campfires at night gave the impression of "an army . . . camping near." They entered no houses along the way, probably because of the universal affliction of the Confederate soldiers—body lice.

About twenty-five miles from Washington, Georgia, Pelham went on alone, and Malone moved more slowly with a companion, who was very sick with pneumonia. At one house along the road, they stopped to seek shelter. Malone wanted to be sure his companion would receive care while he went on ahead in order to obtain some sort of conveyance. The woman of the house refused the request. Malone's comment: "The damned heifer!" All was not lost, however, as they met a man who had two horses; he loaned them to Malone and his sick companion so that they could ride on into Washington, where he was able to get proper medical attention for the ill veteran. From here, Malone went by rail to Montgomery, Alabama, his original destination. By a roundabout route, he finally reached his home in Athens, Georgia. It was a long journey, all the way from the Canadian border to the Deep South, but Malone made it.[30]

For some reason, a former member of Ashby's cavalry by the name of Simpson did not receive transportation for his homeward journey from Johnson's Island to Augusta County, Virginia. Perhaps he refused to take the oath of allegiance, but in any event, he was at liberty to make his way as best he could. Penniless, he walked as far as Indiana. At some unnamed town, he went into the local hotel, hoping to meet somebody who would help him. Here he came upon a group of men, including a Union officer, at the bar of the hotel. The officer loudly proclaimed that he had taken a vow to kill everyone he met of Ashby's unit. Simpson, without thinking, announced that he was one of Ashby's cavalrymen. The officer pulled out his pistol and fired three times. Either the officer was a poor shot or his aim was affected by whatever he had drunk, because he only lightly wounded the ex-Confederate. The Ashby veteran grappled for the pistol and shot and killed the officer. Arrested and thrown into prison, he spent several months awaiting trial. When the trial was held, Simpson was acquitted, and then he started again for his Virginia home. He arrived in Lynchburg by train from Tennessee and received assistance from local people who knew him. From Lynchburg he went on to his home, some seven miles from Staunton, in Augusta County. These experiences occurred in 1866, so, as the local Lynchburg paper said, Simpson was perhaps "the last 'rebel' in gray [to] come back to his home."[31]

Pvt. John Thompson, a member of the Jeff Davis Artillery, was wounded and captured in the last battle of the Army of Northern Virginia, on April 9, 1865. The soldiers in blue took him to a Federal hospital in Farmville, Virginia. In all the confusion and excitement of those hectic days, Thompson was able to escape his captors. Once free, he set out to join Gen. Joseph E. Johnston's army in North Carolina. The nature of his wound is not revealed; although apparently serious enough to warrant attention in a hospital, it was not severe enough to keep him from escaping and making his way to the remaining Confederate force in the eastern theater. Here, he was included in the surrender of that last force, and during the next few weeks, he seemed to be on a tour of Federal prisoner-of-war facilities in the East. Taken to Fort Delaware, he went on to Elmira, New York; then to Newport News, Virginia; and finally, he arrived at Point Lookout, on the southern tip of Maryland's eastern shore. Here, Thompson was released and paroled, thus ending his war experiences.[32]

Men returning home from camps such as Elmira, Point Lookout, and Johnson's Island had a variety of experiences. All types of transportation were put to use—both passenger and freight trains, chartered steamboats, and even, in some cases, coastal ships. William Durrett remembered that his train trip from Johnson's Island to his home in Sumner County, Tennessee, via Cincinnati, was "pleasant . . . [I] was not molested during my trip." W. T. Askew said that he had been "treated fine along the road," but Jessie Broadeway recalled that during his train ride through the North, he "nearly starved." One Tennessee soldier, incarcerated at Point Lookout, Maryland, made his way to New York City in order to obtain transportation on a vessel bound for Mobile, Alabama. "The ship was blown away" in a severe storm; no one drowned, although several men died afterwards, presumably from exposure or injuries received during the incident.[33]

Another prisoner of the Federal forces found himself at Point Lookout at the end of the war. W. J. Andrews of Company K, 23rd South Carolina Volunteers, also used different forms of transportation, including a handcar on the railroad. He started his return to South Carolina in a rather standard fashion, by steamer to Charleston. Then he took the railroad, bound first for Orangeburg and then for his home in Sumter, but the bridge across the Congaree River had been burned out, thus ending the rail travel for the time. A local man with a boat took Andrews and his companions across the river, but not without a fare being paid. The fare was finally agreed upon: "a good pair of blankets and about 50 cents worth of tobacco." Once across the river, they were able to proceed by handcar to Kingsville. At this point, they received free passage to Sumter and home.[34]

After beginning his prisoner status in October 1864 near Woodstock, Virginia, George M. Neese, a gunner in Chew's Battery of Stuart's Horse Artillery, Army of Northern Virginia, made quite a trek through northern Virginia and into Maryland, finally ending up, along with thousands of his peers, at Point Lookout. Early in May 1865, after the surrender of Appomattox, the entire camp registered to take the oath of allegiance to the United States. His June 29 diary entry reads, "About 20,000 released since June 9." He was released that very day. Since he had taken the oath, he received free transportation by boat and railroad. The next day, he passed Fortress Monroe, and the steamer made its way up the James River. When night fell, the boat stopped at Harrison's Landing; the next morning, after waiting for high tide, they reached Richmond. At this point, he was able to switch to rail transportation and left by train for Gordonsville. Once there, the men started out on foot. A kind woman in the area provided the group with a bucket of buttermilk. Still on foot, Neese went through Madison

Court House, his only food "berries and cherries." Another sympathetic housewife gave him some pears. On this diet of fruit, he crossed the Blue Ridge Mountains and went into Page County. At a farmhouse, he had his "first square meal . . . in nine months, and [it was his] first time at a table in fourteen months." On July 4, he was on top of Massanutten Mountain. The next day, he arrived home, still carrying the blanket he had taken to war with him. Ironically, his home was only about twenty miles from Woodstock, the place of his capture some nine months earlier.[35]

Toward the end of the conflict in Virginia, Martin Brett received a wound at Cedar Creek in October 1864. Back on duty in time for the siege of Petersburg, Brett was unable to keep up with his comrades, who were withdrawing after an unsuccessful attack on Fort Steadman, and thus became a prisoner on March 25. Via General Grant's headquarters, where he was "reviewed" by President Lincoln, together with Generals Grant and Meade, Brett then took up residence at Point Lookout, Maryland, along with "40,000 prisoners." He mentions that there was a "great influx [of prisoners] during the latter days of combat." Rations were "pretty tough," and the drinking water was "very bad." There were some places in camp where "tolerabaly good drinking water could be had if one could get a permit." At Point Lookout, the prisoners were at first under guard of black troops, but after a time, these soldiers were replaced by white troops. On June 24, Brett took the oath and was sent by boat to Richmond, just as George Neese was a few days later. After receiving rations and transportation, Brett headed for his home in Georgia. Since the railroads were "badly torn up from Richmond south . . . [I] rode a little and walked more." July 6 saw him in Atlanta; from here, he went on to LaGrange, almost on the border with Alabama. He had friends who lived ten or twelve miles out in the country, and for two or three weeks, Brett recuperated with them. Once recovered from his travels, he headed back to Atlanta, then as now the railroad hub of the South, in order to take a train to his home district. By foot march, he finished his journey home to Drayton, about halfway between Macon and Albany, in Dooly County, Georgia.[36]

Two months after Lee's surrender at Appomattox, going by the fictitious name of Robert Cannon, a veteran asked, "Why did the government retain us in prison?" "All the Confederate armies had disbanded," he continued, so what was the point of the prisoners still being held in camps—in Cannon's case, Point Lookout, Maryland? Shortly after he asked this question, the men in his group took the oath, and thus he started out by means of a steamer to Richmond and, from there, went on to his home. He was another one of the soldiers captured during the final days of combat, just prior to the surrender.[37]

Pvt. Daniel Holt of Company K, 16th Mississippi Infantry Regiment, became a prisoner in the Petersburg area in August 1864. He was at Point Lookout until November 1, 1864. Although strictly speaking, his trip home was not a part of demobilization as such, his travels and modes of transportation were typical of the travel means used a few months later by thousands of his comrades in arms. It is quite certain that there was no improvement in the various forms of transportation between November 1864 and May 1865; if anything, they deteriorated.

Holt began his journey aboard a ship bound for Savannah. He then started to travel by railroad. It took four different railroads in order for him to reach Montgomery, Alabama, where he was able to bathe, obtain fresh clothing, and rest for a week at the home of an uncle. The next leg of his journey was by boat on the Alabama River to Selma, Alabama. He wanted to take the Alabama and Mississippi Railroad to Demopolis, but the railroad was "out of commission." The only practical alternative was road marching. He and "a Negro valet . . . a fine fellow," started out. Walking about twenty-four miles a day and camping out at night, they finally arrived in Meridian, Mississippi. In order to reach Jackson, they boarded a train, but "the roadbed was in such a bad fix that it was a foolish venture to travel at night," and they had to stop frequently to take on wood. When they reached the Pearl River, passengers had to get off the train and cross the river on "a flimsy, makeshift of a bridge that barely cleared the water." Holt finally got to Jackson and walked to the State House. His plan was to go by train on yet another railroad to Summit and then to walk to Woodville, sixty-six miles farther. He was able to go as far as Hazelhurst and then continued to Woodville by buggy, together with a friend. The two men traveled with two other buggies for mutual protection from local marauders. Two nights' travel saw Holt finally at home.[38]

Yet another Confederate soldier, captured in the last days of the Army of Northern Virginia, ended up at Point Lookout, Maryland. Julius Leinbach of the 26th North Carolina Regimental Band, a Moravian organization of musicians, was a casualty at Hatcher's Run on April 5, 1865. For almost three months, he sustained life in the prison camp, living in crowded, filthy conditions, with no privacy and with restrictions on water consumption. The usual fare, according to Leinbach, was a piece of bread in the morning and about 1 P.M., a piece of meat or decaying codfish and a pint of soup. Conditions were so bad that men eagerly sought assignment to the sanitary police detail because in that way they could obtain a double ration. "Some [prisoners] set traps at the cook-house for rats to add to their bill of fare." Finally, on June 28, 1865, Leinbach was paroled and discharged. He set out by train for High Point, North Carolina, then went on by foot on his way to Salem. On the road he had a stroke of luck: He met his brother with a buggy and, best of all, with food! July 2 saw him at home. His journey did not take too long, but considering the living conditions he had left, it must have seemed a long trip indeed.[39]

Prison camp conditions and the experiences of prisoners on their way to prison camps help explain the eagerness of the men to get away from the camps and get on the road home. In addition, they help explain the men's appreciation for the least little assistance, be it food, clothing, shelter, or transportation on their journeys home. David E. Johnston, a youth in Company D, 7th Virginia Infantry Regiment, is a case in point. On the 150-mile trek that he and his companions made to Point Lookout, food was at a premium. He related how the men and their guards came upon a drove of cattle destined for the Union Army. The guards butchered some of the animals and handed out some of the meat to the prisoners, who ate it "blood raw, without salt, while marching." This raw diet was the first food they had been given in about two weeks. He described the extremely limited food rations in camp: "eight ounces of bread per day, a thin slice of bacon or salt pork, almost transparent, and a pint cup of very thin bean soup." The men were always hungry. Johnson had weighed 165 pounds when he entered the camp; when he left at the end of June, his weight was down to 127 pounds. The prison camp population was more than 23,000 in an area of twenty-two acres. With such a concentration of men and such poor food, it is no wonder that deaths, according to Johnston, "from April to July were more than 6,800!"[40]

Johnston was one of the lucky ones; he survived and received his parole and discharge. He went by steamer to Richmond, as did so many others. He had no money, no food, and no place to stay. He slept in the yard of the Chimborazo Hospital for a time. He started by train from the Danville station in Richmond and "slowly, due to an old, broken-down engine, made [his] way to Burkeville and then Farmville." Yet another train took him to a point six miles short of Lynchburg; he then boarded a packet boat and arrived at Lynchburg on July 1. Two days later, he boarded still another train and headed west to the foot of the Allegheny Mountains. Here, the railroad was broken, so Johnston made his way on foot through the Allegheny Tunnel to the depot at Christiansburg. Still on foot, he begged some bread and milk, crossed the New River, and arrived at his home on July 5, 1865. His long journey, beset with all manner of noncombat perils, was at last over.[41]

Hiram Smith Williams, although born in New Jersey, served the Confederacy in a variety of ways. At first he was in the 40th Alabama Volunteer Infantry Regiment. Since he was a skilled craftsman, he was placed on detached service (then as now a soldier's dream assignment) to work as a naval carpenter in Mobile, Alabama. In February 1864, he was sent back to the regiment but immediately transferred to the Pioneer (Engineer) Corps. Eight months later, he was with his regiment and became a prisoner of war on March 19, 1865, at Bentonville, North Carolina. He arrived at Point Lookout, Maryland, just about the time that General Lee was surrendering his army to General Grant. As is so often the case, rumor took over. Rumors were circulating that 3,000 prisoners were to be shot in retaliation for Lincoln's assassination; all prisoners who arrived in camp after March 25 were to be transferred to Elmira, New York; and prisoners were to be paroled "tomorrow." "Tomorrow" stretched out through April, May, and June, into July. On the last day of July 1865, all the men obtained their release, except for a few officials of the Confederacy. Williams was back in Alabama "within a few months."[42]

A Virginia native with many family connections in the Lower Valley of the Shenandoah, John O. Casler was a private in Company A, 33rd Regiment of the Virginia Infantry, a part of the famous Stonewall Brigade. Captured near Winchester early in February 1865 and sent to Fort McHenry in the Baltimore Harbor, Casler received aid from an uncle from (West) Virginia, who provided him with some money and also clothing. On May 1, he took the oath of allegiance to the United States and began his trip home. An uncle in Baltimore helped him with additional funds and suitable clothing. From Baltimore, he took a train to Winchester, where he went to the home of yet another uncle, who lived some fifteen miles from Winchester. From here, Casler was able to visit with his relatives in the neighboring counties. After spending some time making the rounds of his family, he went back to Winchester and started up the Valley, finally arriving at Harrisonburg, his home.[43]

"The end of this long and bloody war is certainly drawing to a close and that very rapidly. And what an awful close it is going to be." So reads the March 27, 1865, diary entry made by Pvt. Henry Robinson Berkeley. At that time, he had been a prisoner for almost a month, following his capture near Waynesboro, Virginia, on March 2. His unit was part of Gen. Jubal Early's command, and its defeat at Waynesboro was the end of the Confederate military presence in the Shenandoah Valley. Berkeley's travels as a prisoner were fairly typical: a road march to Winchester, then on by train to Harpers Ferry, Baltimore, and Fort McHenry. After two days, he was transferred to Fort Delaware, on Pea Patch Island in the Delaware River, near the junction of the Chesapeake-Delaware Canal and Chesapeake Bay. "Our Yankee guards are fairly kind; but I find some who are fiends incarnate." Like all prisoners of war, Berkeley was interested in the war news. "The Philadelphia Inquirer is the only newspaper which the Yanks will allow." From this source, as well as rumors and reports from the guards, the prisoners learned about the surrenders. According to Berkeley, at this time there were about 6,000 enlisted men and about 1,500 officers held at Fort Delaware.

At first, almost everyone refused to take the hated oath of allegiance, but at the end of April, they obtained a copy of the *Richmond Whig.* This issue of the newspaper revealed a long list of prominent people of Richmond who had taken the oath. With this news, most of the prisoners hesitated no longer; they took the oath.[44]

Distance from home was one of the factors that determined the order of departure; length of time in prison was the other. Men from the remote areas of the Confederacy as well as men who had been in prison the longest were released first. On June 11, men from Mississippi, Alabama, Florida, and South Carolina began their journeys home. On June 16, the Georgians started home, and the North Carolina men departed on June 20.

Berkeley had taken the oath and left the same day as the North Carolina soldiers. He received three days' rations of hardtack and pork, and took passage on a Baltimore-bound boat, which went through the Chesapeake and Delaware Canal. In Baltimore, he transferred to a large steamboat; he reached Richmond about sunset on June 23. At this point, he obtained permission to leave the contingent in order to travel on his own. The next day, he boarded a train for Staunton, and thus he reached home.[45]

One of the North Carolina contingent was Lt. E. L. Cox of Company C, 68th North Carolina Infantry Regiment. He had been a prisoner since

Old Capitol Prison, Washington, D.C., used for both civilian and military prisoners

July 1, 1864, and had made the rounds of several camps—from Camp Hamilton, Virginia, to Point Lookout, Maryland; a stay in the Old Capitol Prison, in the nation's capital; and finally, Fort Delaware. Following his release, when he arrived in Baltimore, he and his companions, all officers, were "well received by the citizens. Many of our number has received full outfits of clothing and plenty of money. All are in high spirits." A combination of "poor accommodations and many of the men being drunk" made a very disagreeable steamer trip to Fortress Monroe. After transferring to Norfolk, he went on to North Carolina, where he "was received with open arms."[46]

Two other Confederate officers, Capt. Henry C. Dickinson of Company A, 2nd Virginia Cavalry, and Capt. Robert E. Park of the 12th Alabama Infantry Regiment, both at Fort Delaware, remarked again and again at the extreme pressure exerted on them to swear the oath of allegiance. Submission to the oath was a gradual process, for the most part, as many of the men tried to hold out as long as they could. But as the news of the surrenders filtered into the camp, more and more of the prisoners submitted. For Dickinson, the crucial moment was the capture of Jefferson Davis; Park held out longer, until after Mosby surrendered. Once they swore the oath, the men were free to go home.[47]

Some of the Confederate prisoners incarcerated at Fort Delaware were part of a rather infamous transfer of men to Morris Island, outside of Charlestown, South Carolina, in August 1864. The purpose of the transfer was to place the prisoners in a position of danger from Confederate artillery in retaliation for the Confederate threat to place Union officer prisoners near a hospital in order to deter shelling by Union forces. Nothing came of this incident, except that some of the men spent eighteen days on a ship, en route to Charleston.

Once back in Fort Delaware, Capt. W. H. Morgan, a man of Northern birth, remained there until May 21, 1865. His brother, who lived in Brooklyn, had somehow arranged for a special order in Washington for Morgan's release. The captain's brother arrived at the fort with the order, and the two went to Brooklyn, where Captain Morgan spent two weeks. He left New York City by steamer, bound for Norfolk, and then proceeded up the James River to Richmond. Via the Richmond and Danville Railroad, he started for Lynchburg. He could only go as far as Burkeville due to a break in the line. He went on to Farmville by wagon, and then back on the train to another break in the railroad. Finally, by canal boat, he arrived in Lynchburg. The next day, Morgan traveled the remaining twenty-one miles to his home in Campbell County. Thus ended yet another journey of mixed transportation modes.[48]

Another captain, Henry E. Handerson, an assistant adjutant general, was likewise part of the shipment of prisoners to Charleston as a deterrent to the shelling. When he finally took the oath of allegiance at Fort Delaware, it was after Jefferson Davis had been captured. This event convinced him that the Confederacy had been destroyed. He went by steamer to Philadelphia and there became a free man.[49]

A private in the 19th Mississippi Infantry Regiment, Matthew Jack Davis, captured in May 1864 and sent to Fort Delaware, remained there until the end of the war. He and two fellow prisoners obtained their freedom, but with no money and no transportation, only the well-worn clothing on their backs, this group had some 1,500 miles to travel, and none of the three men knew anyone north of the Mason-Dixon Line. Taken to New Castle, Delaware, they wandered through town. Suddenly they spotted a waving handkerchief and quickly found themselves guests of a widow and her daughter, whose son, and brother, was in the Confederate Army. An eight-year-old girl had recognized the men as liberated prisoners and alerted the ladies in the neighborhood. They were treated to "a nice supper," and then about a dozen women, all Southern sympathizers, greeted them. The men accepted invitations to dinner for the next few days and started to look for work. Local sympathizers of the Southern cause paid for their lodging at a local hotel and paid for train tickets to Philadelphia. Here they went to a large, fine hotel, armed with a letter of reference. The owner of the hotel suggested another hotel for them, at his expense. The men were not successful in locating work; only one had a trade, that of brick molder, while the other two had been farmers.

At this point, they decided to look for farm work out in the country, but there they met with "rebuffs, insults and abuse." After seeking work in vain for a week, the three veterans arrived in Wilmington, Delaware, tired, hungry, and desperate, as they had had no food that day and had slept in the woods. Twenty discharged Union soldiers took the three Confederates into their camp and fed them. In Wilmington, the tradesman was able to find work in a local brickyard. The owner, whose wife had been born and raised in Vicksburg, Mississippi, helped them with some funds and also gave them a letter to U.S. senator George R. Riddle of Delaware. Senator Riddle arranged for transportation, but Davis was overcome by the heat in the brickyard, so the three men went back to New Castle to stay with the people who had first befriended them, until Davis recovered. Once recovered, and given some cash and decent suits, Davis and his companions went to Baltimore and then on to Washington, where they were supposed to obtain the transportation the senator had arranged. While in Washington, they were among the spectators at the Grand Review of the Federal troops. After looking in vain for the proper officer and the transportation arrangements, they decided to go right to the top. They called on Gen. Ulysses S. Grant, and the men got results! Grant took the three men to the War Department and directed Secretary Stanton to arrange the necessary papers. In one hour, everything was set, and they were on their way home.

Since they were to travel on the B & O Railroad, they had to backtrack to Baltimore. While in Baltimore waiting for their train, the three ex-prisoners took part in an argument that broke out between "over-ardent Unionists and rebel sympathizers." The argument got out of hand, the police were summoned, and the ringleader of the Northern contingent was arrested, along with several of his supporters.

Their departure time was 10 P.M. The next day saw them through Harpers Ferry; then it was on to Cincinnati and Columbus, Ohio, through Indiana and Illinois to Cairo, Illinois, where they met some of their fellow prisoners who had left Fort Delaware ten days ahead of them. At Cairo, they boarded a steamer, which took them to Memphis. The men pooled their funds and found that they had $43 among them. The entire group had a good breakfast, and then Davis and his two fellow travelers, who now had no money due to their generosity at breakfast, started to walk home, a distance of some 100 miles. It was, indeed, "a long journey home."[50]

One rather unique prisoner-of-war experience was that of Constantine A. Hege, a soldier in the 48th North Carolina Infantry Regiment. Captured in October 1863 and confined in Old Capitol Prison in Washington, D.C., in January 1864 Hege was "anxiously awaiting an opportunity of taking the oath of allegiance to the United States and live a free man." Released on July 14, he went to New York and then to Bethlehem, Pennsylvania, where he got a job in a "zink work" for the princely sum of $1.25 per day. Some clergy friends aided him; prior to his wartime service, he had been a student at Davidson College in North Carolina. (Although that school was generally thought of as a Presbyterian institution, the facts that Hege came to Bethlehem and that he came from North Carolina make it quite likely that he was a Moravian.) After laboring in the "zink work" for some time, he was employed at the Bethlehem Iron Works with quite a raise in pay; he now earned $1.80 per day. Since his board with a Moravian family was only $3 per week, he seemed to make out rather well financially. Late in June 1865, he wrote to his mother: "If you do [call me a Yankee] all right. I consider that more an honor than a disgrace."[51]

A category of prisoners of war that is relatively unknown consists of the "galvanized" soldiers of both sides. Though the Confederacy did not attempt such a plan until very late in the war, the Federal program began earlier in the war and was rather successful. In short, prisoners who desired to avoid the rigors of prison camps could volunteer for service on the western frontier. It was clearly understood that these "galvanized Yankees," sometimes known as "transfugees" or "whitewashed Rebs," would not be required to serve in the East against their old comrades. Approximately 6,000 Confederates availed themselves of this opportunity to serve in the Federal forces; some six regiments were ultimately organized. A similar Confederate program began late in 1864 but fell apart and completely failed in the waning months of the war.

One such "galvanized Yankee" was James A. P. Fancher, originally of the 16th Tennessee Infantry Regiment, C.S.A. Taken prisoner in Tennessee in January 1864, Fancher went to Rock Island, Illinois. After nine months in prison, Fancher opted to serve the North, enlisting in Company F, 3rd U.S. Volunteer Infantry Regiment. He served in Kansas and Colorado, primarily guarding wagon trains. He gained his discharge at the end of November 1865 at Fort Leavenworth, Kansas. Men who had been enlisted from prisons were entitled to transportation home, according to an October 17, 1865, War Department order. Thus Fancher made his way back to Tennessee by way of St. Joseph and St. Louis, Missouri.[52] It would be interesting to know the reactions of the relatives and friends of these "galvanized Yankees" upon their return home.

The history of the 3rd Mississippi Infantry Regiment, C.S.A., contains a fitting summary of Confederate demobilization as it pertained to Confederate veterans returning from Northern prisons: "The weary scarecrow survivors slowly made their way homeward over back country roads from the Carolinas and Alabama. Several more weeks passed before those incarcerated in Northern prison camps were released to make their individual home treks." The men generally moved in small groups of natives of the same state in order to facilitate donations of food and other forms of assistance. The returning soldiers depended upon "Yankee-drawn rations, charitable donations from citizenry and some thievery."[53] Thus in the months that followed the surrenders, Confederate prisoners of war slowly and gradually, sometimes painfully, but always optimistically, made their way to their Southern homes.

CHAPTER ELEVEN

Demobilization of Hospital Patients

There's just one thing,
I hope I never get sent to the hospital.
You don't get well when you go to the hospital.
I'd rather be shot and killed quick.
                    —Stephen Vincent Benét

With General Order No. 77, dated April 28, 1865, which specifically targeted the reduction of expenses of maintaining the ongoing military establishment, the demobilization process for hospital patients began. Paragraph VI ordered as follows:

> All volunteer soldiers (patients) in hospitals, except veteran volunteers, veterans of the First Army Corps (Hancock), and enlisted men of the Veteran Reserve Corps, who require no further medical treatment, be honorably discharged from service with immediate payment.

The order went on to state: "Paperwork for discharge/payment of soldiers to be processed without delay, so that this order may be carried into effect immediately."[1] No doubt the patients in the many hospitals welcomed the note of urgency, but how well this aspect of the directive was followed is another matter.

The Veteran Reserve Corps consisted of officers and men who had been wounded and/or were physically unfit for full combat duty. These troops were used in noncombatant roles, such as aides in hospitals or guards for military storage areas and prisoner-of-war camps.

Two weeks had just elapsed when the intent of General Order No. 77 was expanded by a War Department letter dated May 16, 1865:

> All patients, even if they require further medical treatment, if they are physically able to travel and desire to be discharged, and all men still in hospitals recently transferred to the Veteran Reserve Corps [to be discharged] as soon as the interest of the public service will permit.

As if to emphasize that this change in procedure was important and should be implemented without delay, the letter went on to say even more explicitly: "The order for the discharge from hospitals should be liberally interpreted."[2]

For the soldier patients in the Confederate hospitals, there was no provision made for their demobilization, just as there was no formal program for the rest of the Confederate soldiers. Large numbers of Confederate soldiers were in hospitals at the end of the hostilities. While an exact total is not available, in Richmond alone at war's end there were some 5,000 soldiers receiving care in nine hospitals.[3] Though this was perhaps the largest concentration of wounded and ill soldiers in one area, it was not the only such concentration. All the major cities of the South that had escaped devastation and capture by Sherman were hospital centers.

One such Confederate veteran, Col. William C. Oates of the 48th Alabama Infantry Regiment, had lost his right arm as a result of a combat wound received fighting on the James River in August 1864. Sent home as an invalid in November, by January 1865 he had recovered to the extent that he was able to report for duty in Richmond. He wanted to serve at the front again, but his wound would not permit such service. At that point, he received a furlough to his home in Abbeville, Alabama. In February, just a few weeks prior to the surrenders and the resulting large flow of returning soldiers, Oates started southward from Richmond. By train, he got as far as Abbeville, South Carolina. He then used a carriage to make his way toward Washington, Georgia. Next, he switched to a two-horse wagon as far as the Savannah River, where he was ferried across, thus arriving in Georgia. The next leg of the journey was by foot, to Crawfordsville, Milledgeville, and on to Macon. Here he was able to board a train and so reached his home in Abbeville, Alabama.[4] Although Colonel Oates's journey home did not

occur in connection with the postwar demobilization, it provides an accurate glimpse into the difficulties of travel in the moribund Confederacy.

Capt. Henry A. Chambers, a native of North Carolina, was a casualty
in the April 1, 1865, battle of Five Forks, Virginia. He attempted to reach
Petersburg but was intercepted by the Union forces and forced to turn
north. He reached the area of Amelia Court House, then traveled on to
Farmville and then the Appomattox area, arriving there on April 8, the day
before Lee's capitulation to Grant. Chambers required medical aid and
reported to a Federal hospital, where he signed a parole. The next day, he
was taken to Farmville, on the way to Burkeville. He traveled by "Yankee
ambulance" and spent the entire day on the road. "Our Yankee companions were very civil to us," he noted in his diary. After two days in the hospital at Burkeville, he went by train to Petersburg, his original destination.
Upon his arrival at Petersburg, he went to the home of some friends, and
after two days, he was ordered by the Federal authorities to remain in the
private home; he was also able to draw Federal rations. Late in April,
Chambers was released from the care of the Union doctors and allowed to
return to his North Carolina home.[5] Likely the volume of wounded soldiers under the care of the Union hospital system necessitated his being
treated as an outpatient. Possibly also his wound, while requiring medical
attention, was not serious enough to warrant hospitalization.

John H. Worsham of Company F, 21st Virginia Infantry Regiment,
confined to bed in his Richmond home as the result of a severe wound
received at Third Winchester on September 19, 1864, observed the paroled
Confederates returning to the capital. His articulate and frequently quoted
recollections described the scene:

> A majority of them literally had nothing but the ragged clothing on
> their backs. They did not even have a change of clothing. While
> some of the soldiers had their land, that was all they had. If one had
> stock, farming utensils, or provisions, he was an exception.[6]

William Walker Ward, whose military career spanned the entire war,
served as a private, first sergeant, captain, lieutenant colonel, and finally
colonel in command of his regiment, the 9th Tennessee Cavalry, John Hunt
Morgan's brigade. During his career, he experienced being a prisoner of
war and was also wounded in the skirmish at Bull's Gap, Tennessee, on

October 16, 1864. His status as prisoner of war, which began when he surrendered at Buffington Island on the Ohio River, July 19, 1863, took him to Cincinnati, Johnson's Island in Lake Erie, then on to the state prison in Columbus, Ohio. His "tour" of prisons next took him to Fort Delaware, where he was finally exchanged on August 4, 1864. He went back to his old command, which was then near Jonesboro, Tennessee. After his wound, he recuperated near Wytheville, Virginia; this was his location at the end of the war. His diary stopped just short of the surrenders, ending with Ward hearing the rumors of the fall of Richmond and Petersburg. Once recovered, Ward returned to Tennessee.[7]

Confederate soldier Joshua Hilary Hudson was seriously wounded at the Battle of Five Forks on April 1, 1865, just a few days before the surrender at Appomattox. His wound was so severe that many of the officers and men in his unit believed he had been killed. A field ambulance transported him to Ford's Station, a trip of about seven miles that required six hours. Here he was placed in a private home for care. On April 3, he was captured by Federal soldiers. Federal medical personnel nursed Hudson in the private house; his recuperation lasted for six weeks. At that point, Gen. Joshua L. Chamberlain paroled him. The first leg of his homeward journey took him to Greensboro, North Carolina, where he had to enter a hospital for three days. Again he started out, this time for Charlotte, North Carolina. Because of a break in the railroad, he was forced to walk several miles. On the way, he was fed by local people. By chance, he met his regimental commanding officer, who was startled and pleased to find Hudson alive. Finally, Hudson arrived at his home in Bennettsville, South Carolina, close to the North Carolina boundary.[8]

Another casualty of the Five Forks Battle was an Englishman named Francis W. Dawson, who had served in Gen. Fitzhugh Lee's cavalry. Following his wounding and a transfer to Richmond, Dawson was there at the time of Lee's surrender. He recovered sufficiently to travel, but he first needed a parole. Applying to the provost marshal, he received his parole, but that was about all he had in his possession. His total assets consisted of a postage stamp and some change from a $5 bill. He splurged with these funds: "The first luxuries that I bought were cigars and oranges." Early in June, he wrote to his mother in England: "I have not a sixpence in the world and at present I cannot obtain any. Confederate money I had an abundance of but that is only valuable as waste paper." Dawson remained in this country, taking a variety of odd jobs, and ultimately went on the staff of a Charleston, South Carolina, newspaper.[9]

Gilbert Moxley Sorrell's wartime service was almost exclusively in the capacity of a staff officer for Gen. James Longstreet. In October 1864, Sorrell was promoted to brigadier general and placed in command of a brigade in Gen. William Mahone's division, Gen. A. P. Hill's Corps. On February 7, 1865, Sorrell was seriously wounded at Hatcher's Run. Already bearing a wound in his leg from duty in front of Petersburg, this time he was shot through his right lung. He was evacuated to Richmond and then sent to Big Lick, near Roanoke, for hospitalization and recuperation. After recovering to the extent that he could resume active service, he was on his way back to his unit when, at Lynchburg, he learned of the surrender at Appomattox. As he was a native of Savannah, he started in that direction. On the way, his wound reopened, and he was forced to return to Roanoke to recuperate. When finally able to travel, he boarded a train for Lynchburg, where he was paroled formally. Traveling with his brother, Sorrell made his way to Richmond, using a variety of modes of transportation—railroad, army wagon, and road marching. He later wrote that the "route was tedious and wearying." The only funds the two men had amounted to $15, three half eagles in gold. This sum was put to good use.

In Richmond at last, Sorrell remarked about the quantity and quality of the Union Army's equipment, clothing, draft animals, uniforms, and so forth. The brothers prepared to go to Baltimore, but because of Sorrell's weakened condition, they felt the only way to travel was by sea. They took the required oath of allegiance to the United States, but Sorrell was refused a permit to leave by boat. Some friends, however, were able to smuggle the brothers aboard. From Baltimore, they went on to New York City, where they arranged for passage on a steamer bound for Savannah. Although the steamer was "small, crowded, most uncomfortable," and the seas were rough, the two brothers finally arrived in Savannah.[10]

Even though the status of the hospital patients differed from that of the soldiers still on active duty, their experiences on the way home were remarkably similar. The major differences in treatment accorded the Union and Confederate patients reflected the differences in available material resources. As the war progressed and reached its climax, hospital care of the Northern men had vastly improved, while conditions for the men in gray had declined in every respect, with medicine, food, transportation, and clothing all in short supply or totally lacking. But as in the case of all the other veterans, they were glad to be on their way home.

CHAPTER TWELVE

Demobilization of Black Troops

And I wants to be free. I want to see my chillun
Growin' up free, and all bust out of Egypt.
I wants to be free like an eagle in de air,
Like an eagle in de air.
—Stephen Vincent Benét

The Civil War is a conflict that is well known for its many firsts. Many of these innovations became permanent elements in subsequent military history, affecting the fields of organization, weapons, modes of transportation, and so forth. One of these lasting changes was the introduction of black soldiers to the Union Army.

It is true that the Confederacy, in its death throes, did legislate a limited use of black slaves in service, but this experiment lasted just a few weeks, and then the war was over. It was the Union that definitively utilized black males in active service in the army. In so doing, the army was copying the practice of the U.S. Navy, as black men had served, apparently without discrimination, in the navy even prior to the war. Likewise, African-American men had served in the army during the Revolutionary War and the War of 1812, but not in the war with Mexico. Advocates of black men serving as soldiers questioned why they were satisfactory and acceptable to Generals Washington and Jackson but not to Generals McClellan and Halleck.

Abraham Lincoln was under constant pressure from both the abolitionist legislators and influential people, as well as from such people as Frederick Douglass. Though he was not the only person who actively campaigned for the military use of black manpower, Douglass's eloquent voice was perhaps the most effective. He recruited African-American regiments during the war, once the government opened its recruiting policy to the enlistment of black troops. His family's contribution to the ranks consisted of two of his sons, who served in the 54th Massachusetts Colored Infantry Regiment, the unit made famous by the recent motion picture *Glory,* which culminated with the regiment's participation in the attack on Fort Wagner, South Carolina, in July 1863.

Once the preliminary Emancipation Proclamation was made public, the countdown began to its effective date, January 1, 1863. The Emancipation Proclamation was effective only in those areas under the control of the Confederates—that is, the areas still in a state of rebellion—and it did not free slaves in other parts of the country. Limited though it may have been in scope, the very existence of such a proclamation showed that freedom of the slaves was a priority of the Federal government, one that seemed almost to overshadow the original objective of the war—restoration and preservation of the Union. With this step taken, the doors were opened to enlistment of black men for army service.

Terminology has changed over the years since the Civil War. At the time, members of the African-American race were known as colored, and this term was part of the designations of several units.

The contribution made to the war effort by African-American personnel in combat and other services was far from a token representation. While the figures vary slightly according to various authors and sources, one of the better estimates shows that black troops accounted for almost 10 percent of the Union Army. There were approximately 179,000 enlisted men and slightly more than 7,100 officers in the military service. Perhaps the most significant measure of the contribution made to the war effort by African-Americans is the total number of deaths of black men while serving in the army: 37,300.[1] While most of the officers placed in command of the African-American troops were white, there were at least two black majors and twenty-nine black captains. One author summarized that the black commissioned officers totaled "not more than one hundred Negroes (excluding chaplains)." The Congressional Medal of Honor was awarded to at least fourteen African-American soldiers during the war.[2] Considering that many of the black soldiers had been slaves only months prior to their service, the total numbers and attainment of rank reflect an almost miraculous revolution.

On the Confederate side, there were a few black men who actually enlisted in the service. Six of these men are known by name, although "there were undoubtedly other Black men in Confederate service, particularly those who were 'passing' [for white] before the war, but their names remain unknown."[3] In addition, there were at least four black camp servants who joined in actual combat on the Confederate side. There were many hundreds, perhaps even thousands, of African-Americans who served the Confederate forces as cooks, freight handlers, teamsters, pioneers or engineers in construction of fortifications, and railroad workers. Some historians claim these men as members of the armed forces, but they were almost entirely slaves loaned or hired out to the government. The use of blacks in these noncombat functions released significant white manpower, which the Confederates put to military use.

Although Union recruitment and enlistment of white soldiers was discontinued just days after the surrender at Appomattox, this action did not affect the recruitment and enlistment of black soldiers, especially in Kentucky, which was specifically exempted from the general order. African-American units represented the first soldiers to enter the cities of Charleston, South Carolina, and Richmond. In Richmond, a dramatic reunion occurred between an elderly black woman and Chaplain Garland H. White, who served with the 28th U.S. Colored Infantry. Born a slave, White had run away as a young boy and escaped to Canada. The elderly woman turned out to be his mother.[4]

African-American soldiers served in the occupation forces in the South. Statistically, black soldiers represented a disproportionately high portion of the occupation forces, as white soldiers, generally having served longer, had been demobilized earlier, thus increasing the percentage of black troops to the total occupation force. Maj. Gen. Henry W. Halleck, in his capacity as commanding general of the Federal occupation forces in Virginia, decided to send his black troops to Texas. An entire corps of black soldiers, the XXV Corps, was transferred to Texas as part of the occupation force and also as part of the show of military strength on the Mexican frontier. Prior to this mass transfer, the XXV Corps moved from Richmond to Petersburg, and thus out of the ex-Confederate capital. It is possible that a dislike of black troops on the part of Maj. Gen. E. O. C. Ord prompted this move. Ord, who had assumed command of the occupation forces in Richmond, had superseded Maj. Gen. Godfrey Weitzel, the commanding general of the

XXV Corps. All black troops in the Richmond area were then transferred into the XXV Corps; as a result, after the departure of the corps to Texas, there were no black troops in the immediate area of Richmond.[5] "Many of these black troops . . . reacted violently to the move." One regiment, the 29th Connecticut Colored Infantry, mutinied in Texas, prompted to some extent by a rumor that they were to be taken to Cuba and there sold into slavery.[6]

When the African-American soldiers received pay equal to that of the white troops, their families ceased to receive the ration allowance. The troops were expected to be able to support their families out of their pay. Even before the pay rates were standardized for white and black troops, there was at least one element of equality in the pay situation: Pay for black soldiers was just as much in arrears as it was for white soldiers. This delay, sometimes as long as eight to ten months, meant that the troops were hard-pressed to provide funds for their families.[7]

Another problem affecting the black troops was that of illness. The 115th U.S. Colored Infantry suffered greatly on the way to Texas. Problems of poor sanitation and spoiled or insufficient food plagued them; fever broke out, and an average of twelve men died daily. Scurvy also "reached epidemic proportions" among black troops. It had begun during the last months of the war, and by midsummer 1865, an estimated 60 percent of the XXV Corps troops suffered from the disease. By mid-August, shipments of fresh vegetables and fruit finally caught up with the unit, resulting in a dramatic decline in the incidence of scurvy.[8]

Other problems affected troops of both races—inactivity, idleness, discontent, boredom, and frustration recognize no distinction of race or color. "Public drunkenness, loathsome diseases of a private nature, [and] loose moral behavior" were also in evidence. Even some of the officers had lost interest in military service; they seemed to feel that their jobs had ended with the surrenders. Apparently enticed by the "easy marks," there were instances of unscrupulous officers defrauding soldiers of their pay and savings.[9]

Some of the officers tried to impose stricter, more rigorous discipline on their troops, with the predictable unfavorable reaction. There were harsh punishments for infractions that were merely the result of inconsiderate treatment. Acts of mutiny were matched by executions; in Jacksonville, Florida, shooting broke out in October 1865. Scores of arrests followed, together with five executions.[10]

At the other end of the spectrum were officers who instituted programs of education and religious study. Many black soldiers, heretofore illiterate, used their occupation time to learn to read and write. Many of the troops made known their desire for "two more boxes besides the cartridge box—the ballot and jury boxes."[11]

Some of the white officers sought demobilization as soon as possible. Most of them had served three or more years, even longer than many officers in the all-white units. They felt that they had received unfair treatment because of their willingness to serve in black units. Black enlisted men likewise were eager for separation from service. Many of them wanted to stay in the South in order to search for family members who had been sold and transported to distant areas of the South before and during the war. Men with families in the North wanted to return to their homes and start earning a living in order to provide for their families. Initially, however, some officers and men elected to remain in service as long as possible. The pay was good and by that date was on time. In time, the novelty of army life wore off, and generally, a year of reconstruction and occupation duty was enough, as by that late date almost all of the officers and men wanted to return to civilian life. Many men considered reconstruction service "a bitter pill to swallow."[12]

Letters and diaries are understandably fewer for black soldiers due to the high rate of illiteracy. The few letters that are available reveal many interesting aspects of their final months in service, their desire to be discharged, and ultimately, their participation in the demobilization process. When the long-awaited demobilization orders finally came through, there were sometimes mixed emotions about the forthcoming separation from service. They were citizen-soldiers for the most part, yet the friendships of their peers and attachments to units were strong, and demobilization would end these. Military life was so intense and concentrated that sometimes it seemed the soldiers had never experienced any other lifestyle. There were "certain trepidations about facing the 'real world.'"

Another factor that entered into the demobilization process was the army regulation that required units to be mustered out of service in the same locations as their musters in had occurred.[13] This requirement resulted in extensive travel for some units, especially those that were in the Deep South or on the Mexican frontier when demobilization orders came through.

Sgt. Peter Vogelsang, regimental
quartermaster, 54th Massachusetts
Colored Infantry Regiment

A member of the famous 54th Massachusetts Infantry, Sgt. Peter Vogelsang, served as quartermaster sergeant of his regiment. From April to August
1865, the unit was in and around Charleston, South Carolina. Sergeant
Vogelsang was an exceptional person and an outstanding soldier, so much so
that despite the prejudice and even protest resignations of some of the white
officers, he was commissioned to serve as regimental quartermaster, an
extremely important position. As the unit was about to be demobilized,
Vogelsang was responsible for checking the supplies, equipment, and
accounts of the regiment. On August 20, the 54th Regiment was officially
mustered out of service, even though the unit had been mustered into service in Boston, and the next day, the soldiers boarded transport ships and set
sail for Boston. A week later, they arrived at their destination, a final report
was made, and the troops received their pay. On September 2, 1865, there
was a final parade in Boston that Gov. John A. Andrew and other dignitaries
reviewed. Thus ended the federal service of one of the best-known units in
the Union Army and definitely the most outstanding colored unit, the 54th
Massachusetts Colored Infantry Regiment.[14]

Lt. Col. Benjamin W. Thompson had been the provost marshal general
of the Department of the South, but he went home with his old unit, the
32nd U.S. Colored Infantry Regiment, a Pennsylvania outfit. Since the

regularly assigned colonel of the regiment was absent, Thompson was assigned the task of taking the regiment home. In his memoirs, he wrote:

> In August 1865 an order came for the muster out of a certain number of colored regiments and the 32nd was chosen. Colonel Baird being absent at the time, I took charge of the right wing of the regiment and embarked on the steamer <u>George McClellan</u> for New York. In New York City we indulged in a march down Broadway, and with our twenty drummer boys, the same little black fellows who went out with us, we attracted considerable attention. . . . From New York we went to Philadelphia, arriving there on Sunday morning, and were marched through the town to Camp Cadwallader, where, on the 29th of August, '65, I became a private citizen.[15]

All travel was not accomplished with the apparent ease and dispatch experienced by the 54th Massachusetts and the 32nd Pennsylvania. While the 43rd U.S. Colored Infantry Regiment was en route in heavy seas from Brownsville, Texas, to New Orleans, the ship sprang a leak. The pumps were ineffective, and the incoming water extinguished the boiler fires. It became necessary to lighten the ship; this was accomplished by throwing overboard the horses and goods. It was still necessary for the men to bail the ship for two days. Luckily, the ship ran aground on a sandbar near the entrance to the Mississippi River. A tug towed the ship to New Orleans, and the journey was completed by train.[16]

The 56th U.S. Colored Infantry Regiment was en route in two steamers from Helena, Arkansas, to St. Louis in August 1866. During the journey, there was an outbreak of cholera, and several soldiers died. The illness was not at first diagnosed, and when the ships arrived at St. Louis, the commanding officer kept the troops aboard; at this point, the proper diagnosis was made. The vessels were ordered to the quarantine area by Maj. Gen. William T. Sherman, and while there, an officer and 178 enlisted men died from the disease. The city of St. Louis, however, was spared a full-blown cholera epidemic, thanks to the foresight of the commanding general.[17]

One recurring theme in the letters is the request for information about relatives. Sgt. Olmstead Massey, a member of the 76th U.S. Colored Infantry Regiment in New Orleans, had been sold at the age of seventeen and was sent to the Deep South from Virginia. He placed ads in newspapers in the hope of locating his mother. Whether or not he succeeded is not indicated in the letters.[18]

A quartermaster sergeant of the 29th Connecticut Colored Infantry Regiment, Alex Newton, described his homeward journey. His unit had seen combat in Virginia and then had been sent to Texas, there to take up station on the Rio Grande. In October 1865, the regiment was mustered out and marched to Brownsville, Texas, where it was joined by the 9th U.S. Colored Infantry Regiment. After a parade through Brownsville, the two regiments moved to the coast and embarked on steamers for New Orleans. The sea voyage to New York City lasted one month; the ships arrived at the Hudson River pier on November 22. After a night in barracks in the Battery area, the troops boarded steamers for Hartford, Connecticut, arriving the next morning. The mayor of the city, joined by an official welcoming committee, greeted the soldiers on their arrival. After a parade through the city, the men stacked arms, unslung their knapsacks, and had "a fine repast . . . prepared by white and colored citizens of Hartford" at the city hall. After being joined by the 31st U.S. Colored Infantry Regiment, there was yet another parade, together with greetings from both the mayor and the governor of Connecticut. November 25 saw the troops paid off, disbanded, and on their way home.[19]

One letter writer, identified only as Hannibal, was a member of the 5th U.S. Colored Infantry Regiment, an Ohio unit. This regiment ended what Hannibal called "the shooting war" at Wilmington, North Carolina, but this war was to be followed by "a moral war." In a very definite understatement, Hannibal rather gently remarked that there was "a tendency for old relations with . . . [the] peculiar institution to surface." When the regiment arrived at Columbus, Ohio, it was greeted with speeches in which their bravery, bearing, and discipline were highly praised, but as Hannibal pointed out, there was "no elective franchise." He further noted that the black man was good enough to fight with whites but not to vote with them.[20]

The ballot box was much on the minds of the African-American veterans, with good reason. Having suffered all the dangers of active military service, not to be able to vote, as befitted patriotic citizens, seemed a gross injustice. Orderly Sgt. I. N. Triplett of the 60th U.S. Colored Infantry Regiment, a Davenport, Iowa, outfit, returned from the war in October 1865. He actively worked toward getting the vote for his peers, but he, along with thousands of others, had to wait for the passage of the Fifteenth Amendment to the Constitution in 1869. Just a few days after he was sep-

arated from military service, Triplett presented a resolution to the Iowa legislature in which he said, "He who is worthy to be trusted with the musket
can and ought to be trusted with the ballot."[21] As these two letters were
dated in the first week of November 1865, it is obvious that the veterans
wasted no time in making known their feelings about the right to vote.

Hardship cases abounded, and special circumstances and appropriate
requests were outlined in the letters. The dates of the letters are interesting,
as they reflect the time element that intensified the requests for special consideration.

A member of the 56th U.S. Colored Infantry Regiment, the Missouri
regiment that suffered the cholera outbreak, wrote to the secretary of war
from Helena, Arkansas, on May 15, 1866, before the regiment moved out:

> There has severl redgements who enlisted one year after we did
> mustered out and gone home. We stood on the bank and shed
> teers to think that we who had batled for our country over two
> years should still be retained and deprived of the priviledge of see-
> ing those who are so dear to us.[22]

Two weeks later, a black soldier from Kentucky wrote to both the president and the secretary of war on behalf of six men in the 116th U.S. Colored Infantry, from White's Ranch, Texas, that the men had done their duty,
were worried about their families at home, and were unable to forward
funds to the families, having noted that "my own family is liven in old Kentucky under just as much slave as the was when I left her or before the war
broke out." He ended by requesting that the officers observe the laws and
regulations, implying that this would ensure their timely demobilization.[23]

Some wrote about their illnesses or wounds. A sergeant from Iowa
wrote repeatedly to the secretary of war of his failing health and the fact that
he was the sole support of his aged mother and his one child. A first sergeant
in the 4th U.S. Colored Infantry Regiment, Alex Shaw, said that he had
been "badly wonded very badley for life." He went on to say that "I don't
think my countary needs me anay longer—if so I will be willing to seve."[24]

In January 1866, while stationed at Morris Island, South Carolina, an
anonymous black soldier from South Carolina addressed a letter to the commander of the Department of South Carolina. He explained that he had
gone from slavery into the army and that he expected to get out at the end
of the war. Speaking for his fellow soldiers, he explained that their families

were in need and that the men were ready to go to work in order to provide proper homes for their families. He ended his letter with a plea: "So please if you can do any good for us do it in the name of god. It is a mejority of men of the 33rd Regt, USCT." It would appear that the men of the regiment made a poor choice of advocate to act on their behalf, as the commanding officer of the regiment, who endorsed the letter, included a statement in which he described the writer as "the most troublesome man in the regiment; he has deserted four times, and has repeatedly been confined and punished for writing similar documents to Superior Head Quarters . . . which upon investigation have always been found groundless."[25]

The secretary of war must have received a large quantity of mail, if the extant letters from the black troops represent a fair sample. An anonymous soldier wrote in July 1865 from New Bern, North Carolina, to ask for a shortening of time for the men who "have done . . . [their] duty as men and soldiers." Since there was no more fighting, and also since many of the men were farmers and mechanics who could find employment, he reasoned that the men of the 1st, 4th, 5th, and 6th Regiments should be discharged. "Please do all you can for these four regiments."[26]

Another anonymous writer, this one a black soldier from Missouri, directed a letter the following month to the secretary of war. From Chattanooga, he wrote, referring to the men of the 44th, 16th, and 18th Regiments, many of whom had not seen their families for two years or more. "There wives is scatered about over world without pertioction in suffernce condishtion. The grets duites that is performed at this place is poleasing ground." He went on to say that "since there is no fighting on this side of the Rior Grand," he felt that the men should be able to attend to their families' needs. He and the others were perfectly willing to fight in the U.S. "The[y] all say the[y] will do it without truble. Recording to there enlistments there time is out for the war is over. They enlist 3 years or during the war[;] the war is over." As a final emphasis, he closed the letter by saying, "The war is over[,] there times is out."[27]

In a beautifully worded and perfectly spelled letter, musician Elijah Reeves of the 5th Massachusetts Colored Cavalry Regiment, wrote from Clarksville, Texas, to his U.S. senator from Michigan, Zachariah Chandler, in September 1865, asking Chandler to use his influence with the War Department to speed up his discharge process. He too mentioned that the war was over; peace "has again brightened our sky," he wrote. His plea was made on behalf of his grandmother and several orphan sisters, all of whom depended upon him financially. Chandler did recommend Reeves's discharge from his regiment, but by the time the request was made to the War Department, the regiment was already en route to Boston for final payment and discharge.[28]

From their letters, it is obvious that many of the African-American soldiers thought that the demobilization process was taking too long to reach them. The soldiers who were serving in the South saw firsthand the suffering and needs of the destitute black refugees and how they lacked proper food, clothing, and shelter. A large number of the black soldiers had relatives in the South, and thus it was all too easy to imagine that their own family members were suffering in like fashion. The soldiers also feared for their families' safety. Even the whereabouts of their families was a source of concern and worry for the troops, as all too many families had been wrenched apart by the sale of slaves as well as the fortunes of war.

Within five months of the major surrenders, the War Department had processed for discharge nearly one-third of the black volunteers; within eighteen months of the same date, more than 90 percent of the volunteers had been discharged. In July 1865 there were about 123,000 black soldiers on active duty. By October of the same year, the number had decreased to 83,000. A year later, in the fall of 1866, there were less than 13,000 black soldiers still in active service. By the next fall, all of the African-American veterans, other than those who opted to transfer to regular units in order to remain in the army, had been discharged.

Like their white peers, so too did the black veterans, especially the officers and noncommissioned officers, enter into leadership roles once they arrived home and began to adjust to life as a civilian once more. These discharged veterans were "in [the] front ranks in the struggle for land, economic autonomy, and racial justice."[29]

The demobilization of the units of colored troops brought to an end a great experiment, one that was totally successful. These men made a most significant contribution to the war effort, measured not in dollars and cents, but in human lives and suffering.

CHAPTER THIRTEEN

Conclusion

Comrades and cause,
Station and riches lost,
And all the ills that flock
When fortune's fled.
—Herman Melville

B ecause of the widely disparate demobilizations of the Union and Confederate forces, any conclusions drawn may not seem properly applicable to both the North and the South. Yet, there are characteristics
common to both armies of the opposing forces.

Five factors seem particularly significant: the number of men processed;
the speed with which the process was accomplished; for the Union, the
simultaneous programs of demobilization and troop redeployment and even,
in some cases, continuation of combat; the vital role of the railroads; and
the provision of a model for demobilization following subsequent wars.

Demobilization for the Union forces was a well-organized and rapidly
executed means of returning to civilian life just over a million volunteer soldiers. This total represents an impressive number. As of May 1, 1865, just
three weeks after the Appomattox surrender, 1,034,064 volunteer soldiers,
both white and black, were in the Union Army and were slated for mustering out and final discharge. A year and a half later, on November 1,
1866, the comparable number was only 11,043, slightly more than 1 percent of the previous figure. Well over a million volunteers had been
processed out of service during those eighteen months. The bulk of these
discharges, some 801,000, had taken place by the middle of November
1865, a mere six and a half months after the program was approved.[1]

Equally impressive is the timing of the demobilization program. The hostilities were still ongoing when demobilization began. The final surrender did not take place until June 23, 1865; by that time, thousands of Union soldiers had entered the demobilization pipeline, on their way home. Similarly, thousands of ex-Confederates were either already home or still on the road. In addition, significant redeployments of troops took place in order to provide for the garrisoning of key points in the defeated South, as well as to establish a formidable force on the Mexican frontier to checkmate Napoleon III's ambitious hopes for an empire in that country. Personnel, transportation facilities, and military supplies were in great demand in order to accomplish these objectives. In fact, they represented competition to the demobilization program, yet that program proceeded at full speed.

Railroad transportation, so important in the combat phase of the conflict, both from strategic and tactical viewpoints, was absolutely necessary to the demobilization of the Union forces, and where available, it was used equally effectively by the returning Southern soldiers. Without railroads, the program would have taken many more months to complete. The logistical requirements of a nonrailroad demobilization would have been enormous, greater than those necessary to maintain armies in the field. The wartime experience in moving large bodies of troops paid handsome dividends in the 1865–66 demobilization. It is interesting to observe that even with the tremendous demobilization demands on the transportation systems, which seriously strained the capacity of the railroads as well as river and oceangoing vessels, the civilian economy escaped serious interference. As inconsistent as this statement may appear, when one considers that every available type of rolling stock and vessel was used to return veterans to their home areas, it is obvious that any adverse impact on the civilian economy was minimal. Men were moved in boxcars, coal cars, flatcars, and all categories of vessels; had the government relied only on genuine passenger facilities, the program would have taken longer to accomplish.

The knowledge and experience gained through moving large numbers of men to and from and within war zones, and then in postcombat demobilization, were extremely valuable in establishing a pattern or blueprint that was used to good advantage in later wars, especially World War II. Certainly, the number of troops in service during the Indian and Spanish-American Wars did not even approach the Civil War statistics. In World War I, "the war to end all wars," approximately 4 million soldiers served in the army, but almost three times that number wore army khaki in World War II.[2] When it came time to demobilize these millions of men, the Civil War experiences were of great importance and value.

Following the combat phases of the Civil War, there were constant redeployments of smaller units to accommodate the requirements of the occupation phase. This type of relocation was a constant occurrence throughout Reconstruction. Such redeployment set a pattern that was repeated on a much larger scale following World War II. In occupied Germany of 1945–46, there was constant redeployment of troops. As time passed, increased numbers of men qualified for discharge; these discharges meant that units became smaller, and as entire units were sent home, remaining units had to assume control of ever-increasing areas of responsibility and control. This constant shifting of units and personnel quite accurately paralleled the same phenomenon of the post–Civil War days.

Still another pattern can be traced to the Civil War program of demobilization. Provisional organizations were established to facilitate the movement of large numbers of men following the combat phase. As larger units reduced their forces, temporary or provisional organizations were established. Some form of military command had to be utilized in order to move troops from one area to another, especially if the parent unit remained in the first location. Records of the returning soldiers had to be prepared in order to accomplish the final steps of paying off the troops and discharging them. So, too, following World War II, men eligible for immediate discharge were often placed in one unit, and then that unit itself was shipped home. In later months, after the initial flow of troops eligible for discharge had begun to lessen, provisional detachments were made up to accommodate smaller groups of men who were processed through the pipeline. Depending upon the size of the ships to be used, these provisional companies and battalions existed just as long as it took to move the men back to the continental United States.

Field rendezvous points were established at the close of the Civil War. Records were checked, uniforms and equipment replaced as necessary, preliminary physical examinations carried out, and the men generally prepared for the return trip home. At the end of World War II, similar rendezvous camps were established in Europe, most, if not all, on the western coast of France. These were the famous "cigarette camps." Someone had struck upon the names of popular cigarettes to denote the individual camps, and the names stuck. Many of these camps were located in seaside resorts, as they had the hotel capacity necessary to house the returning veterans. As in the Civil War, the men were prepared for their homeward journeys, which in this case were on the high seas. Initially, some of the large liners and troop ships were used, but as time went on and the number of men to be returned declined, the famous Liberty ships were placed in use as troop carriers.

Once back in the continental United States, the men were sent to army camps and posts throughout the country. This phase of the World War II demobilization paralleled the state rendezvous points of the Civil War days. These points were generally located near areas of high population density, thus facilitating the final phase of demobilization.

Comparable figures for the Confederates who served in the army are rather vague and indistinct; estimates of the total number of men enlisted in the Confederate Army vary from 600,000 to 1.5 million, both volunteers and conscripts.[3] Exactly how many soldiers were still on active duty at the end of the war is just as vague and indistinct, since so many records were destroyed in the final days, and the desertions, both genuine and technical, further confused figures. Estimates that some 174,000 Confederate soldiers were surrendered are certainly understated, especially because of the thousands of desertions that occurred in those final days and hours of the conflict. Regardless of the exact figure, the demobilization of even a few hundred thousand soldiers represented a major social relocation of people in the South. The impact of this relocation was intensified by the total collapse of transportation, agricultural, political, financial, and social structures throughout the South. The demobilization process radically affected the South far more than the North.

What little literature exists concerning Confederate demobilization frequently uses terms such as "straggle," "flow," or "melt" to convey the sense of men moving across the landscape in anything but a military formation. As the accounts reveal, the tendency was for men to travel in groups small enough to encourage local people to donate food and yet large enough to discourage any violence on the part of roving gangs. For the most part, there was no semblance of military organization among the returning Confederates; they just went home as best they could. Circumstances taxed their ingenuity and resourcefulness to the utmost. Novel and unique routes were used, as well as any and all means of transportation. The challenges faced on the journey home were, in some respects, far more formidable than the perils and excitement of combat.

Sentiments and thoughts concerning military service and actual combat experiences were similar for the men in blue and the men in gray. Both experienced the same kinds of adventures, and their reactions were much the same. The emotional and psychological effects of combat are common to mankind, regardless of their uniforms, political beliefs, or their skin color.

The last words that a Union lieutenant wrote in his diary, as his unit was sent to Columbus, Ohio, to be mustered out, reflect a thoughtful appreciation of his service and the camaraderie that results from military life:

> Strangely enough the word [of our discharge] had already passed around, but even stranger there was little cheering, little celebration. We had expected to be transported with JOY. Perhaps soldiering in a splendid regiment is not so bad. Where would we find civilian friends to compare with soldier comrades?[4]

Robert Stiles, an artillery and staff officer in the Confederate Army, wrote in his recollections many years after the war that "military existence, notwithstanding the horrors that often attended it, grew upon me every day I lived it." For him, life as a soldier manifested itself in several character traits: "service, duty, obedience to command unquestioned, unceasing accountability, and unmeasured responsibility."[5] It is interesting to speculate what Stiles's thoughts were immediately after the surrenders; these feelings of appreciation of his service may have grown over the four decades that had passed. The human memory has a happy facility of straining out the unpleasant and terrible, retaining only the good and pleasant.

Maj. Abner Small of the 16th Maine Infantry found some aspects of the mustering out and separation process unsettling. "At the rendezvous . . . we formed in line, but only to break ranks and say good-bye. That was hard; I prefer not to speak of it; I cannot. Neither can I find words for what I saw in other faces."[6]

A sergeant in the 12th Virginia, James Whitehorne, expressed questions about his return to civilian life:

> The war has been going on so long I can't realize what a man would do now it's over. How can we get interested in farming or working in a store or warehouse when we have been interested day and night for years in keeping alive, whipping the invaders, and preparing for the next fight?[7]

A Vermont veteran remembered "soldiering as a hard life, and a very undesirable one at best." Yet Wilbur Fisk commented that "if a man loves adventure he finds a wide, reckless freedom in soldiering that has a charm for him. . . . I would not exchange such an experience for the noblest fortune in the land."[8] These words were set down on paper just weeks after the end of the war, so they reflect the mixed emotions of a thoughtful ex-soldier as he began his civilian life anew.

As Sgt. Austin Stearns remarked about his service in the 13th Massachusetts Infantry, "The friendships that had been formed and welded through more than twenty battles, long marches and privations incident to a life of a soldier through three years of service will last . . . long."[9]

Another sergeant, Rice C. Bull of the 123rd New York Infantry, had mixed emotions as his service came to an end. In talking about the last meeting of his company before the men departed for their homes, he reflected:

> Surely we all rejoiced that the end had come, that victory was ours and that home was near. But there was after all a sadness deep down in our hearts in this parting hour. We boys had been together for three years; we had formed close friendships; we had slept under the same blanket; we had faced the enemy shoulder to shoulder on the firing line; we had marched side by side; we had borne danger, hardship, and privation alike; thus a comradeship had grown as only such conditions could form. So it was hard to separate and say goodby, one with the other; but we shook hands all around, and laughed and seemed to make merry, while our hearts were heavy and our eyes ready to shed tears.[10]

This eloquent description of the emotions of the final minutes of the unit's existence and the soldiers' shared life represents a fitting close to the demobilization programs of both the Union and Confederate forces. Yet not everyone had a peaceful, emotion-filled transition from military to civilian lifestyles, as the following accounts will attest.

On August 14, 1866, at Petersburg, Virginia, four Confederate soldiers appeared, three from the 52nd Georgia Infantry and the other a member of the 43rd Louisiana Infantry. Ragged was hardly the word to describe their appearance. One man's clothing was held together with string, thread, and even thorns. The other three had parts and pieces of uniforms, both blue and gray. When Petersburg was evacuated in 1865, they were cut off from their units. Vowing never to go home or give up until the Confederacy was completely overwhelmed, they lived in a cave along the Appomattox River. Subsisting on fish and game, some roasting ears, and an occasional "stray" pig, they maintained a crude existence. A local black man assured them that the Confederacy had indeed gone by the boards, so they decided to return to civilization. The local people outfitted them with fresh clothes and treated them to liquor, so much so that when they finally boarded the train to return to their homes, they were "feeling no pain."[11]

Difficulty in reentering civilian life was not confined to Confederates. An article in the April 1, 1882, Washington, D.C., issue of the *National Tribune* describes a rather heart-rending account of a seventeen-year existence outside the normal framework of civilian life. Martin Schwein, a Union veteran, was apprehended as a vagrant by the police in Woodside, New Jersey. Vagrant he truly was, as he had spent seventeen years wandering across the country, from the Great Lakes to the Gulf of Mexico, and from the Atlantic seaboard to the Mississippi River. Living in a tent, still carrying his weapons, and relying upon a camp kettle and his blankets, he was nonetheless in amazingly good health. To say that this man had difficulty adjusting to civilian life is certainly an understatement. Unfortunately, the source for this story does not relate its conclusion.[12]

Everyone obviously was not able to make the transition from military to civilian life in an easy, convenient manner. That so many men were able to do so is an expression of the inestimable value of the citizen-soldier in the time of his country's need. The United States has always maintained a relatively small professional army. In time of national emergencies, these troops have been augmented and far surpassed in numbers by civilians, volunteers and draftees alike. That so many hundreds of thousands of men, both Union and Confederate, were able to rise to the occasion in order to serve and then return peaceably to their civilian pursuits is a tribute to the indomitable spirit, courage, and élan of the American citizen.

EPILOGUE

Bury this destiny unmanifest,
This system broken underneath the test,
Beside John Brown and though he knows his enemy is there
He is too full of sleep at last to care.
                    —Stephen Vincent Benét

In the Union Army, the traditional army tendency for precise records permits tracing the numerical reduction of the 11,034 volunteers still in service as of November 1, 1866. By October 1867, this volunteer force, reduced to a mere 203 officers and enlisted men, consisted almost totally of white personnel, except for twelve African-American commissioned officers still on duty in the Bureau of Refugees, Freedmen, and Abandoned Lands.[1]

The last white volunteer unit, a company of the 1st New Mexico Battalion, was mustered out November 18, 1867; the last black volunteer organization, the 125th U.S. Colored Infantry, was mustered out a month later, December 20, 1867. The very last commissioned officer of the Union volunteer forces was mustered out July 1, 1869. He was also the very last volunteer still in service, as the last enlisted volunteer, a soldier on duty as a War Department messenger, had been discharged the previous October.[2]

Thus the huge volunteer army, an army that was initially viewed with misgivings and hesitation on the part of the professional military personnel, an army that developed and trained to become what Gen. Joseph E. Johnston, an implacable opponent, praised when he said that "there had been no such army in existence since the days of Julius Caesar,"[3] an army that in large part, was responsible for bringing into being Lincoln's "new birth of freedom," became a part of history, a statistic among the annals of warfare.

No such tracing of the disappearance of the volunteer force is possible for the Confederate armed forces. The signatures of both volunteers and conscripts alike appended to the various surrender documents released the soldiers from service. The identity of the last volunteer to serve is just as impossible to pinpoint as it is to designate the very first volunteer in the Confederate Army. This large force of men, drawn from all over the South, and even with some personnel from the North, a force that carried on a

151

four-year-long struggle for its beliefs, undergoing great difficulties because of limited material means and therefore forced to utilize all manner of ingenious substitute goods, likewise faded into history.

Perhaps the most simplistic statement of all concerning the results of this great struggle is the one that differentiates between the concepts of our country before and after the Civil War. Yet this statement expresses a world of meaning in a few words. Where once the emphasis had been on a plural noun, the United *States* of America, after the war the emphasis was centered on the adjective, thus making the plural noun singular in its scope, the *United* States of America.[4]

Union Field Rendezvous Points by Armies

UNION ARMY MUSTERING OUT FIELD RENDEZVOUS POINTS
WAR DEPARTMENT, ADJUTANT GENERAL'S OFFICE
GENERAL ORDERS 94, MAY 15, 1865★

Army Division/Department	Field Rendezvous Point
Middle Military Division	Defenses of Washington, Harpers Ferry, Va. [sic], Cumberland, Md.
Military Division of the James	Richmond, Old Point Comfort, Va.
Department of North Carolina	New Bern, Wilmington, N.C.
Department of the South	Charleston, S.C., Savannah, Ga.
Military Division of West Mississippi	Mobile, Ala., New Orleans, La., Vicksburg, Miss.
Military Division of the Missouri	Little Rock, Ark., St. Louis, Mo.
Department of the Cumberberland	Nashville, Knoxville, Memphis, Tenn.
Department of Kentucky	Louisville, Ky.
Middle Department	Baltimore, Md.

★*O.R.,* ser. III, vol. 5, 20–23.

Union State Rendezvous Points

RENDEZVOUS POINTS FOR THE NORTHERN AND BORDER STATES WAR DEPARTMENT, ADJUTANT GENERAL'S OFFICE CIRCULAR NO. 19, MAY 16, 1865*

State	State Rendezvous Points
Maine	Augusta, Portland, Bangor
New Hampshire	Concord, Manchester
Vermont	Montpelier, Brattleborough, Burlington
Massachusetts	Boston (Readville and Gallupe's Island)
Rhode Island	Providence
New York	New York City (Hart's Island), Albany, Elmira, Buffalo, Rochester, Syracuse, Sackett's Harbor, Plattsburg, Ogdensburg
New Jersey	Trenton
Pennsylvania	Philadelphia, Harrisburg, Pittsburgh
Delaware	Wilmington
Maryland	Baltimore, Frederick
West Virginia	Wheeling
Ohio	Cincinnati, Cleveland, Columbus
Indiana	Indianapolis
Illinois	Springfield, Chicago
Michigan	Detroit, Jackson
Wisconsin	Madison, Milwaukee
Minnesota	Fort Snelling
Iowa	Davenport, Clinton
Kansas	Lawrence, Leavenworth
Missouri	St. Louis
Kentucky	Louisville, Lexington, Covington

*O.R., ser. III, vol. 5, 24–25.

NOTES

INTRODUCTION

1. David J. Eicher, *The Civil War in Books: An Analytical Bibliography* (Urbana: University of Illinois Press, 1997), xxiii.
2. Ibid., xii.
3. Quoted from original works in Jay Luvaas, *The Military Legacy of the Civil War: The European Inheritance* (Chicago: University of Chicago Press, 1959; Lawrence: University Press of Kansas, 1988), 75, 146.
4. Hondon B. Hargrove, *Black Union Soldiers in the Civil War* (Jefferson, NC: McFarland & Company, 1988), 7.
5. James I. Robertson, Jr., *Stonewall Jackson: The Man, the Soldier, the Legend* (New York: Simon & Schuster, 1997), 327.
6. Eric Foner and John J. Garraty, eds., *The Reader's Companion to American History* (Boston: Houghton Mifflin Company, 1991), 510, 750; Albro Martin, *Railroads Triumphant: The Growth, Rejection, and Rebirth of a Vital American Force* (New York: Oxford University Press, 1992), 29; James M. McPherson, *Battle Cry of Freedom: The Civil War Era* (New York: Oxford University Press, 1988), 320.
7. James McPherson, *Battle Cry of Freedom*, 320; Robert C. Black III, *The Railroads of the Confederacy* (University of North Carolina Press, 1952; Wilmington, NC: Broadfoot Publishing Company, 1987), 128.
8. Margaret Mitchell, *Gone with the Wind* (New York: Macmillan Company, 1936), 515.

CHAPTER 1

1. Douglas Southall Freeman, *R. E. Lee* (New York: Charles Scribner's Sons, 1940), vol. 4, 135; Emory M. Thomas, *Robert E. Lee: A Biography* (New York: W. W. Norton, 1995), 365; Geoffrey Perret, *Ulysses S. Grant: Soldier and President* (New York: Random House, 1997), 359.

2. Thomas L. Livermore, *Numbers and Losses in the Civil War in America, 1861–1865* (Boston: N.p., 1900; Carlisle, PA: John Kallman Publishers, 1996), 137; Chris M. Calkins, *The Final Bivouac: The Surrender Parade at Appomattox and the Disbanding of the Armies, April 10–May 20, 1865* (Lynchburg, VA: M. E. Howard, 1988), 40.

3. Shelby Foote, *Red River to Appomattox,* vol. 3 of *The Civil War: A Narrative* (New York: Random House, 1974), 1000.

4. Stewart Sifakis, *Who Was Who in the Civil War* (New York: Facts on File, 1982), 347; E. B. Long, with Barbara Long, *The Civil War Day by Day: An Almanac, 1861–1865* (Garden City, NY: Doubleday, 1971; New York: Da Capo Press, 1985), 683.

5. U.S. War Department, *The War of the Rebellion: A Compilation of the Official Records of the Union and Confederate Armies, 1861–1865,* 70 vols. in 128 parts (Washington, DC: Government Printing Office, 1880–1901), ser. II, vol. 8, 828–29. Hereafter cited as *O.R.*

6. Roy Morris, Jr., "Genius or Devil, Nathan Bedford Forrest Was One of the Civil War's Most Unforgettable Figures," *America's Civil War* 1, no. 3 (September 1988): 6; Foote, *Red River to Appomattox,* 1002.

7. John Allan Wyeth, *Life of General Nathan Bedford Forrest* (New York: Harper and Bros., 1899), 635, as quoted by Mark Boatner, *The Civil War Dictionary* (New York: David McKay Company, 1959), 289. Wyeth's book was issued in a new edition, *That Devil Forrest: Life of Nathan Bedford Forrest* (New York: Harper & Bros., 1959), which was also reprinted (Baton Rouge: Louisiana State University Press, 1989).

8. The official summary of surrendered and paroled Confederates cited in note 5 does not specify all the particulars of each surrender. It is possible that Jones surrrendered to Brig. Gen. Israel Vodges, who commanded a separate brigade in the District of Florida at this time.

9. Bruce S. Allardice, *More Generals in Gray* (Baton Rouge: Louisiana State University Press, 1995), 219–20; Sifakis, *Who Was Who,* 652.

10. John S. Bowman, ed. *The Civil War Almanac* (New York: Facts on File, Inc. [Bison Book], 1982), 267–68; Hondon B. Hargrove, *Black Union Soldiers in the Civil War* (Jefferson, NC: McFarland & Company, 1988), 201–2; Long, *The Civil War Day by Day,* 688.

11. Douglas Hale, *The Third Texas Cavalry in the Civil War* (Norman: University of Oklahoma Press, 1993), 275.

12. Long, *The Civil War Day by Day,* 690; Ezra J. Warner, *Generals in Gray: Lives of the Confederate Commanders* (Baton Rouge: Louisiana State Uni-

versity Press, 1959), 274; Rod Cragg, *The Civil War Quiz and Fact Book* (New York: Harper & Row, 1985), 175; Foote, vol. 3 of *The Civil War,* 1022–23.

13. W. Craig Gaines, *The Confederate Cherokees: John Drew's Regiment of Mounted Rifles* (Baton Rouge: Louisiana State University Press, 1989), 120; Allan Nevins, *The War for the Union: The Organized War to Victory, 1864–1865* (New York: Charles Scribner's Sons, 1971), 360; Foote, *Red River to Appomattox,* 1022.

14. Hargrove, *Black Union Soldiers in the Civil War,* 201–2.

15. Long, *The Civil War Day by Day,* 695.

16. *O.R.,* ser. II, vol. 8, 828–29.

CHAPTER 2

1. *O.R.,* ser. III, vol. 5, 1–3.

2. Edwin M. Stanton, *Report of the Secretary of War, 1865,* vol. 2 (Washington, DC: Government Printing Office, 1866), 898.

3. Ibid., 897–98.

4. *O.R.,* ser. III, vol. 4, 115–16; 578–79.

5. *O.R.,* ser. I, vol. 48 (part 2), 1190–91.

6. Alexis de Tocqueville, *Democracy in America,* vol. 3 (New York: Random House–Vintage Books, 1945), 286–87.

7. *O.R.,* ser. III, vol. 5, 53–54.

8. Ibid., 28. In my experience in the ETO, such a situation of delayed pay did not occur in World War II. Troops were paid with almost total disregard for the tactical situation. The company clerk, having come up from the rear area, together with the company commander, would pay off troops within range of artillery fire, and often within that of small-arms fire.

9. Cooper, who was born in 1798 at New Hackensack, Dutchess County, New York, and graduated in the class of 1815 from the United States Military Academy, married a sister of James M. Mason, who, together with John Slidell, was a major participant in the famous Trent affair. By marriage, Cooper was also the uncle of Fitzhugh Lee, the nephew of Gen. Robert E. Lee. Ezra J. Warner, *Generals in Gray* (Baton Rouge: Louisiana State University Press, 1959), 62–63.

10. Benjamin P. Thomas and Harold M. Hyman, *Stanton: The Life and Times of Lincoln's Secretary of War* (New York: Alfred A. Knopf, 1962), 159, 163, 263, 379, 581; Dumas Malone, ed., *Dictionary of American*

Biography, 20 vols. (New York: Charles Scribner's Sons, 1936), vol. 18, 441–42. Hereafter cited as *DAB.*

11. Gerry is considered a major figure in American political history by virtue of having bequeathed his name to the scheme of redistricting voting precincts in favor of a particular party—gerrymandering.

12. One of Townsend's major accomplishments was the collection of all available war-related papers, thus ensuring the creation of that remarkable historical source, the *Official Records.* As every Civil War historian and author knows, they are essential to an understanding of events. Malone, *DAB,* vol. 18, 615–16.

13. Mark M. Boatner, *The Civil War Dictionary* (New York: David McKay Company, 1959), 878; George W. Cullum, *Biographical Register of the Officers and Graduates of the United States Military Academy from 1802 to 1867,* 2 vols. (New York: James Miller, Publisher, 1879), vol. 2, 341–42.

14. Ida M. Tarbell, "How the Union Army Was Disbanded," *McClure's Magazine* (March 1901), reprinted in *Civil War Times Illustrated* 6, no. 8 (December 1967): 4–9, 44.

15. Richard B. Armstrong, ed., *The Journal of Charles R. Chewing, Company E, 9th Virginia Cavalry, C.S.A.* (Dayton, OH: Butternut and Blue, 1987), 16–17. In 1864, when assigned to Gardner's staff, Chewing termed him "a grand old man"; during 1865, in the final days of the war, Chewing used the expression "Old Gentleman" to describe Gardner. Gardner, born in 1824, was all of forty years old at the war's end!

16. John Q. Anderson, *A Texas Surgeon in the C.S.A.,* Confederate Centennial Series, no. 6 (Tuscaloosa, AL: Confederate Publishing Company, 1957), 110–11.

CHAPTER 3

1. Mark M. Boatner, *Civil War Dictionary* (New York: David McKay Company, 1959), 75; Peggy Robbins, "Desertion: 'The Great Evil of the War,'" *Civil War* 8, no. 5 (September–October 1990): 35, 74.

2. Kenneth Radley, *Rebel Watchdog: The Confederate States Army Provost Guard* (Baton Rouge: Louisiana State University Press, 1989), 252–53; Royce Gordon Shingleton, ed., "South from Appomattox: The Diary of Abner R. Cox," *South Carolina Historical Magazine* 75, no. 4 (October 1974), 239.

3. Robbins, "Desertion," 33, 35, 74; Radley, *Rebel Watchdog,* 159; James I. Robertson, "Military Executions," *Civil War Times Illustrated* 5, no. 2 (May 1966), 36.

4. *O.R.,* ser. IV, vol. 3, 1119.

5. John E. Divine, *8th Virginia Infantry,* The Virginia Regimental Histories Series (Lynchburg: H. E. Howard, 1983), 38; George William Bagby, Scrapbooks, 1862–1865, 5 vols. Virginia Historical Society, mss 5: 7 B 1463, vol. 3, 197; Lawrence R. Laboda, *From Selma to Appomattox: The History of the Jeff Davis Artillery* (Shippensburg, PA: White Mane Publishing Company, 1994), 297, 312.

6. Mary Laswell, ed., *Rags and Hope: The Recollections of Val C. Giles, Four Years with Hood's Brigade, Fourth Texas Infantry, 1861–1865* (New York: Conrad-McCann, 1961), 276.

7. Alwyn Barr, "Polignac's Texas Brigade," *Texas Gulf Coast Historical Association* 8, no. 1 (November 1964): 56.

8. Arthur W. Bergeron, Jr., ed., *The Civil War Reminiscences of Major Silas T. Grisamore, C.S.A.* (Baton Rouge: Louisiana State University Press, 1993), 180, 182; W. H. Tunnard, *A Southern Record: The History of the Third Regiment Louisiana Infantry* (printed for author, 1866; Dayton, OH: Morningside Bookshop, 1970), 337; Bell Irwin Wiley, ed., *Fourteen Hundred and 91 Days in the Confederate Army: A Journal Kept by W. W. Heartsill for Four Years, One Month and One Day, or Camp Life, Day by Day, of the W. P. Lane Rangers from April 19, 1861, to May 20, 1865* (Jackson, TN: McCowat-Mercer Press, 1954), 244.

9. Johnson Hagood, *Memoirs of the War of Secession* (Columbia, SC: State Company, 1910), 371; Bob Womack, *Call Forth the Mighty Men* (Bessemer, AL: Colonial Press, 1987), 507; W. J. Worsham, *The Old Nineteenth Tennessee Regiment, C.S.A.* (Knoxville, TN: N.p., 1902; Oxford, MS: Guild Bindery Press, 1992), 176; John Witherspoon DuBose, *General Joseph Wheeler and the Army of Tennessee* (New York: Neale Publishing Company, 1912), 469–70.

10. Shingleton, ed., "South from Appomattox: The Diary of Abner R. Cox," 238–39; Allen Johnson and Dumas Malone, *Dictionary of American Biography* (New York: Charles Scribner's Sons, 1943), vol. 2, 608; vol. 6, 356–57.

11. Fred A. Bailey, *Class and Tennessee's Confederate Generation* (Chapel Hill: University of North Carolina Press, 1987), 100, 103, 105.

12. Reid Mitchell, *Civil War Soldiers* (New York: Viking Press, 1988), 182–83.

CHAPTER 4

1. Ida M. Tarbell, "How the Union Army Was Disbanded," *McClure's Magazine* (March 1901), reprinted in *Civil War Times Illustrated* 6, no. 8 (December 1967): 6–7.

2. Robert Hale Strong, *A Yankee Private's Civil War,* ed. Ashley Halsey (Chicago: Henry Regnery Company, 1961), 204.

3. In a very real sense, Sherman and his troops made the first visitations to what in later years would become national military parks.

4. Margaret Brobst Roth, *Well, Mary: Civil War Letters of a Wisconsin Volunteer* (Madison: University of Wisconsin Press, 1960), 137–38; Strong, *A Yankee Private's Civil War,* 203–4.

5. Warren Wilkinson, *Mother, May You Never See the Sights I Have Seen* (New York: Harper & Row, 1990), 352–53.

6. Abner Ralph Small, *The Sixteenth Maine Regiment in the War of the Rebellion* (Portland, ME: B. Thurston & Co., 1886), 218.

7. *New York Times,* May 9, 1865; Henry Edward Tremain, *Last Hours of Sheridan's Cavalry: A Reprint of War Memoranda* (New York: Bonnell, Silver & Bowles, 1904), 305; Strong, *A Yankee Private's Civil War,* 210.

8. Thomas L. Livermore, *Days and Events, 1860–1866* (Boston: Houghton Mifflin Company, 1920), 468. Livermore later authored a classic book in Civil War literature, *Numbers and Losses in the Civil War in America.* The data in this book are today considered somewhat unreliable, at least in part, but it has long been a significant source of information on battle casualties.

9. Joshua L. Chamberlain, *The Passing of the Armies* (New York: G. P. Putnam's Sons, 1915), 372–73; Strong, *A Yankee Private's Civil War,* 208; Ruth L. Silliker, ed., *The Rebel Yell and the Yankee Hurrah: The Civil War Journal of a Maine Volunteer* (Camden, ME: Down East Books, 1985), 278; Roth, *Well, Mary,* 5.

10. Livermore, *Days and Events,* 472; Edwin Lyman Ames, Jr., ed., "The Civil War Diaries of Lyman Daniel Ames, 1861–1865" (unpublished typescript, CWTI Collection, USAMHI, Box Am-Ba), 160; Wilkinson, *Mother, May You Never See,* 358.

11. *New York Times,* May 23, 1865.

12. Roth, *Well, Mary,* 145; Silliker, *The Rebel Yell,* 278.

13. Samuel H. Hurst, *Journal: History of the Seventy-third Ohio Volunteer Infantry* (Chillicothe, OH: N.p., 1866), 181; Hartwell Osborn et al., *Trials and Triumphs: The Record of the Fifty-fifth Ohio Volunteer Infantry* (Chicago: A. C. McClurg & Co., 1904), 217.

14. James McPherson, *The Negro's Civil War: How American Negroes Felt and Acted during the War for the Union* (New York: Pantheon Books, 1965), 237; *New York Times,* May 26, 1865.

15. George Cary Eggleston, *A Rebel's Recollections* (New York: Hurd and Houghton, 1875), 243, 245.

16. James Longstreet, *From Manassas to Appomattox: Memoirs of the Civil War in America* (N.p.: J. B. Lippincott Company, 1896; James I. Robertson, Jr., ed., Bloomington, IN: Indiana University Press, 1960), 630–31; Millard J. Miller, *My Grandpap Rode with Jeb Stuart* (Westerville, OH: Privately printed, 1974), 55.

17. H. Grady Howell, Jr., *To Live and Die in Dixie: A History of the Third Mississippi Infantry, C.S.A.* (Jackson, MS: Chickasaw Bayou Press, 1991), 428; John F. Stegeman, *These Men She Gave: Civil War Diary of Athens, Georgia* (Athens: University of Georgia Press, 1964), 142; James I. Robertson, Jr., ed., *One of Jackson's Foot Cavalry: Recollections of John H. Worsham, F Company, 21st Virginia Infantry* (Wilmington, N.C.: Broadfoot Publishing Company, 1987), 189; Noah Andre Trudeau, *Out of the Storm: The End of the Civil War, April–June 1865* (Boston: Little, Brown and Company, 1994), 382.

18. Whitelaw Reid, "Excluding the Rebel," *After the War: A Southern Tour, May 1865–May 1, 1866,* quoted in William B. Hesseltine, ed., *The Tragic Conflict: The Civil War and Reconstruction* (New York: George Braziller, 1962), 464.

19. William C. Davis, *The Orphan Brigade: The Kentucky Confederates Who Couldn't Go Home* (Garden City, NY: Doubleday & Company, 1980), 256.

20. Gilbert E. Govan and James W. Livingood, eds., *The Haskell Memoirs: John Cheves Haskell* (New York: G. P. Putnam's Sons, 1960), 100.

21. William E. Bahlman, "Down in the Ranks," *Journal of the Greenbrier Historical Society* 2, no. 2 (October 1970), 93.

22. *O.R.,* ser. I, vol. 49, part 2, 828.

23. Chamberlain, *The Passing of the Armies,* 340.

CHAPTER 5

1. *O.R.*, ser. III, vol. 5, 25.

2. Ibid., 28–29.

3. Ibid., 48–49.

4. Emil and Ruth Rosenblatt, eds., *Hard Marching Every Day: The Civil War Letters of Private Wilbur Fisk, 1861–1865* (Lawrence: University Press of Kansas, 1992), 330.

5. *O.R.*, ser. III, vol. 5, 56.

6. Ibid., 57.

7. Ibid., 93–94.

8. Ibid., 288–89.

9. *O.R.*, ser. III, vol. 5: 135–36.

10. Allan Nevins, *The War for the Union: War Becomes Revolution, 1862–1863* (New York: Charles Scribner's Sons, 1960), 168; E. B. Long with Barbara Long, *The Civil War Day by Day: An Almanac, 1861–1865* (Garden City: Doubleday, 1971; New York: DaCapo Press, 1985), 727–28.

11. Johnson Hagood, *Memoirs of the War of Secession* (Columbia, SC: State Company, 1910), 372; U. R. Brooks, *Butler and His Cavalry in the War of Secession, 1861–1865* (Columbia, SC: State Company, 1909), 478; D. Augustus Dickert, *History of Kershaw's Brigade* (Newberry, SC: Elbert H. Aull Company, 1899), 531; R. Hugh Simmons, "The Story of the 12th Louisiana Infantry in the Final Campaign in North Carolina with the Confederate Army of Tennessee, January to April 1865" (typescript, USAMHI, 1992), 24; Charles C. Jones, Jr., *History of the Chatham Artillery during the Confederate Struggle for Independence* (Albany, NY: Joel Munsell, 1867), 221.

12. John Will Dyer, "A Confederate Goes Home," *Reminiscences; or, Four Years in the Confederate Army,* quoted in William B. Hesseltine, ed., *The Tragic Conflict,* 241.

13. Samuel G. French, *Two Wars: An Autobiography* (Nashville: Confederate Veteran, 1901), 310.

14. *Richmond News Leader,* April 26, 1967, "Post–War Excitement."

15. Edward S. Gregory, "Homeward Bound," *The Old Dominion* 5, no. 9 (September 15, 1871): 507.

16. H. Grady Howell, Jr., *To Live and Die in Dixie: A History of the Third Mississippi Infantry, C.S.A.* (Jackson, MS: Chickasaw Bayou Press, 1991), 428.

17. John F. Stegeman, *These Men She Gave: Civil War Diary of Athens, Georgia* (Athens: University of Georgia Press, 1964), 142.

18. Fred A. Bailey, *Class and Tennessee's Confederate Generation* (Chapel Hill: University of North Carolina Press, 1987), 106, 108–10.

CHAPTER 6

1. George Edgar Turner, *Victory Rode the Rails: The Strategic Place of the Railroads in the Civil War* (Indianapolis: Bobbs-Merrill Co., 1953; Lincoln: University of Nebraska Press, 1992), 29, 33. Turner describes the opposition of local businesspeople to establishment of direct track connections so that through service could exist. Operators of hotels, warehouses, carting concerns, saloons, restaurants, and liquor stores all objected to any steps that would permit people to pass through the cities without stop or transhipment of goods (p. 38).

2. Albro Martin, *Railroads Triumphant: The Growth, Rejection and Rebirth of a Vital American Force* (New York: Oxford University Press, 1992), 46.

3. Eric Foner and John A. Garraty, eds., *The Reader's Companion to American History* (Boston: Houghton Mifflin Company, 1991), 907; Thomas H. Johnson, ed., *The Oxford Companion to American History* (New York: Oxford University Press, 1966), 612.

4. Angus James Johnston II, *Virginia Railroads in the Civil War* (Chapel Hill: University of North Carolina Press, 1961), 7.

5. Festus P. Summers, *The Baltimore and Ohio in the Civil War* (Indianapolis: Bobbs-Merrill Company, 1939; Gettysburg, PA: Stan Clark Military Books, 1993), 42.

6. Ibid., 52–58; Turner, *Victory Rode the Rails,* 54–56.

7. Thomas Weber, *The Northern Railroads in the Civil War, 1861–1865* (New York: Columbia University–King's Crown Press, 1952), 15, 120, 125–26, 225.

8. Robert C. Black III, *The Railroads of the Confederacy* (Chapel Hill: University of North Carolina Press, 1952; Wilmington, NC: Broadfoot Publishing Company, 1987), 38, 115, 127, 163, 172, 214.

9. James I. Robertson, Jr., *Stonewall Jackson: The Man, the Soldier, the Legend* (New York: Simon & Schuster, 1997), 221.

10. Turner, *Victory Rode the Rails,* 83.

11. *O.R.,* ser. I, vol. 5, 7–8.

12. Ibid., 47.

13. Johnston, *Virginia Railroads,* 17–18.

14. Weber, *Northern Railroads,* 135–36. In addition to his railroad expertise, McCallum was a published poet and had been the architect for St. Joseph's Church in Rochester.

15. Robertson, *Stonewall Jackson,* 435, 698.

16. Jeffrey Lash, *Destroyer of the Iron Horse: General Joseph E. Johnston and Confederate Rail Transport, 1861–1865* (Kent, OH: Kent State University Press, 1991), 3.

17. Ibid., 1.

18. Warner, *Generals in Gray,* 243.

19. Black, *Railroads of the Confederacy,* 109, 119, 121.

20. Turner, *Victory Rode the Rails,* 1.

21. Ibid., 369.

22. *O.R.,* ser. IV, vol. 3, 1092.

23. Martin, *Railroads Triumphant,* 30.

24. George Skoch, "Miracle of the Rails," *Civil War History Illustrated* 31, no. 4 (September–October 1992): 24, 59. It is interesting that the Federals and the Confederates made similar troop movements by railroad at much the same time. Considering the poor condition of Southern railroads during the war, as well as the limited rail facilities in the South at the beginning of the war, the fact that the South was able to make such effective military use of railroads at all is indeed remarkable.

25. Black, *Railroads of the Confederacy,* 180–83, 189–91.

26. Turner, *Victory Rode the Rails,* 269, 376.

27. *O.R.,* ser. III, vol. 5, 303–5.

28. Ibid., 302.

29. *New York Times,* June 23, 1865.

CHAPTER 7

1. Alanson A. Haines, *History of the Fifteenth Regiment, New Jersey Volunteers* (New York: Jenkins & Thomas, 1883), 316–17; Michael Hanifen, *History of Battery B, First New Jersey Artillery* (Ottawa, IL: N.p., 1905; Hightstown, NJ: Longstreet House, 1991), 149.

2. William P. Haines, *History of the Men of Co. F, with Descriptions of the Marches and Battles of the 12th New Jersey Volunteers* (Camden: C. S. McGrath Printer, 1897), 91–93; Samuel Toombs, *Reminiscences of the War, Comprising a Detailed Account of the Experiences of the Thirteenth Regiment New Jersey Volunteers in Camp, on the March and in Battle* (Orange,

NJ: Journal Office, 1878; Hightstown, NJ: Longstreet House, 1994), 223–31.

3. D. P. Conyham, *The Irish Brigade and Its Campaigns,* ed. Lawrence Frederick Kohl (New York: Fordham University Press, 1994), 529, 597.

4. John W. Rowell, *Yankee Artillerymen: Through the Civil War with Eli Lilly's Indiana Battery* (Knoxville: University of Tennessee Press, 1975), 259–61.

5. Bentley Kutz Diary, Harrisburg CWRT Collection, Box Fle–L, USAMHI.

6. John McGowan, Anderson-Capehart-McGowan Family File, Civil War Miscellaneous Collection, USAMHI.

7. Simon Bennage Diary, Civil War Miscellaneous Collection, USAMHI.

8. Daniel Brion Diary, *Civil War Times Illustrated* Collection, USAMHI.

9. James B. Thompson, Typescript of Memoirs, Civil War Miscellaneous Collection, USAMHI.

10. John Levy, Letter to Wife, April 29, 1865, Civil War Miscellaneous Collection, USAMHI.

11. Reese H. Egbert, Letters to His Family, April 21, 1865, and May 3, 1865, Civil War Miscellaneous Collection, USAMHI.

12. Jacob Yarger Diary, Civil War Miscellaneous Collection, USAMHI.

13. John H. Burrill, 2nd New Hampshire Infantry Regiment, Typescript of Letters, *Civil War Times Illustrated* Collection, USAMHI.

14. James W. Cartwright, 56th Massachusetts Infantry Regiment, Letters, *Civil War Times Illustrated* Collection, USAMHI.

15. Arthur B. Wyman Diary, Civil War Miscellaneous Collection, USAMHI.

16. John L. Parker and Robert G. Carter, *History of the Twenty-Second Massachusetts Infantry, the Second Company of Sharpshooters, and the Third Light Battery, in the War of the Rebellion* (Boston: Rand Avery Co., 1887), 535.

17. Lewis Josselyn, Typescript of Memoirs, Civil War Miscellaneous Collection, USAMHI.

18. Warren H. Cudworth, *History of the First Regiment (Massachusetts Infantry)* . . . (Boston: Walker, Fuller & Co., 1866), 486; Asa W. Bartlett, *History of the Twelfth Regiment, New Hampshire Volunteers in the War of the Rebellion* (Concord, NH: Ira C. Evans, 1897), 313–16, 319.

19. William Child, *A History of the Fifth Regiment New Hampshire Volunteers in the American Civil War, 1861–1865* (Bristol, NH: R. W. Musgrove, 1893), 305–6, 308–9.

20. John Day Smith, *The History of the Nineteenth Maine Regiment of Maine Volunteer Infantry, 1862–1865* (Minneapolis: Great Western Printing Company, 1909), 312–14.

21. Edwin B. Houghton, *The Campaigns of the Seventeenth Maine* (Portland, ME: Short & Loring, 1866), 285, 288–91.

22. Henry W. Gay, Letter to Parents, August 11, 1865, Civil War Miscellaneous Collection, USAMHI; John O'Connell, Print of Handwritten Memoir, Civil War Miscellaneous Collection, USAMHI.

23. William Henry Walling, Typescript of Letters to His Sister, Civil War Miscellaneous Collection, USAMHI; Andrew Boyd Diary, as reported in George H. Washburn, *A Complete Military History and Record of the 108th Regiment New York Volunteers from 1862 to 1865* (Rochester, NY: E. R. Andrews, 1894), 146; Theodore W. Skinner, Letters to Friends at Home, Civil War Miscellaneous Collection, USAMHI.

24. Adolphus P. Wolf, Typescript of Letters, *Civil War Times Illustrated* Collection, USAMHI.

25. Edward H. Reynolds Diary, *Civil War Times Illustrated* Collection, USAMHI.

26. James F. Greathouse, Letter to George S. Marks, July 11, 1865, Civil War Miscellaneous Collection, USAMHI.

27. Theodore B. Gates, *The Ulster Guard (20th New York State Militia) and the War of the Rebellion* (New York: Benjammin H. Tyrrel, 1879), 553, 555–56.

28. Edwin F. Bryant, *History of the Third Regiment of Wisconsin Veteran Volunteer Infantry, 1861–1865* (Madison, WI: Veterans Association of the Regiment, 1891), 330–33, 336, 341–42, 344.

29. Asa Beak Smith, Typescript of Civil War Recollections, Civil War Miscellaneous Collection, USAMHI.

30. *O.R.,* ser. III, vol. 5, 217.

31. Wilkinson, *Mother, May You Never See,* 353.

32. Aaron E. Bachman, Unpublished Memoirs, Harrisburg CWRT Collection, USAMHI, Box A–Fil. This shows that red tape in the army is not a twentieth-century phenomenon.

33. W. H. Newlin, *A History of the Seventy-third Regiment of Illinois Infantry Volunteers* (N.p.: Regimental Reunion Association of Survivors, 1890), 527–29.

34. Robert Tilney, *My Life in the Army: Three Years and a Half with the Fifth Army Corps, Army of the Potomac, 1862–1865* (Philadelphia: Ferris & Leach, 1912), 241–45.

35. Lucius C. Cox Letters, Civil War Miscellaneous Collection, USAMHI.
36. Newlin, *Seventy-third Illinois,* 529; Thomas D. Marbaker, *History of the Eleventh New Jersey Volunteers from Its Organization to Appomattox* (Trenton: MacCrellish & Quigley, 1898), 313; William Bircher, *A Drummer-Boy's Diary: Comprising Four Years of Service with the Second Regiment Minnesota Veteran Volunteers, 1861 to 1865* (St. Paul: St. Paul Book and Stationery Company, 1898), 193.
37. Byron R. Abernathy, ed., *Private Elisha Stockwell, Jr., Sees the Civil War* (Norman: University of Oklahoma Press, 1958), 190–93.
38. Theodore Gerrish, *Army Life: A Private's Reminiscences of the Civil War* (Portland, ME: Hoyt, Fogg & Donham, 1882), 304–8.
39. Aaron S. Tucker Diary. Civil War Miscellaneous Collection, USAMHI.
40. Edward Davis Townsend, *Anecdotes of the Civil War in the United States* (New York: D. Appleton and Company, 1884), 247–48; Judson W. Bishop, *The Story of a Regiment: Being a Narrative of the Service of the Second Regiment Minnesota Veteran Volunteer Infantry in the Civil War of 1861–1865* (St. Paul: St. Paul Book and Stationery Company, 1890), 191; Newlin, *Seventy-third Ilinois,* 529.
41. Stephen H. Smith Diary, Civil War Miscellaneous Collection, USAMHI.
42. Marbaker, *Eleventh New Jersey,* 315.
43. Brian A. Bennett, *Sons of Old Monroe: A Regimental History of Patrick O'Rorke's 140th New York Volunteer Infantry* (Dayton, OH: Morningside House, 1992), 563–74. Payday has always been an anticipated moment in military life, even when in combat, with no way to spend the money, except perhaps gambling.
44. Letters of Maj. George Shuman to His Wife, Harrisburg CWRT Collection, USAMHI, Box S–Z.
45. *New York Times,* June 12 and 23, 1865. Lengthy delays in pay were not limited to the Civil War; the officers and men of the U.S. Army went a full year without pay in 1877, according to Stephen E. Ambrose, *Upton and the Army* (Baton Rouge: Louisiana State University Press, 1964; paperback edition, 1993), 112.
46. Camille Baquet, *History of the First Brigade, New Jersey Volunteers from 1861 to 1865* (Trenton: MacCrellish & Quigley, 1910; Gaithersburg, MD: Ron R. Van Sickle Military Books, 1988), 193; Letters of Daniel Faust to His Wife, Harrisburg CWRT Collection, USAMHI, Box A–Fil; Letters of Bentley Kutz to His Wife, Harrisburg CWRT Collection, USAMHI, Box Fle–L.

47. Daniel Sterling, Prints of Handwritten Letters, *Civil War Times Illustrated* Collection, USAMHI.

48. William H. H. Gripman, Letter to His Sister, September 5, 1865, Civil War Miscellaneous Collection, USAMHI.

49. Lewis G. Schmidt, *A Civil War History of the 47th Regiment of Pennsylvania Veteran Volunteers* (Allentown, PA: Privately published, 1986), 741.

50. Shuman, Letters to His Wife. Here, Shuman refers to the surrender agreement, initially accepted by Sherman but rejected by Washington officials, as mentioned in chapter 1. As a result of this rejection and subsequent modification, there were ill feelings between Sherman and his superiors, especially Secretary of War Edward M. Stanton.

51. Ibid.

52 Henry Rinker, Letters Home, Harrisburg CWRT Collection, Box M–Z, USAMHI.

53. Ames, The Civil War Diaries of Lyman Daniel Ames, 164–65.

54. Peter Boyer Letters, Harrisburg CWRT Collection, USAMHI, Boyer Family File.

55. William H. Martin Papers, Harrisburg CWRT Collection, USAMHI.

56. George B. Jennys's Letters in William Mangold Collection, Harrisburg CWRT Collection, USAMHI.

57. Fergus Elliott Diary, *Civil War Times Illustrated* Collection, USAMHI.

58. Ernest H. Jacob Diary, *Civil War Times Illustrated* Collection, USAMHI.

59. Stephen P. Chase Diary, *Civil War Times Illustrated* Collection (uncatalogued), USAMHI.

60. Editorial, *New York Times,* June 4, 1865.

61. *New York Times,* June 10, 15, and 23, 1865.

62. Gerish, *Army Life,* 304–5; Marbaker, *Eleventh New Jersey,* 313.

63. Bircher, *Drummer-Boy's Diary,* 192; *New York Times,* June 13, 1865.

64. Strong, *Yankee Private's Civil War,* 214–18.

65. Samuel Calvin Jones, *Reminiscences of the Twenty-second Iowa Volunteer Infantry* (Iowa City: S. C. Jones, 1907), 115–17.

66. *New York Times,* June 19, 20, 22, and 25, 1865.

67. Nicholas J. DeGraff, 115th Infantry Regiment, New York Volunteer Infantry, War Diary and Reminiscences, *Civil War Times Illustrated* Collection, USAMHI.

CHAPTER 8

1. Lt. William N. Ashley, Ashley Family Papers, Civil War Miscellaneous Collection, USAMHI.
2. Arnold Gates, ed., *The Rough Side of War: The Civil War Journal of Chesley A. Mosman* (Garden City, NY: Basin Publishing Co., 1987), x, 367, 406.
3. Charles E. Perkins, Typescript of Letters, *Civil War Times Illustrated* Collection (uncatalogued), USAMHI.
4. William L. Richter, *The Army in Texas during Reconstruction, 1865–1870* (College Station, TX: Texas A & M University Press, 1987), 25–30.
5. Henry G. Shedd Diary, *Civil War Times Illustrated* Collection, USAMHI.

CHAPTER 9

1. Special Order (unnumbered), April 9, 1865, Hq. Armies of the Confederate States, Virginia Historical Society, MSS 2, J 6475b.
2. Special Order (unnumbered), April 10, 1865, Hd.Qrs. Armies of the U. S., Virginia Historical Society, MSS 2, J 6425b.
3. Millard J. Miller, *My Grandpap Rode with Jeb Stuart* (Westerville, OH: Privately printed, 1974), 55.
4. William Forbes II, *Hauling Brass: Capt. Croft's Flying Battery, Columbus, Georgia* (Dayton, OH: Morningside House, 1993), 268.
5. James Longstreet, *From Manassas to Appomattox: Memoirs of the Civil War in America* (N.p.: J. B. Lippincott Company, 1896; James I. Robertson, ed., Bloomington: Indiana University Press, 1960), 630–31; Whitelaw Reid, "Excluding the Rebel," in William B. Hesseltine, ed., *The Tragic Conflict: The Civil War and Reconstruction* (New York: George Braziller, 1962), 464.
6. Stanley F. Horn, *The Army of Tennessee: A Military History* (Indianapolis: Bobbs-Merrill Company, 1941), 428, quoted in H. Grady Howell, Jr., *Going to Meet the Yankees: A History of the "Bloody Sixth" Mississippi Infantry, C.S.A.* (Jackson, MS: Chickasaw Bayou Press, 1981), 269.
7. John Watson Morton, *The Artillery of Nathan Bedford Forrest's Cavalry* (Nashville: Publishing House of the M. E. Church, South, 1909), 320.
8. Horn, *Army of Tennessee,* 428; Morton, *Artillery,* 320; Edward A. Moore, *The Story of a Cannoneer under Stonewall Jackson* (Lynchburg, VA: J. P. Bell Company, 1910), 306–7.

9. "The Last Six Days of the Grand Old Army of Northern Virginia: A Graphic Sketch by an Englishman (Francis Lowley)," *London Fortnightly Review,* in George William Bagby, *Scrapbooks, 1862–1865,* 5 vols. (Richmond: Virginia Historical Society, mss. 5, 7B1463, 1–5), vol. 3, 194–97.

10. George C. Underwood, *History of the Twenty-Sixth Regiment of the North Carolina Troops in the Great War, 1861–1865* (Goldsboro, NC: Nash Brothers; Wendell, NC: Broadfoot's Bookmark, 1978), 91.

11. Bagby, *Scrapbooks,* "Last Six Days"; Underwood, *Twenty-Sixth North Carolina,* 91; Horn, *Army of Tennessee,* 428, quoted in Howell, *Going to Meet the Yankees,* 269.

12. Chris M. Calkins, *The Final Bivouac: The Surrender Parade at Appomattox and the Disbanding of the Armies, April 10–May 20, 1865* (Lynchburg, VA: M. E. Howard, 1988), 34.

13. Ibid., 18, 42.

14. Gary W. Gallagher, ed., *Fighting for the Confederacy: The Personal Recollections of General Edward Porter Alexander* (Chapel Hill: University of North Carolina Press, 1989), 544–45; Natalie Jenkins Bond and Osman Latrobe Coward, eds., *The South Carolinians: Colonel Asbury Coward's Memoirs* (New York: Vantage Press, 1968), 179.

15. William H. Runge, ed., *Four Years in the Confederate Artillery: The Diary of Private Henry Robinson Berkeley* (Richmond: Virginia Historical Society, 1991), 124; "A Civil War Diary Being an Account of the Life and Times of a Confederate Soldier," *Jacksonville (Florida) Times-Union and Journal,* July 6, 1975, Harrisburg CWRT Collection, Box M–Z, USAMHI; Douglas Hale, *The Third Texas Cavalry in the Civil War* (Norman, OK: University of Oklahoma Press, 1993), 273.

16. Calkins, *Final Bivouac,* 2.

17. Ibid., 51.

18. Ibid., 2, 47, 51, 55, 59–60, 70.

19. Stuart H. Buck, ed., "With Lee after Appomattox: Personal Experiences from Diary of Samuel C. Lovell," *Civil War Times Illustrated* 17, no. 7 (November 1978): 42–43.

20. John B. Gordon, *Reminiscences of the Civil War* (New York: Charles Scribner's Sons, 1904), 454.

21. Gregory A. Coco, *The Civil War Infantryman: In Camp, on the March, and in Battle* (Gettysburg, PA: Thomas Publications, 1996), 148.

22. John C. Breckinridge, "A Rebel Leader's Flight," *Civil War Times Illustrated* 6, no. 3 (June 1967): 4–10. This article is based on a letter to Breckinridge's son, Owen, and is in the John Taylor Wood Papers, Southern Historical Collection, University of North Carolina. Also, William C. Davis, "John C. Breckinridge," *Civil War Times Illustrated* 6, no. 3 (June 1967), 11–18.

23. Jubal A. Early, *A Memoir of the Last Year of the War for Independence in the Confederate States of America Containing an Account of the Operations of His Commands in the Years 1864 and 1865* (Toronto: Lovell & Gibson, 1866), 138; Ezra J. Warner, *Generals in Gray: Lives of the Confederate Commanders* (Baton Rouge: Louisiana State University Press, 1959), 79–80.

24. T. Harry Williams, *P. G. T. Beauregard: Napoleon in Gray* (Baton Rouge: Louisiana State University Press, 1955), 256.

25. Richard Taylor, *Destruction and Reconstruction: Personal Experiences of the Late War in the United States* (Edinburgh, Scotland: William Blackwood and Sons, 1879), 302–7.

26. John Witherspoon DuBose, *General Joseph Wheeler and the Army of Tennessee* (New York: Neale Publishing Company, 1912), 469–70.

27. Calkins, *Final Bivouac,* 48–50.

28. Noah Andre Trudeau, *Out of the Storm: The End of the Civil War, April–June 1865* (Boston: Little, Brown and Company, 1998), 382.

29. Bob Womack, *Call Forth the Mighty Men* (Bessemer, AL: Colonial Press, 1987), 512–13.

30. Robert Grier Stephens, Jr., ed., *Intrepid Warrior: Clement Anselm Evans* (Dayton, OH: Morningside Press, 1992), 556.

CHAPTER 10

1. *O.R.,* ser. II, vol. 8, 603.

2. Ibid., 624. It is obvious that much of this report was composed during the final days of the Confederacy's existence. One wonders what type of reception the report would have received if it had ever been submitted.

3. Lonnie R. Speer, *Portals to Hell: Military Prisons of the Civil War* (Mechanicsburg, PA: Stackpole Books, 1997), 287.

4. *O.R.,* ser. II, vol. 8, 641.

5. Ibid., 288–89.

6. Ibid., 296, 311; Speer, *Portals to Hell,* 35, 311.

7. William Marvel, *Andersonville: The Last Depot* (Chapel Hill: University of North Carolina Press, 1994), 235–40.

8. Jerry Potter, "The *Sultana* Disaster: Conspiracy of Greed," *Blue & Gray Magazine* 7, no. 6 (August 1990): 8, 17.

9. Gene Erick Salecker, *Disaster on the Mississippi: The Sultana Explosion, April 27, 1865* (Annapolis, MD: Naval Institute Press, 1996), 20.

10. Ibid., 12.

11. Ibid., 65.

12. Ibid., 24.

13. Ibid., 74–77.

14. Ibid., 163.

15. Ibid., 210.

16. *O.R.,* ser. III, vol. 5, 3; *New York Times,* June 21 and 25, 1865.

17. Speer, *Portals to Hell,* 280.

18. *O.R.,* ser. II, vol. 8, 500–1, 504.

19. K. M. Kostyal, ed., *Field of Battle: The Civil War Letters of Major Thomas J. Halsey* (Washington, DC: National Geographic Society, Book Division, 1996), 136–38, 148.

20. Brian A. Bennett, *Sons of Old Monroe: A Regimental History of Patrick O'Rorke's 140th New York Volunteer Infantry* (Dayton, OH: Morningside House, 1992), 567.

21. Bailey, Fred A. *Class and Tennessee's Confederate Generation* (Chapel Hill: University of North Carolina Press, 1987), 112.

22. Letter from Confederate Soldier, July 20, 1863, Lewis Leigh Collection, Book 28, Item no. 53, USAMHI.

23. Charles D. Spurlin, ed., *The Civil War Diary of Charles A. Leuschner* (Austin, TX: Eakin Press, 1992), 50–54, 119 (n. 79).

24. Andrew Davidson Long, *Stonewall's "Foot Cavalryman"* (Austin: TX: Steck Company, 1965), 30–36.

25. Henry Clay Mettem, "Civil War Memoirs of the First Maryland Cavalry, C.S.A.," *Maryland Historical Magazine* 53 (1963): 161–68.

26. Alfred R. Gibbons, *The Recollections of an Old Confederate Soldier* (Shelbyville, MO: Herald Print, 1931), 2, 13–19, 21, 31.

27. Bell Irvin Wiley, ed., *Four Years on the Firing Line* (Jackson, TN: McCowat-Mercer Press, 1963), 216–18, 237, 239.

28. John H. Lewis, *Recollections from 1860 to 1865* (Washington, DC: Peake & Company, Publishers, 1895), 86–87, 91.

29. Capt. F. M. Imboden to His Sister, May 18, 1865, Lewis Leigh, Jr. Collection, Book 28, Item no. 27, USAMHI.

30. Thomas H. Malone, *Memoir of Thomas H. Malone* (Nashville: Baird-Ward, 1928), 186–87, 190–92, 197, 205, 211.

31. "A Returned Confederate," *Lynchburg News,* reported in the *Montevallo (Alabama) Star,* September 26, 1866.

32. Lawrence R. Laboda, *From Selma to Appomattox: The History of the Jeff Davis Artillery* (Shippensburg, PA: White Mane Publishing Company, 1994), 316.

33. Bailey, *Class and Tennessee's Confederate Generation,* 112.

34. W. J. Andrews, *Sketch of Company K, 23rd South Carolina Volunteers, in the Civil War from 1862–1865* (Richmond: Whittet & Shepperson, n.d.; Sumter, SC: Wilder & Weard, n.d.), 29.

35. George M. Neese, *Three Years in the Confederate Horse Artillery* (Dayton, OH: Press of the Morningside Bookshop, 1983), 322, 333, 353–62.

36. Martin Brett, "Reminiscences" (typescript, 1897), Fredericksburg and Spotsylvania National Military Park, Virginia, BV 26.

37. Robert Cannon (pseudonym), "an ex-Boy," *Where Men Only Dare to Go; or, The Story of a Boy Company (C.S.A.)* (Richmond: Whittet & Shepperson, 1885), 236–37.

38. Thomas D. Cockrell and Michael B. Ballard, eds., *A Mississippi Rebel in the Army of Northern Virginia: The Civil War Memoirs of Private Daniel Holt* (Baton Rouge: Louisiana State University Press, 1995), 307, 332, 337–42.

39. Harry A. Hall, *A Johnny Reb Band from Salem: The Pride of Tarheelia* (Raleigh: North Carolina Confederate Centennial Commission, 1963), 104, 106–8. Although Moravians are traditionally pacificists, some men from Moravian backgrounds fought in both armies. There was a concentration of Moravian settlers in parts of North Carolina, and it was in the Tarheel units that these men were found. Moravians were also centered in areas of Pennsylvania and Maryland and thus furnished men to Union outfits.

40. David E. Johnston, *The Story of a Confederate Boy in the Civil War* (Portland, OR: Glass & Prudhomme Company, 1914), 337–41.

41. Ibid., 343–45.

42. Lewis N. Wynne and Robert A. Taylor, eds., *This War So Horrible: The Civil War Diary of Hiram Smith Williams* (Tuscaloosa: University of Alabama Press, 1993), 8–9, 13–16, 18, 134–37.

43. John O. Casler, *Four Years in the Stonewall Brigade* (Girard, KS: Appeal Publishing Company, 1906), 284, 288–89. This second edition was revised, corrected, and improved by Maj. Jed Hotchkiss.

44. William H. Runge, ed., *Four Years in the Confederate Artillery: The Diary of Private Henry Robinson Berkeley* (Richmond: Virginia Historical Society, 1991), 112, 130, 135.

45. Ibid., 121, 126–44.

46. Lt. E. L. Cox Diary, Company C, 68th North Carolina Infantry, Virginia Historical Society, mss. 5, 1 C 8394:1.

47. Anny Lewis Dickinson Brown Morris, ed., *Diary of Capt. Henry C. Dickinson C.S.A.* (Denver: Press of the Williamson-Haffner Co., n.d.), 171, 185–87; Robert E. Park, "Diary of Captain Robert E. Park, Twelfth Alabama Regiment," *Southern Historical Society Papers,* vol. 3 (January–June 1877) repr. Kraus Reprint Co., 1977: 244–54.

48. W. H. Morgan, *Personal Reminiscences of the War of 1861–5* (Lynchburg: J. P. Bell Company, 1911), 231–36, 250–53, 269–70.

49. Genevieve Miller, ed., *Yankee in Gray: The Civil War Memoirs of Henry E. Handerson, with a Selection of His Wartime Letters* (Cleveland: Press of Western Reserve University, 1962), 76, 82–83.

50. Matthew Jack Davis, "A Long Journey Home," *Civil War Times Illustrated* 36, no. 2 (May 1997): 14–16, 50–52, 54–55.

51. Letter of Constantine A. Hege, Lewis Leigh Collection, Book 11, USAMHI.

52. Boatner, *The Civil War Dictionary,* 322; James M. Templeton, Jr., "Time Lapse: A Soldier for Two Countries," *Civil War Times Illustrated* 34, no. 1 (March–April 1995): 90; J. J. Fox, "History: Brook's Battalion: The Experiment That Failed," *Blue & Gray Magazine* 2, no. 2 (November 1984): 40–43; James A. P. Fancher Diary, Civil War Miscellaneous Collection, USAMHI.

53. H. Grady Howell, Jr., *To Live and Die in Dixie: A History of the Third Mississippi Infantry, C.S.A.* (Jackson, MS: Chickasaw Bayou Press, 1991), 428.

CHAPTER 11

1. Ibid., 1280.

2. Ibid., 25.

3. Ernest B. Furguson, *Ashes of Glory: Richmond at War* (New York: Alfred A. Knopf, 1996), 352.

4. William C. Oates, *The War between the Union and Confederacy and Its Lost Opportunities* (New York: Neale Publishing Co, 1905; Dayton, OH: Morningside Bookshop, 1985), 430–31.

5. Thilbert H. Pearce, ed., *Diary of Captain Henry A. Chambers* (Wendell, NC: Broadfoot's Bookmark, 1983), xxxvi, 258–65.

6. James I. Robertson, Jr., ed., *One of Jackson's Foot Cavalry: Recollections of John H. Worsham, F Company, 21st Virginia* (Wilmington, NC: Broadfoot Publishing Company, 1987), 183, 189.

7. R. B. Rosenburg, ed., *"For the Sake of My Country": The Diary of Colonel W. W. Ward, Ninth Tennessee Cavalry, Morgan's Brigade, C.S.A.* (Murfreesboro, TN: Southern Heritage Press, 1992), 6–17.

8. Joshua Hilary Hudson, *Sketches and Reminiscences* (Columbia, SC: State Company, 1903), 66ff, 71–72.

9. Francis W. Dawson, *Reminiscences of Confederate Service, 1861–1865* (Charleston, SC: News and Courier Book Presses, 1882; Bell I. Wiley, ed., Baton Rouge: Louisiana State University Press, 1980), 144–46, 150–51, 172, 210.

10. Gen. G. Moxley Sorrell, *Recollections of a Confederate Staff Officer* (New York: Neale Publishing Company, 1905), 265–67, 275, 278–81.

CHAPTER 12

1. James M. McPherson, *The Negro's Civil War: How American Negroes Felt and Acted during the War for the Union* (New York: Pantheon Books, 1965), 237, 239.

2. *The Civil War Book of Lists* (Conshohocken, PA: Combined Books, 1993, 1994), 167–70. McPherson (*Negro's Civil War,* 237) claims Congressional Medals of Honor were awarded to seventeen colored soldiers and four black sailors.

3. *Civil War Book of Lists,* 169 (footnote).

4. Ernest B. Furguson, *Ashes of Glory: Richmond at War* (New York: Alfred A. Knopf, 1996), 346.

5. Ibid., 353.

6. Joseph T. Glatthaar, *Forged in Battle: The Civil War Alliance of Black Soldiers and White Officers* (New York: Free Press, 1990), 219.

7. Ibid., 219.

8. Ibid., 220–21.

9. Ibid., 221.

10. Ibid., 222–23.

11. Ibid., 227.
12. Ibid., 229–32.
13. Ibid., 232–33.
14. Edwin S. Redkey, ed., *A Grand Army of Black Men: Letters from African-American Soldiers in the Union Army, 1861–1865* (New York: Cambridge University Press, 1992), 281–84.
15. Benjamin W. Thompson, "Memoirs" (Typescript, CWTI Collection, USAMHI).
16. Glatthaar, *Forged in Battle*, 233.
17. Ibid., 233–34.
18. Redkey, *Grand Army of Black Men*, 284 (ltr. 126).
19. Ibid., 285–87 (ltr. 127).
20. Ibid., 288–93 (ltr. 128).
21. Ibid., 293.
22. Ira Berlin, Joseph P. Reidy, and Leslie S. Rowland, eds., *Freedom: A Documentary History of Emancipation, 1861–1867: Selected from the National Archives of the United States. Ser. 2: The Black Military Experience* (New York: Cambridge University Press, 1982; repr. 1983), 778–79 (ltr. 340).
23. Ibid., 779–81 (ltr. 341).
24. Ibid., 775–77 (ltr. 338).
25. Ibid., 777–78 (ltr. 339).
26. Ibid., 772–73 (ltr. 335).
27. Ibid., 773–74 (ltr. 336).
28. Ibid., 774–75 (ltr. 337).
29. Ibid., 765, 767, 770.

CHAPTER 13

1. *O.R.*, ser. III, vol. 4, 1012–29.
2. Mark S. Hoffman, ed., *The World Almanac and Book of Facts, 1992* (New York: Pharos Books, 1991), 702.
3. Ibid., 702.
4. Gregory A. Coco, *The Civil War Infantryman: In Camp, on the March, and in Battle* (Gettysburg, PA: Thomas Publications, 1996), 148.
5. Ibid., 150.
6. Ibid.
7. Ibid., 151.

8. Ibid., 150.

9. Ibid., 152.

10. Ibid.

11. *Petersburg (Virginia) Index,* August 15, 1866, quoted in *Blue & Gray Magazine* 14, no. 3 (winter 1997): 5.

12. Coco, *Civil War Infantryman,* 153.

EPILOGUE

1. *O.R.,* ser. III, vol. 5, 1047.

2. Ibid., (footnote).

3. Quoted in Benjamin W. Bacon, *Sinews of War: How Technology, Industry, and Transportation Won the Civil War* (Novato, CA: Presidio Press, 1997), 216.

4. McPherson, *Battle Cry of Freedom,* 859.

BIBLIOGRAPHY

UNPUBLISHED MATERIALS

United States Army Military History Institute, Carlisle Barracks, Carlisle, Pennsylvania

Civil War Times Illustrated Collection:
Ames, Lyman Daniel, Typescript of diary
Barker, William H. H., Typescript of autobiography
Brion, Daniel, Diary
Brown, William H., Letters
Burrill, John H., Typescript of letters
Cartwright, James W., Letters
Chase, Stephen P., Typescript of diary
Craw, Robert Burns, Typescript of memoirs
DeGraff, Nicholas J., Diary & reminiscences
Elliott, Fergus, Typescript of diary
Heffelfinger, Jacob, Diary
Hurter, Henry, Typescript of diary
Jacob, Ernest H., Print of pocket diary
Johnson, Clarence A., Prints of letters
Oesterle, Frederick W., Typescript of memoirs
Parkinson, Joseph, Print of diary
Parsens, Charles Moses, Typescript of memoirs
Perkins, Charles E., Typescript of letters
Reynolds, Edward H., Typescript of diary
Shedd, Henry G., Typescript of diary
Sterling, Daniel, Prints of letters
Sturgis, Eben P., Prints of letters
Thompson, Benjamin W., Typescript of memoirs
Wolf, Adolphus P., Typescript of letters

Harrisburg Civil War Round Table Collection:
Bachman, Aaron E., Memoirs
Boyer, Peter, Letters
Brown, John, Transcript of diary
Eddington, W. R., Memoirs
Faust, Daniel, Letters
Jennys, George B., Letters
Kutz, Bently, Letters
Martin, William H., Papers
Rinker, Henry, Letters
Shuman, George, Letters
Talley, William R., Newspaper clipping
Williamson, Elbert Madison, Biographical account
Woodward, William H., Letters

Civil War Miscellaneous Collection:
Ashley, William N., Letter
Bennage, Simon, Print of diary
Cox, Lucius C., Letters
Ebgert, Reese H., Letters
Fancher, James A. P., Typescript of diary
Finley, Thomas Y., Diary
Foster, Brigham, Letters
Gay, Henry W., Letters
Greathouse, James F., Letter
Gripman, William H. H., Letter
Hoyt, Henry R., Letter
Josselyn, Lewis, Typescript of memoirs
Levy, John, Letter
Lusk, William H., Print of discharge
Marks, Samuel J., Letters
McGowan, John, Letter
O'Connell, John, Print of memoirs
Rock, Thomas, Letter
Skinner, Theodore W., Letters
Smith, Asa Beak, Typescript of "Civil War Recollections"
Smith, Stephen H., Typescript of diary
Thompson, James B., Typescript of memoirs
Tucker, Aaron S., Diary

Turner, Aaron S., Original pocket diary
Walling, William Henry, Letters
Williams, James, Letter
Wyman, Arthur B., Pocket diary
Yarger, Jacob, Pocket diary

Lewis Leigh, Jr. Collection:
Anonymous soldier, Letter (Book 28–#53)
(Illegible), Hanford, Account of experiences (Book 32–#66)
Hege, Constantine A., Letters
Imboden, F. M., Letter to sister

Virginia Historical Society, Richmond, Virginia
Archer, Richard, Diary
Bagby, George William, Scrapbooks
Cox, E. L., Diary
Johnston, Samuel, Pass, Hq., Dept. of Washington, XXII Corps
Scott, Dr. James McClure, War record
Special Order, April 9, 1865, Hq., Armies of C.S.A.
Special Order, April 10, 1865, Hq., Armies of the U.S.
Turrentine, James Alexander, Diary for 1865
Vincent, John Bell, Diary 1864–1865

Fredericksburg and Spotsylvania National Military Park, Fredericksburg, Virginia
Brett, Martin, Typescript of reminiscences

NEWSPAPERS AND MAPS

Chatham Record, Pittsboro, North Carolina, 1924, n.p.
Index, Petersburg, Virginia, August 15, 1866.
Montevallo Star, Montevallo, Alabama, September 26, 1866.
New York Times, May and June 1865, passim.
Richmond News Leader, Richmond, Virginia, April 26, 1867.
Times-Union and Journal, Jacksonville, Florida, July 6, 1975.
ADC The Map People. *ADC's State Road Map of Maryland and Delaware.* Alexandria, Virginia: Langenscheidt Publishing Group, 1991.
Map of Baltimore, Washington, D.C., and Vicinity, Rand, McNally & Company, 1972.

JOURNAL ARTICLES

Alexander, Ted. "The Chippewa Sharpshooters of Company K." *Civil War,* vol. 10, no. 5 (September–October 1992): 24–26.

Bahlmann, William E. "Down in the Ranks." *Journal of the Greenbrier Historical Society,* vol. 2, no. 2 (October 1970): 41–93.

Bahnson, Henry T. "The Last Days of the War." *North Carolina Booklet,* vol. 2, no. 12 (April 1903): 3–22.

Barr, Alwyn. "Polignac's Texas Brigade." *Texas Gulf Coast Historical Association,* vol. 8, no. 1 (November 1964): 56.

Bradwell, I. G. "Making Our Way Home from Appomattox." *Confederate Veteran,* vol. 29 (March 1921): 102–3.

Breckinridge, John C. "A Rebel Leader's Flight." *Civil War Times Illustrated,* vol. 6, no. 3 (June 1967): 4–10.

Buck, Stuart H., ed. "With Lee after Appomattox: Personal Experiences from Diary of Samuel C. Lovell." *Civil War Times Illustrated,* vol. 17, no. 7 (November 1978): 42–43.

Colston, Frederick M. "Recollections of the Last Months in the Army of Northern Virginia." *Southern Historical Society Papers,* vol. 38 (January–December 1910): 1–15.

Crenshaw, Edward. "Diary of Captain Edward Crenshaw of the Confederate States Army." *Alabama Historical Quarterly,* vol. 2, no. 4 (winter 1940): 465–82.

Davis, Matthew Jack. "A Long Journey Home." *Civil War Times Illustrated,* vol. 36, no. 2 (May 1997): 14–16, 50–52, 54–55.

Davis, William C. "John C. Breckinridge." *Civil War Times Illustrated,* vol. 6, no. 3 (June 1967): 11–18.

———. "On the Road to Appomattox by Major General William Mahone." *Civil War Times Illustrated,* vol. 9, no. 9 (January 1971): 4–11, 42–49.

Fortin, Maurice S., ed. "Colonel Hilary A. Herbert's 'History of the Eighth Alabama Volunteer Regiment, C.S.A.'" *The Alabama Historical Quarterly,* vol. 39, nos. 1, 2, 3, 4 (1977).

Fox, J. J. "History: Brook's Battalion: The Experiment That Failed." *Blue & Gray Magazine,* vol. 2, no. 2 (November 1984): 40–43.

Gregory, Edward S. "Homeward Bound." *The Old Dominion,* vol. 5, no. 9 (September 15, 1871): 506–10.

Hargis, O. P. "We Kept Fighting and Falling Back." *Civil War Times Illustrated,* vol. 7, no. 8 (December 1968): 37–42.

Mettem, Henry Clay. "Civil War Memoirs of the First Maryland Cavalry, C.S.A." *Maryland Historical Magazine,* vol. 53 (1963): 139–70.

Montgomery, Walter A. "Appomattox and the Return Home." *North Carolina Regiments, 1861–1865,* vol. 5: 1–13.

Morris, Roy. "Genius or Devil, Nathan Bedford Forrest Was One of the Civil War's Most Unforgettable Figures." *America's Civil War,* vol. 1, no. 3 (September 1988): 6–12.

Park, Robert E. "Diary of Captain Robert E. Park, Twelfth Alabama Regiment." *Southern Historical Society Papers,* vol. 3 (January–June, 1877); repr. Kraus Reprint Co., 1977: 244–54.

Potter, Jerry. "The *Sultana* Disaster: Conspiracy of Greed." *Blue & Gray Magazine,* vol. 7, no. 6 (August 1990): 8–24.

Robbins, Peggy. "Desertion: The Great Evil of the War." *Civil War,* vol. 8, no. 5 (September–October 1990): 30–35, 74.

Robertson, Frank S. "Reminiscences of the Years 1861–1865." *The Historical Society of Washington County, Virginia Bulletin,* series 2, no. 23 (1986): 34–38.

Robertson, James I. "Military Executions." *Civil War Times Illustrated,* vol. 5, no. 2 (May 1966): 34–39.

Rudolph, Jack. "The Grand Review." *Civil War Times Illustrated,* vol. 19, no. 7 (November 1980): 34–43.

Shingleton, Royce Gordon, ed. "South from Appomattox: The Diary of Abner R. Cox." *South Carolina Historical Magazine,* vol. 75, no. 4 (October 1974): 238–44.

Skoch, George. "Miracle of the Rails." *Civil War Times Illustrated,* vol. 31, no. 4 (September–October 1992): 22, 24, 56–59.

Stonebraker, John R. "Munford's Marylanders Never Surrendered to Foe." *Richmond Times-Dispatch,* February 6, 1910, repr. *Southern Historical Society Papers,* vol. 37 (1909): 309–12.

Tarbell, Ida M. "How the Union Army Was Disbanded." *McClure's Magazine* (March 1901); repr. *Civil War Times Illustrated,* vol. 6, no. 8 (December 1967): 4–9.

———. "Disbanding the Confederate Army." *McClure's Magazine* (April 1901); repr. *Civil War Times Illustrated,* vol. 6, no. 9 (January 1968): 10–19.

Templeton, James M., Jr. "Time Lapse: A Soldier for Two Countries." *Civil War Times Illustrated*, vol. 34, no. 1 (March–April 1995): 90.

Ward, James A. "Mississippi's Southern Railroad: Study in Perils and Perseverance." *Railroad History Bulletin*, Bulletin 144 (spring 1981): 24–49.

BOOKS

Abernethy, Byron R., ed. *Private Elisha Stockwell, Jr. Sees the Civil War.* Norman: University of Oklahoma Press, 1958.

Allardice, Bruce S. *More Generals in Gray.* Baton Rouge: Louisiana State University Press, 1995.

Ambrose, Stephen E. *Halleck: Lincoln's Chief of Staff.* Baton Rouge: Louisiana State University Press, 1962; repr. pb. edition, 1996.

———. *Upton and the Army.* Baton Rouge: Louisiana State University Press, 1964; pb. edition, 1993.

American Heritage, eds. *The American Heritage Pictorial Atlas of United States History.* New York: American Heritage Publishing Co.: 1966.

Anderson, Ephraim McDowell. *Memoirs: Historical and Personal, Including the Campaigns of the First Missouri Brigade.* St. Louis: Times Printing Company, 1868; repr. Dayton, Ohio: The Press of Morningside Bookshop, 1972.

Anderson, John Q. *A Texas Surgeon in the C.S.A.* (Confederate Centennial Series, no. 6). Tuscaloosa, Alabama: Confederate Publishing Company, Inc., 1957.

Andrews, Andrew J. *A Sketch of the Boyhood Days of Andrew J. Andrews of Gloucester County, Virginia, and His Experience as a Soldier in the Late War between the States.* Richmond: The Hermitage Press, Inc., 1905.

Andrews, W. J. *Sketch of Company K, 23rd South Carolina Volunteers, in the Civil War, from 1862–1865.* Richmond: Whittet & Shepperson, n.d.; repr. Sumter, South Carolina: Wilder and Ward, n.d.

Armstrong, Richard B., ed. *The Journal of Charles R. Chewing, Company E, 9th Virginia Cavalry, C.S.A.* Baltimore: Butternut and Blue, 1987.

Bacon, Benjamin W. *Sinews of War: How Technology, Industry, and Transportation Won the Civil War.* Novato, CA: Presidio Press, 1997.

Bailey, Fred A. *Class and Tennessee's Confederate Generation.* Chapel Hill: The University of North Carolina Press, 1987.

Bailey, Thomas A. *A Diplomatic History of the American People.* New York: Appleton-Crofts, 1964.

Banes, Charles H. *History of the Philadelphia Brigade.* Philadelphia: J. B. Lippincott & Co., 1876.

Baquet, Camille. *History of the First Brigade, New Jersey Volunteers from 1861 to 1865.* Trenton: MacCrellish & Quigley, 1910; repr. Gaithersburg, Maryland: Ron R. Van Sickle Military Books, 1988.

Bartlett, Asa W. *History of the Twelfth Regiment, New Hampshire Volunteers in the War of the Rebellion.* Concord, New Hampshire: Ira C. Evans, 1897.

Baumgartner, Richard A., ed. *William Pitt Chambers: Blood & Sacrifice: The Civil War Journal of A Confederate Soldier.* Huntington, West Virginia: Blue Acorn Press, 1994.

Benedict, George Grenville. *A Short History of the 14th Vermont Regiment.* Bennington, Vermont: C. M. Pierce, 1887.

Bennett, Brian A. *Sons of Old Monroe: A Regimental History of Patrick O'Rorke's 140th New York Volunteer Infantry.* Dayton, Ohio: Morningside House, Inc., 1992.

Benson, Susan Williams, ed. *Berry Benson's Civil War Book: Memoirs of a Confederate Scout and Sharpshooter.* Athens, Georgia: University of Georgia Press, 1962.

Bergeron, Arthur W., Jr., ed. *The Civil War Reminiscences of Major Silas T. Grisamore, C.S.A.* Baton Rouge: Louisiana State University Press, 1993.

Berlin, Ira, Joseph O. Reidy, and Leslie S. Rowland, eds. *Freedom: A Documentary History of Emancipation, 1861–1867, Selected from the National Archives of the United States—Series II: The Black Military Experience.* New York: Cambridge University Press, 1982; repr. 1983.

Bernard, George S., ed. *"Last Days of Lee and His Paladins"—War Talks of Confederate Veterans.* Petersburg, Virginia: Fenn & Owen, Publishers, 1892.

Bevier, R. S. *History of the First and Second Missouri Confederate Brigades, 1861–1865, and from Wakarusa to Appomattox.* St. Louis: Bryan, Brand & Company, 1879.

Bircher, William. *A Drummer-Boy's Diary: Comprising Four Years of Service with the Second Regiment Minnesota Veteran Volunteers, 1861 to 1865.* St. Paul: St. Paul Book and Stationery Company, 1889.

Bishop, Judson W. *The Story of a Regiment: Being a Narrative of the Service of the Second Regiment Minnesota Veteran Volunteer Infantry in the Civil War of 1861–1865.* St. Paul: St. Paul Book and Stationery Company, 1890.

Black, Robert C., III *The Railroads of the Confederacy.* Chapel Hill: The University of North Carolina Press, 1952; repr. Wilmington, North Carolina: Broadfoot Publishing Company, 1987.

Blackford, Charles Minor, III, ed. *Letters from Lee's Army or Memoirs of Life In and Out of the Army in Virginia during the War between the States.* New York: Charles Scribner's Sons, 1947.

Blackford W. W. *War Years with Jeb Stuart.* New York: Charles Scribner's Sons, 1945.

Blake, Henry N. *Three Years in the Army of the Potomac.* Boston: Lee and Shepard, 1865.

Boatner, Mark Mayo, III. *The Civil War Dictionary.* New York: David McKay Company, Inc., 1959.

Bond, Natalie Jenkins, and Osmun Latrobe Coward, eds. *The South Carolinians: Colonel Asbury Coward's Memoirs.* New York: Vantage Press, 1968.

Booth, G. W. *Personal Reminiscences of a Maryland Soldier in the War between the States, 1861–1865.* Baltimore: Fleet, McGinley & Co., 1898.

Bowman, John S., ed. *The Civil War Almanac.* New York: Facts on File, Inc. (Bison Book), 1982.

Brooks, U. R. *Butler and His Cavalry in the War of Secession, 1861–1865.* Columbia, South Carolina: The State Company, 1909.

Brown, Norman D., ed. *One of Cleburne's Command: The Civil War Reminiscences and Diary of Capt. Samuel T. Foster, Granbury's Texas Brigade C.S.A.* Austin, Texas: University of Texas Press, 1980.

Bruce, Robert V. *Lincoln and the Tools of War.* Indianapolis: Bobbs-Merrill, 1956; repr. Urbana, Illinois: University of Illinois Press, 1989.

Bryant, Edwin F. *History of the Third Regiment of Wisconsin Volunteer Infantry, 1861–1865.* Madison, Wisconsin: Veterans Association of the Regiment, 1891.

Buck, Samuel D. *With the Old Confeds: Actual Experiences of a Captain in the Line.* Baltimore: H. E. Houck & Co., 1925.

Buckley, Cornelius M., ed. and trans. *A Frenchman, A Chaplain, A Rebel: The War Letters of Père Louis-Hippolyte Gache, S.J.* Chicago: Loyola University Press, 1981.

Caldwell, J. F. J. *The History of a Brigade of South Carolinians, Known First as "Gregg's," and Subsequently as "McGowan's Brigade."* Philadelphia: King and Baird, Printers, 1866; repr. Dayton, Ohio: Morningside Bookshop, 1974.

Calhoun, Capt. William L. *History of the 42nd Regiment, Georgia Volunteers, Confederate States Army, Infantry;* repr. University, Alabama: Confederate Publishing Co., 1977.

Calkins, Chris M. *The Final Bivouac: The Surrender Parade at Appomattox and the Disbanding of the Armies, April 10–May 20, 1865.* Lynchburg, Virginia: M. E. Howard, Inc., 1988.

Cammack, John Henry. *Personal Recollections of Private John Henry Cammack: A Soldier of the Confederacy, 1861–1865.* Huntington, West Virginia: Paragon Ptg. & Pub. Co., n.d.

Cannon, Robert (pseudonym), "an ex-Boy." *"Where Men Only Dare to Go"; or, The Story of a Boy Company (C.S.A.).* Richmond: Whittet & Shepperson, 1885.

Carter, Robert Goldthwaite. *Four Brothers in Blue or Sunshine and Shadows of the War of the Rebellion: A Story of the Great Civil War from Bull Run to Appomattox.* Austin, Texas: University of Texas Press, 1978.

Casler, John O. *Four Years in the Stonewall Brigade.* Girard, Kansas: Appeal Publishing Company, 1906; 2nd edition, revised, corrected, and improved by Maj. Jed Hotchkiss.

Cater, Douglas John. *As It Was: Reminiscences of a Soldier of the Third Texas Cavalry and the Nineteenth Louisiana Infantry.* Austin, Texas: State House Press, 1990.

Chamberlain, Joshua Lawrence. *The Passing of the Armies.* New York: G. P. Putnam's Sons, 1915.

Chamberlaine, William W. *Memoirs of the Civil War between the Northern and Southern Sections of the United States of America, 1861 to 1865.* Washington, D.C.: Press of Byron S. Adams, 1912.

Chamberlayne, C. G., ed. *Ham Chamberlayne—Virginian: Letters and Papers of an Artillery Officer in the War for Southern Independence, 1861–1865.* Richmond: Press of the Dietz Printing Co., Publishers, 1932.

Child, William. *A History of the Fifth Regiment New Hampshire Volunteers in the American Civil War, 1861–1865.* Bristol, New Hampshire: R. W. Musgrove, 1893.

Cockrell, Thomas D., and Michael B. Ballard, eds. *A Mississippi Rebel in the Army of Northern Virginia: The Civil War Memoirs of Private Daniel Holt.* Baton Rouge: Louisiana State University Press, 1995.

Coco, Gregory A. *The Civil War Infantryman: In Camp, On the March, and in Battle.* Gettysburg: Thomas Publications, 1996.

Coffman, Edward M. *The Old Army: A Portrait of the American Army in Peacetime, 1784–1898.* New York: Oxford University Press, 1986.

Connelly, Thomas Lawrence. *Autumn of Glory: The Army of Tennessee, 1862–1865.* Baton Rouge: Louisiana State University Press, 1971.

Cooling, Benjamin Franklin. *Symbol, Sword, and Shield: Defending Washington during the Civil War.* Shippensburg, Pennsylvania: White Mane Publishing Company, Inc., 1975; 2nd rev. edition, 1991.

Cudworth, Warren H. *History of the First Regiment (Massachusetts Infantry)....* Boston: Walker, Fuller & Co., 1866.

Cullum, George W. *Biographical Register of the Officers and Graduates of the U.S. Military Academy, from 1802 to 1869.* Vol. II: 1841–1867. New York: James Miller, Publisher, 1879.

Curtis, Orson Blair. *History of the Twenty-Fourth Michigan of the Iron Brigade, Known as the Detroit and Wayne County Regiment.* Detroit: Winn & Hammond, 1891; repr. Gaithersburg, Maryland: Olde Soldier Books, 1988.

Cutrer, Thomas W., ed. *Longstreet's Aide: The Civil War Letters of Major Thomas J. Goree.* Charlottesville, Virginia: University Press of Virginia, 1995.

Davis, William C. *The Orphan Brigade: The Kentucky Confederates Who Couldn't Go Home.* Garden City, New York: Doubleday & Company, Inc., 1980.

———. *Diary of a Confederate Soldier: John S. Jackman of the Orphan Brigade.* Columbia, South Carolina: University of South Carolina Press, 1990.

Dawson, Francis W. *Reminiscences of Confederate Service, 1861–1865.* Charleston, South Carolina: The News and Courier Book Presses, 1882.

Dawson, Joseph G. *Army Generals and Reconstruction: Louisiana, 1862–1877.* Baton Rouge: Louisiana State University Press, 1982.

Dayton, Ruth Woods, ed. *The Diary of a Confederate Soldier: James E. Hall.* N.p., 1961.

de Tocqueville, Alexis. *Democracy in America.* Vol. III. New York: Random House (Vintage Books), 1945.

Devereux, T. P. "The Homeward March after Stacking Arms at Appomattox" in *Recollections and Reminiscences, 1861–1865 through World War I.* South Carolina Division, United Daughters of the Confederacy, 1990.

Dickert, D. Augustus. *History of Kershaw's Brigade.* Newberry, South Carolina: Elbert H. Aull Company, 1899.

Divine, John E. *8th Virginia Infantry.* The Virginia Regimental Histories Series. Lynchburg, Virginia: H. E. Howard, Inc., 1983.

Douglas, Henry Kyd. *I Rode with Stonewall.* Chapel Hill: The University of North Carolina Press, 1940.

DuBose, John Witherspoon. *General Joseph Wheeler and the Army of Tennessee.* New York: The Neale Publishing Company, 1912.

Dunlap, Leslie W., ed. *"Your Affectionate Husband, J. F. Culver," Letters Written during the Civil War.* Iowa City: Friends of the University of Iowa Libraries, 1978.

Dunning, William A. *Reconstruction: Political and Economic, 1865–1877.* New York: Harper & Brothers, 1907.

Dyer, John Will. "A Confederate Goes Home" in *Reminiscences; or, Four Years in the Confederate Army* in William B. Hesseltine, ed., *The Tragic Conflict: The Civil War and Reconstruction.* New York: George Braziller, 1962.

Early, Jubal A. *A Memoir of the Last Year of the War for Independence in the Confederate States of America, Containing an Account of the Operations of His Commands in the Years 1864 and 1865.* Toronto: Lovell & Gibson, 1866.

Editors of Combined Books. *The Civil War Book of Lists.* Conshohocken, Pennsylvania: Combined Books, Inc., 1993, 1994.

Eicher, David J. *The Civil War in Books: An Analytical Bibliography.* Urbana: University of Illinois Press, 1997.

Eggleston, George Cary. *A Rebel's Recollections.* New York: Hurd and Houghton, 1875.

Emilio, Luis F. *A Brave Black Regiment: The History of the 54th Massachusetts, 1863–1865.* Boston, n.p., 1894, 2nd edition; repr. New York: DaCapo Press, 1995.

Fletcher, W. A. *Rebel Private—Front and Rear: Experiences and Observations from the Early Fifties and through the Civil War.* Beaumont, Texas: Press of the Green Print, 1908.

Foner, Eric, and John A. Garraty, eds. *The Reader's Companion to American History.* Boston: Houghton Mifflin Company, 1991.

Foote, Shelby. *The Civil War: A Narrative.* Vol. 3: *Red River to Appomattox.* New York: Random House, 1974.

Forbes, William, II. *Hauling Brass: Capt. Croft's Flying Artillery Battery, Columbus, Georgia.* Dayton, Ohio: Morningside House, Inc., 1993.

Franklin, John Hope. *Reconstruction: After the Civil War.* The Chicago History of American Civilization. Chicago: The University of Chicago Press, 1961.

Freeman, Douglas Southall. *R. E. Lee.* Vol. IV. New York: Charles Scribner's Sons, 1940.

French, Samuel G. *Two Wars: An Autobiography.* Nashville: Confederate Veteran, 1901.

Furguson, Ernest B. *Ashes of Glory: Richmond at War.* New York: Alfred A. Knopf, 1996.

Gaines, W. Craig. *The Confederate Cherokees: John Drew's Regiment of Mounted Rifles.* Baton Rouge: Louisiana State University Press, 1989.

Gallagher, Gary W., ed. *Fighting for the Confederacy: The Personal Recollections of General Edward Porter Alexander.* Chapel Hill: The University of North Carolina Press, 1989.

Gallaway, B. P. *The Ragged Rebel: A Common Soldier in W. H. Parson's Texas Cavalry, 1861–1865.* Austin, Texas: University of Texas Press, 1988.

Gates, Arnold, ed. *The Rough Side of War: The Civil War Journal of Chesley A. Mosman.* Garden City, New York: The Basin Publishing Company, 1987.

Gates, Theodore B. *The Ulster Guard (20th New York State Militia) and the War of the Rebellion.* New York: Benjamin H. Tyrrel, 1879.

George, Henry. *History of the 3d, 7th, 8th, and 12th Kentucky, C.S.A.* Louisville, Kentucky: C. T. Dearing Printing Co., Inc., 1911.

Gerrish, Theodore. *Army Life: A Private's Reminiscences of the Civil War.* Portland, Maine: Hoyt, Fogg & Donham, 1882.

Gibbons, Alfred R. *The Recollections of an Old Confederate Soldier.* Shelbyville, Missouri: Herald Print, 1931.

Gill, John. *Reminiscences of Four Years as a Private Soldier in the Confederate Army, 1861–1865.* Baltimore: Sun Printing Office, 1904.

Glatthaar, Joseph T. *Forged in Battle: The Civil War Alliance of Black Soldiers and White Officers.* New York: The Free Press, 1990.

Gordon, John B. *Reminiscences of the Civil War.* New York: Charles Scribner's Sons, 1904.

Gordon, Sarah H. *Passage to Union: How the Railroads Transformed American Life, 1829–1929.* Chicago: Ivan R. Dee, 1996.

Govan, Gilbert E., and James W. Livingood, eds. *The Haskell Memoirs: John Cheves Haskell.* New York: G. P. Putnam's Sons, 1960.

Gragg, Rod. *The Civil War Quiz and Fact Book.* New York: Harper & Row, 1985.

Hagood, Johnson. *Memoirs of the War of Secession.* Columbia, South Carolina: The State Company, 1910.

Haines, Alanson A. *History of the Fifteenth Regiment, New Jersey Volunteers.* New York: Jenkins & Thomas, 1883.

Haines, William P. *History of the Men of Co. F, with Descriptions of the Marches and Battles of the 12th New Jersey Volunteers.* Camden, New Jersey: C. S. McGrath Printer, 1897.

Hale, Douglas. *The Third Texas Cavalry in the Civil War.* Norman, Oklahoma: University of Oklahoma Press, 1993.

Hall, Harry H. *A Johnny Reb Band from Salem: The Pride of Tarheelia.* Raleigh: The North Carolina Confederate Centennial Commission, 1963.

Hanifen, Michael. *History of Battery "B," First New Jersey Artillery.* Ottawa, Illinois: n.p., 1905; repr. Hightstown, New Jersey: Longstreet House, 1991.

Hargrove, Hondon B. *Black Union Soldiers in the Civil War.* Jefferson, North Carolina: McFarland & Company, 1988.

Harwell, Richard Barksdale, ed. *A Confederate Diary of the Retreat from Petersburg, April 3–20, 1865.* Atlanta, Georgia: The Library of Emory University, 1953.

Haynes, William G., Jr., ed. *The Field Diary of a Confederate Soldier.* Darien, Georgia: The Ashantilly Press, 1963.

Heitman, Franklin B. *Historical Register of the United States Army from Its Organization—September 29, 1789, to September 29, 1889.* Washington, D.C.: The National Tribune, 1890.

Hennessy, John. *The First Battle of Manassas: An End to Innocence, July 18–21, 1861.* The Virginia Civil War Battles and Leaders Series. Lynchburg, Virginia: H. E. Howard, Inc., 1989.

Hoffman, Mark S., ed. *The World Almanac and Book of Facts—1992.* New York: Pharos Books, 1991.

Horn, Stanley F. *The Army of Tennessee: A Military History.* Indianapolis: The Bobbs-Merrill Company, 1941.

Houghton, Edwin B. *The Campaigns of the Seventeenth Maine.* Portland, Maine: Short & Loring, 1866.

Howell, H. Grady, Jr. *Going to Meet the Yankees: A History of the "Bloody Sixth" Mississippi Infantry, C.S.A.* Jackson, Mississippi: Chickasaw Bayou Press, 1981.

———. *To Live and Die in Dixie: A History of the Third Mississippi Infantry, C.S.A.* Jackson, Mississippi: Chickasaw Bayou Press, 1991.

Hudson, Joshua Hilary. *Sketches and Reminiscences.* Columbia, South Carolina: The State Company, 1903.

Huntington, Samuel P. *The Soldier and the State: The Theory and Politics of Civil-Military Relations.* The Belknap Press of Harvard University Press, 1957.

Hurst, Samuel H. *Journal: History of the Seventy-Third Ohio Volunteer Infantry.* Chillicothe, Ohio: n.p., 1866.

Ingeresoll, Lurton Dunham. *Iowa and the Rebellion: A History of the Troops Furnished by the State of Iowa to the Volunteer Armies of the Union, Which Conquered the Great Southern Rebellion of 1861–1865.* 3rd ed. Philadelphia: J. P. Lippincott & Co., 1867.

Johnson, Allen, and Dumas Malone. *Dictionary of American Biography.* Vol. 2. New York: Charles Scribner's Sons, 1943; also, 1936 edition, vol. 18.

Johnson, Thomas H., ed. *The Oxford Companion to American History.* New York: Oxford University Press, 1966.

Johnston, Angus James, II. *Virginia Railroads in the Civil War.* Chapel Hill: The University of North Carolina Press, 1961.

Johnston, David E. *The Story of a Confederate Boy in the Civil War.* Portland, Oregon: Glass & Prudhomme Company, 1914.

Jones, Benjamin W. *Under the Stars and Bars: A History of the Surry Light Artillery.* Richmond: Everett Waddey Company, 1909; repr. Dayton, Ohio: Morningside Bookshop, 1975.

Jones, Charles C., Jr. *History of the Chatham Artillery during the Confederate Struggle for Independence.* Albany, New York: Joel Munsell, 1867.

Jones, J. B. *A Rebel War Clerk's Diary at the Confederate States Capital.* Vol. 2. Philadelphia: J. B. Lippincott Company, 1866; repr. n.p.: Time-Life Books, Inc., 1982.

Jones, Samuel Calvin. *Reminiscences of the Twenty-Second Iowa Volunteer Infantry.* Iowa City, Iowa: S. C. Jones, 1907; repr. Iowa City: Camp Pope Bookshop, 1993.

Jordan, David M. *Winfield Scott Hancock: A Soldier's Life.* Bloomington, Indiana: Indiana University Press, 1988.

Kent, Arthur A. *Three Years with Company K: Sergt. Austin C. Stearns, 13th Mass. Infantry.* Cranbury, New Jersey: Associated University Presses, Inc., 1976.

Ketchum, Richard M., ed. *The American Heritage Picture History of the Civil War.* New York: American Heritage Publishing Company, Inc., 1960.

Kirwan, A. D., ed. *Johnny Green of the Orphan Brigade: The Journal of a Confederate Soldier.* Louisville, Kentucky: The University of Kentucky Press, 1956.

Kohl, Lawrence Frederick, ed. *The Irish Brigade and Its Campaigns by D. P. Conynham.* New York: Fordham University Press, 1994.

Kostyal, K. M. *Field of Battle: The Civil War Letters of Major Thomas J. Halsey.* Washington, D.C.: Book Division, National Geographic Society, 1996.

Krick, Robert K. *Lee's Colonels: A Biographical Register of the Field Officers of the Army of Northern Virginia.* Dayton, Ohio: Morningside House, Inc., 1992.

Laboda, Lawrence R. *From Selma to Appomattox: The History of the Jeff Davis Artillery.* Shippensburg, Pennsylvania: White Mane Publishing Company, Inc., 1994.

Lash, Jeffrey N. *Destroyer of the Iron Horse: General Joseph E. Johnston and Confederate Rail Transport, 1861–1865.* Kent, Ohio: The Kent State University Press, 1991.

Laswell, Mary, ed. *Rags and Hope: The Recollections of Val[erius] C. Giles, Four Years with Hood's Brigade, Fourth Texas Infantry, 1861–1865.* New York: Coward-McCann, Inc., 1961.

Leech, Margaret. *Reveille in Washington, 1860–1865.* New York: Grosset & Dunlap, 1941.

Lewis, John H. *Recollections from 1860 to 1865.* Washington, D.C.: Peake & Company, Publishers, 1895.

Livermore, Thomas L. *Numbers and Losses in the Civil War in America, 1861–1865.* Boston: n.p., 1900; repr. Carlisle, Pennsylvania: John Kallman, 1996.

———. *Days and Events, 1860–1866.* Boston: Houghton Mifflin Company, 1920.

Long, Andrew Davidson. *Stonewall's "Foot Cavalryman."* Austin, Texas: The Steck Company, 1965.

Long, E. B., with Barbara Long. *The Civil War Day by Day: An Almanac, 1861–1865.* Garden City, New York: Doubleday, 1971; repr. New York: DaCapo Press, Inc., 1985.

Longstreet, James. *From Manassas to Appomattox: Memoirs of the Civil War in America.* Philadelphia: J. B. Lippincott Company, 1896; repr. James I. Robertson, ed. Bloomington, Indiana: Indiana University Press, 1960.

Loving, Jerome M., ed. *Civil War Letters of George Washington Whitman.* Durham, North Carolina: Duke University Press, 1975.

Luvaas, Jay. *The Military Legacy of the Civil War: The European Inheritance.* Chicago: The University of Chicago Press, 1959; repr. Lawrence, Kansas: University Press of Kansas, 1988.

Madison, James H. *Eli Lilly: A Life, 1885–1977*. Indianapolis: Indiana Historical Society, 1989.

Malone, Thomas H. *Memoir of Thomas H. Malone*. Nashville: Baird-Ward, 1928.

Marbaker, Thomas D. *History of the Eleventh New Jersey Volunteers from Its Organization to Appomattox*. Trenton: MacCrellish & Quigley, 1898.

Martin, Albro. *Railroads Triumphant: The Growth, Rejection, and Rebirth of a Vital American Force*. New York: Oxford University Press, 1992.

Marvel, William. *Andersonville: The Last Depot*. Chapel Hill: The University of North Carolina Press, 1994.

Marzalek, John F. *Sherman: A Soldier's Passion for Order*. New York: The Free Press, 1993.

McCaffrey, James M. *This Band of Heroes: Granbury's Texas Brigade, C.S.A.* Austin, Texas: Eakin Press, 1985.

McCarthy, Carlton. *Detailed Minutiae of Soldier Life in the Army of Northern Virginia, 1861–1865*. Lincoln, Nebraska: University of Nebraska Press, 1993.

McConnell, Stuart. *Glorious Contentment: The Grand Army of the Republic, 1865–1900*. Chapel Hill: The University of North Carolina Press, 1992.

McMorries, Edward Young. *History of the First Regiment Alabama Volunteer Infantry, C.S.A.* (Bulletin No. 2: State of Alabama Archives and History). Montgomery, Alabama: The Brown Printing Company, 1904.

McMurray, W. J. *History of the Twentieth Tennessee Regiment Volunteer Infantry, C.S.A.* Nashville: The Publication Committee, 1904.

McPherson, James M. *The Negro's Civil War: How American Negroes Felt and Acted during the War for the Union*. New York: Pantheon Books (Random House), 1965.

———. *Battle Cry of Freedom: The Civil War Era* (Oxford History of the United States, vol. 4). New York: Oxford University Press, 1988.

———. *Drawn with the Sword: Reflections on the American Civil War*. New York: Oxford University Press, 1996.

———. *For Cause and Comrade: Why Men Fought in the Civil War*. New York: Oxford University Press, 1997.

Meade, Edwin B., ed. *Memoirs: Early Life and Civil War Days of Captain Edwin E. Bouldin*. Danville, Virginia: J. T. Townes Ptg. Co., 1968.

Melville, Herman. *Battle-Pieces and Aspects of the War: Civil War Poems*. New York: n.p., 1866; repr. New York: DaCapo Press, 1995.

Meyers, Augustus. *Ten Years in the Ranks—U.S. Army.* New York: The Stirling Press, 1914; repr. New York: Arno Press, 1979.

Miller, Genevieve, ed. *Yankee in Gray: The Civil War Memoirs of Henry E. Handerson, with a Selection of His Wartime Letters.* Cleveland, Ohio: The Press of Western Reserve University, 1962.

Miller, Millard J. *My Grandpap Rode with Jeb Stuart.* Westerville, Ohio: privately printed, 1974.

Mitchell, Reid. *Civil War Soldiers.* New York: Viking Press, 1988.

Mixson, Frank M. *Reminiscences of a Private.* Camden, South Carolina: J. J. Fox, n.d.; repr. 1990.

Moore, Edward A. *The Story of a Cannoneer under Stonewall Jackson.* Lynchburg, Virginia: J. P. Bell Company, Inc., 1910.

Morgan, W. H. *Personal Reminiscences of the War of 1861–5.* Lynchburg, Virginia: J. P. Bell Company, Inc., 1911.

Morison, Samuel Eliot. *The Oxford History of the American People.* New York: Oxford University Press, 1965.

Morris, Anny Lewis Dickinson Brown, ed. *Diary of Capt. Henry C. Dickinson, C.S.A.* Denver: Press of the Williamson-Haffner Co., n.d.

Morton, John Watson. *The Artillery of Nathan Bedford Forrest's Cavalry.* Nashville: Publishing House of the M. E. Church, South, 1909.

Munson, John W. *Reminiscences of a Mosby Guerrilla.* New York: Moffat, Yard & Co., 1906; repr. Washington, D.C.: Zenger Publishing Co., Inc., 1983.

Nash, Eugene Arus. *A History of the Forty-Fourth Regiment New York Volunteer Infantry in the Civil War, 1861–1865.* Chicago: R. R. Donnelley and Sons Company; repr. Dayton, Ohio: Morningside Press, 1988.

Neese, George M. *Three Years in the Confederate Horse Artillery.* Dayton, Ohio: Press of the Morningside Bookshop, 1983.

Nevins, Allen. *The War for the Union: War Becomes Revolution, 1862–1863.* New York: Charles Scribner's Sons, 1960.

———. *The War for the Union: The Organized War to Victory, 1864–1865.* New York: Charles Scribner's Sons, 1971.

Newlin, W. H. *A History of the Seventy-Third Regiment of Illinois Infantry Volunteers.* N.p.: Regimental Reunion Association of Survivors, 1890.

Nisbet, James Cooper. *Four Years on the Firing Line.* Bell Irwin Wiley, ed. Jackson, Tennessee: McCowat-Mercer Press, 1963.

Noggle, Burl. *The Fleming Lectures, 1937–1990: A Historiographical Essay.* Baton Rouge: Louisiana State University Press, 1992.

Nolan, Allan T. *The Iron Brigade: A Military History.* New York: The Macmillan Company, 1961; repr. 3rd edition: Berrien Springs, Michigan: Hardscrabble Books, 1983.

Oates, William C. *The War between the Union and the Confederacy and Its Lost Opportunities.* New York: Neale Publishing Co., 1905; repr. Dayton, Ohio: Morningside Bookshop, 1985.

Osborn, Hartwell, et al. *Trials and Triumphs: The Record of the Fifty-Fifth Ohio Volunteer Infantry.* Chicago: A. C. McClurg & Co., 1904.

Owen, William Miller. *In Camp and Battle with the Washington Artillery of New Orleans: A Narrative of Events during the Late Civil War from Bull Run to Appomattox and Spanish Fort.* Boston: Ticknor and Company, 1885.

Owens, W. M. *A Soldier's Story of the War, Including the Marches and Battles of the Washington Artillery and of Other Louisiana Troops.* New Orleans: Clark & Hofeline, Book Printers, 1874.

Parker, John L., and Robert G. Carter. *History of the Twenty-Second Massachusetts Infantry, the Second Company Sharpshooters, and the Third Light Battery, in the War of the Rebellion.* Boston: Rand Avery Co., 1887.

Pearce, Thilbert H., ed. *Diary of Captain Henry A. Chambers.* Wendell, North Carolina: Broadfoot's Bookmark, 1983.

Perrett, Geoffrey. *Ulysses S. Grant: Soldier and President.* New York: Random House, 1997.

Phisterer, Frederick. *Statistical Record of the Armies of the United States.* New York, 1883; repr. Carlisle, Pennsylvania: John Kallman, Publishers, 1996.

Polley, Joseph B. *Hood's Texas Brigade: Its Marches, Its Battles, Its Achievements.* New York: The Neale Publishing Company, 1910.

Pullen, John J. *The Twentieth Maine: A Volunteer Regiment in the Civil War.* Philadelphia: J. B. Lippincott Company, 1957.

Radley, Kenneth. *Rebel Watchdog: The Confederate States Army Provost Guard.* Baton Rouge: Louisiana State University Press, 1989.

Randall, J. G., and David Donald. *The Civil War and Reconstruction.* Boston: Little, Brown and Company, 1961; 2nd edition, 1969.

Redkey, Edwin S., ed. *A Grand Army of Black Men: Letters from African-American Soldiers in the Union Army, 1861–1865.* New York: Cambridge University Press, 1992.

Reese, Timothy J. *Sykes' Regular Infantry Division, 1861–1864: A History of Regular United States Infantry Operations in the Civil War's Eastern Theater.* Jefferson, North Carolina: McFarland & Company, 1990.

Reid, Whitelaw. "Excluding the Rebel" in *After the War: A Southern Tour, May 1865–May 1, 1866* in Hesseltine, William B., ed. *The Tragic Conflict: The Civil War and Reconstruction.* New York: George Braziller, 1962.

Reid-Green, Marcia, ed. *Letters Home—Henry Mattrau of the Iron Brigade.* Lincoln: University of Nebraska Press, 1993.

Rennolds, Edwin H. *A History of the Henry County Commands Which Served in the Confederate States Army.* Jacksonville, Florida: Sun Publishing Company, 1904; repr. Kennesaw, Georgia: Continental Book Company, 1961.

Rhodes, Robert Hunt, ed. *All for the Union: The Civil War Diary and Letters of Elisha Hunt Rhodes.* New York: Orion Books, 1985.

Richter, William L. *The Army in Texas during Reconstruction, 1865–1870.* College Station, Texas: Texas A & M University Press, 1987.

Robertson, James I., Jr., ed. *One of Jackson's Foot Cavalry: Recollections of John H. Worsham, F Company, 21st Virginia Infantry.* Wilmington, North Carolina: Broadfoot Publishing Company, 1987.

————. *Stonewall Jackson: The Man, the Soldier, the Legend.* New York: Simon & Schuster, 1997.

Roper, Peter W. *Jedediah Hotchkiss: Rebel Mapmaker and Virginia Businessman.* Shippensburg, Pennsylvania: White Mane Publishing Company, Inc., 1992.

Rosenblatt, Emil and Ruth, eds. *Hard Marching Every Day: The Civil War Letters of Private Wilbur Fisk, 1861–1865.* Lawrence, Kansas: University Press of Kansas, 1983, 1992.

Rosenburg, R. B., ed. *"For the Sake of My Country": The Diary of Colonel W. W. Ward, Ninth Tennessee Cavalry, Morgan's Brigade, CSA.* Murfreesboro, Tennessee: Southern Heritage Press, 1992.

Roth, Margaret Brobst, ed. *Well, Mary: Civil War Letters of a Wisconsin Volunteer.* Madison: The University of Wisconsin Press, 1960.

Rowell, John W. *Yankee Cavalrymen: Through the Civil War with the Ninth Pennsylvania Cavalry.* Knoxville: The University of Tennessee Press, 1971.

————. *Yankee Artillerymen: Through the Civil War with Eli Lilly's Indiana Battery.* Knoxville: The University of Tennessee Press, 1975.

Runge, William H., ed. *Four Years in the Confederate Artillery: The Diary of Private Henry Robinson Berkeley.* Richmond: Virginia Historical Society, 1991.

Salecker, Gene Eric. *Disaster on the Mississippi: The* Sultana *Explosion, April 27, 1865*. Annapolis, Maryland: Naval Institute Press, 1996.

Sawyer, Franklin. *A Military History of the 8th Regiment Ohio Volunteer Infantry: Its Battles, Marches, and Army Movements*. Cleveland: Fairbanks & Co., 1881.

Schmidt, Lewis G. *A Civil War History of the 47th Regiment of Pennsylvania Veteran Volunteers*. Allentown, Pennsylvania: privately published by author, 1986.

Seville, William P. *History of the First Regiment, Delaware Volunteers*. Wilmington: Historical Society of Delaware, 1885.

Shaver, Lewellyn A. *A History of the Sixtieth Alabama Regiment, Gracie's Alabama Brigade*. Montgomery, Alabama: Barrett & Brown, Publishers, 1867.

Sifakis, Stewart. *Who Was Who in the Civil War*. New York: Facts on File Publications, 1988.

Silliker, Ruth L., ed. *The Rebel Yell & the Yankee Hurrah: The Civil War Journal of a Maine Volunteer*. Camden, Maine: Down East Books, 1985.

Simmons, R. Hugh. *The Story of the 12th Louisiana Infantry in the Final Campaign in North Carolina with the Confederate Army of Tennessee, January to April, 1865*. Typescript, 1992.

Simons, Ezra D. *A Regimental History: The One Hundred and Twenty-Fifth New York State Volunteers*. New York: Judson Printing Co., 1988.

Small, Abner Ralph. *The Sixteenth Maine Regiment in the War of the Rebellion*. Portland, Maine: B. Thurston & Co., 1886.

Smith, John Day. *The History of the Nineteenth Maine Regiment of Maine Volunteer Infantry, 1862–1865*. Minneapolis: Great Western Printing Co., 1909.

Smith, William Alexander. *The Anson Guards: Company C Fourteenth Regiment North Carolina Volunteers, 1861–1865*. Charlotte, North Carolina: Stone Publishing Co., 1914.

Sorrel, Gen. G. Moxley. *Recollections of a Confederate Staff Officer*. New York: The Neale Publishing Company, 1905.

Sparrow, John C. *History of Personnel Demobilization in the United States Army*. Pamphlet No. 20–210. Washington, D.C.: Department of the Army, 1952.

Speer, Lonnie R. *Portals to Hell: Military Prisons of the Civil War*. Mechanicsburg, Pennsylvania: Stackpole Books, 1997.

Spurlin, Charles D., ed. *The Civil War Diary of Charles A. Leuschner.* Austin, Texas: Eakin Press, 1992.

Stanton, Edwin M., secretary of war. *Report of the Secretary of War.* Washington, D.C.: Government Printing Office, 1866.

Starr, John W., Jr. *Lincoln and the Railroads.* New York: Dodd, Mead & Company, 1927.

Stegeman, John F. *These Men She Gave: Civil War Diary of Athens, Georgia.* Athens: University of Georgia Press, 1964.

Stephens, Robert Grier, Jr., ed. *Intrepid Warrior: Clement Anselm Evans.* Dayton, Ohio: Morningside Press, 1992.

Stocker, Jeffrey D., ed. *From Huntsville to Appomattox: R. T. Coles's History of the 4th Regiment, Alabama Volunteer Infantry, C.S.A., Army of Northern Virginia.* Knoxville: University of Tennessee Press, 1996.

Stover, John F. *History of the Baltimore and Ohio Railroad.* West Lafayette, Indiana: Purdue University Press, 1987.

Strong, Robert Hale. *A Yankee Private's Civil War.* Ashley Halsey, ed. Chicago: Henry Regnery Company, 1961.

Summers, Festus P. *The Baltimore and Ohio in the Civil War.* New York: George Putnam's Sons, 1939; repr. Gettysburg: Stan Clark Military Books, 1993.

Tanner, Robert G. *Stonewall in the Valley: Thomas J. "Stonewall" Jackson's Shenandoah Valley Campaign, Spring 1862.* New York: Doubleday & Company, Inc., 1976; repr. rev. expanded ed. Mechanicsburg, Pennsylvania: Stackpole Books, 1996.

Taylor, George Rogers, and Irene D. Neu. *The American Railroad Network, 1861–1890.* New York: Arno Press, 1981.

Taylor, Richard. *Destruction and Reconstruction: Personal Experiences of the Late War in the United States.* Edinburgh, Scotland: William Blackwood and Sons, 1879.

Thomas, Benjamin P., and Harold M. Hyman. *Stanton: The Life and Times of Lincoln's Secretary of War.* New York: Alfred Knopf, 1962.

Thomas, Emory M. *Robert E. Lee: A Biography.* New York: W. W. Norton, 1995.

Thompson, William T., Jr. *Family Letters by Dr. John Herbert Claiborne, April 1864–April 1865.* Petersburg, Virginia: reproduced privately, 1961.

Tilney, Robert. *My Life in the Army: Three Years and a Half with the Fifth Army Corps, Army of the Potomac, 1862–1865.* Philadelphia: Ferris & Leach, 1912.

Toombs, Samuel. *Reminiscences of the War, Comprising a Detailed Account of the Experiences of the Thirteenth Regiment New Jersey Volunteers in Camp, on the March, and in Battle.* Orange, New Jersey: Journal Office, 1878; repr. Hightstown, New Jersey: Longstreet House, 1994.

Tower, R. Lockwood, ed., with John S. Belmont. *Lee's Adjutant: The Wartime Letters of Colonel Walter Herron Taylor, 1862–1865.* Columbia, South Carolina: University of South Carolina Press, 1995.

Townsend, Edward Davis. *Anecdotes of the Civil War in the United States.* New York: D. Appleton and Company, 1884.

Tremain, Henry Edwin. *Last Hours of Sheridan's Cavalry: A Reprint of War Memoranda.* New York: Bonnell, Sliver & Bowers, 1904.

Trudeau, Noah Andre. *Out of the Storm: The End of the Civil War, April–June, 1865.* Boston: Little, Brown and Company, 1994.

Trulock, Alice Rains. *In the Hands of Providence: Joshua L. Chamberlain and the American Civil War.* Chapel Hill: University of North Carolina Press, 1992.

Tunnard, W. H. *A Southern Record: The History of the Third Regiment Louisiana Infantry.* Baton Rouge: Printed for the Author, 1866; repr. Dayton, Ohio: Morningside Bookshop, 1970.

Turner, George Edgar. *Victory Rode the Rails: The Strategic Place of the Railroads in the Civil War.* Indianapolis, Bobbs-Merrill, 1953; repr. Lincoln: University of Nebraska Press, 1992.

Underwood, George C. *History of the Twenty-Sixth Regiment of the North Carolina Troops in the Great War, 1861–1865.* Goldsboro, North Carolina: Nash Brothers; repr. Wendell, North Carolina: Broadfoot Bookmark, 1978.

United States War Department. *The War of the Rebellion: A Compilation of the Official Records of the Union and Confederate Armies, 1861–1865.* Washington, D.C.: Government Printing Office, 1880–1901, 70 vols. in 128 parts.

———. *Atlas to Accompany the Official Records of the Union and Confederate Armies.* Washington, D.C.: Government Printing Office, 1891–1895. Originally published in 3 vols; repr. Hong Kong: Fairfax Press, 1978, in 1 vol.

Warner, Ezra J. *Generals in Gray: Lives of the Confederate Commanders.* Baton Rouge: Louisiana State University Press, 1959.

———. *Generals in Blue: Lives of the Union Commanders.* Baton Rouge: Louisiana State University Press, 1964.

Washburn, George H. *A Complete Military History and Record of the 108th Regiment New York Volunteers from 1862 to 1865.* Rochester, New York: E. R. Andrews, 1894.

Weber, Thomas. *The Northern Railroads in the Civil War, 1861–1865.* New York: Columbia University Press, 1952.

Weigley, Russell F. *History of the United States Army.* New York: The Macmillan Company, 1967.

Welch, Spencer Glasgow. *A Confederate Surgeon's Letters to His Wife.* New York: The Neale Publishing Company, 1911; repr. Marietta, Georgia: Continental Book Company, 1954.

Welker, David A., ed. *A Keystone Rebel: The Civil War Diary of Joseph Garey, Hudson's Battery, Mississippi Volunteers.* Gettysburg: Thomas Publications, 1997.

Wert, Jeffry D. *From Winchester to Cedar Creek: The Shenandoah Campaign of 1864.* South Mountain Press, 1987; repr. Mechanicsburg, Pennsylvania: Stackpole Books, 1997.

Wheeler, Richard. *Witness to Appomattox.* New York: Harper & Row, 1989.

Wiley, Bell Irwin, *The Life of Johnny Reb: The Common Soldier of the Confederacy.* Indianapolis: The Bobbs-Merrill Company, 1943.

———. *The Life of Billy Yank: The Common Soldier of the Union.* Indianapolis: The Bobbs-Merrill Company, 1951.

———, ed. *Fourteen Hundred and 91 Days in the Confederate Army: A Journal Kept by W. W. Heartsill for Four Years, One Month, and One Day; or, Camp Life, Day by Day, of the W. P. Lane Rangers from April 19, 1861, to May 20, 1865.* Jackson, Tennessee: McCowat-Mercer Press, 1954.

———, ed. *Kentucky Cavaliers in Dixie: Reminiscences of a Confederate Cavalryman—George Dallas Mosgrove.* Jackson, Tennessee: McCowat-Mercer Press, Inc., 1957.

Wilkinson, Warren. *Mother, May You Never See the Sights I Have Seen.* New York: Harper & Row, 1990.

Williams, T. Harry. *P. G. T. Beauregard: Napoleon in Gray.* Baton Rouge: Louisiana State University Press, 1955.

Wills, Ridley, II. *Old Enough to Die.* Franklin, Tennessee: Hillsboro Press, 1996.

Womack, Bob. *Call Forth the Mighty Men.* Bessemer, Alabama: Colonial Press, 1987.

Woodward, C. Vann. *The Future of the Past*. New York: Oxford University Press, 1989.

Worsham, W. J. *The Old Nineteenth Tennessee Regiment, C.S.A.* Knoxville, Tennessee: n.p., 1902; repr. Oxford, Mississippi: The Guild Bindery Press, 1992.

Wynne, Lewis N, and Robert A. Taylor, eds. *This War So Horrible: The Civil War Diary of Hiram Smith Williams.* Tuscaloosa, Alabama: University of Alabama Press, 1993.

INDEX